# DEVELOPING COUNTRIES IN THE INTERNATIONAL ECONOMY

# Developing Countries in the International Economy

## Selected Papers

Sanjaya Lall

*Oxford University Institute of*
*Economics and Statistics*

338.91
L19d

*First published 1981 by*
THE MACMILLAN PRESS LTD
*London and Basingstoke*
*Companies and representatives*
*throughout the world*

*Printed in Hong Kong*

**British Library Cataloguing in Publication Data**

Lall, Sanjaya
  Developing countries in the international
  economy
  1. Underdeveloped areas – Foreign economic
  relations
  I. Title
  382.1′09172′4          HF1413

  ISBN  0–333–28875–0

This book is dedicated
to
Sushila, Gyanshila and Sahdeo Singh Jayaswal

# Contents

# Preface

This book presents a selection of published and unpublished papers on some aspects of development. It is not a comprehensive examination of the international economic problems of the Third World, but a series of studies, empirical and conceptual, on which I have worked over the past five years in relation with my main field of interest, the multinational (or transnational) corporation. In the main the papers focus on the external relations of manufacturing industry, but the range of topics covered is fairly wide, and the collection should prove useful to all those who are interested in the general problems of development. It is intended to complement another collection of my papers (*The Multinational Corporation: Nine Essays*), specifically on the multinational corporation.

The first two papers deal with some conceptual problems in the analysis of the process of development. One is a critique of the 'dependence' theories which became popular as all-embracing explanations of the process of development (or the lack thereof) in the mid-1970s. The other discusses some of the limitations of orthodox welfare economics in analysing development problems, and shows how some of the controversies which still rage over the basic issues of development can be traced to differences over these fundamental methodological premises.

The two papers in Part Two deal with international investment. The first of these is a review article which analyses different approaches to the analysis of multinational corporations. The second presents a study of multinationals in the food-processing industry, with special attention to the operations of Unilever. Unfortunately, this paper was written well before the publication of D. K. Fieldhouse's scholarly book on *Unilever Overseas*, and it was not feasible to change my paper to take his findings into account. Nevertheless, my analysis was addressed to rather different issues from Fieldhouse's and retains interest despite the appearance of his detailed historical study.

Part Three comprises two papers on technology transfer, one a brief literature survey and research agenda, and the other an analysis of the international patent system. The book ends, in Part Four, with two papers on exports by developing countries. The first of these reviews relates the growth of manufactured exports by the 'newly industrialising countries' (NICs). It describes the main countries and products involved, surveys the recent literature on the comparative advantage of developing countries and identifies the main agents (domestic or multinational companies) responsible for the expansion of these exports. While it does not deal with the issue of protectionism or the institutional structure of trade (both adequately treated in the literature), it should help to plug a gap in the reading available, which does not seem adequately to cover this important phenomenon. The last paper deals with an interesting new development—the entrance of developing country enterprises as exporters of advanced industrial technology—in the international scene. The evidence on which it is based is (necessarily) patchy and anecdotal, but the issues raised, in terms of the changing comparative advantage of developing countries, their technological advance and the prospects of intra-Third World trade, may be of great significance.

A large number of colleagues helped me to prepare these papers; specific acknowledgements are made in each essay. I would also like to record my gratitude to the Director and the staff of the Institute of Economics and Statistics for their help and encouragement.

The author and publishers wish to thank Mr Mario Luiz Possas, for permission to use the table based on sources from CACEX, Banco do Brasil, and Visão (1974) estimated by IPEA, Brazil, and reproduced in his work 'Employment Effects of Multinational Enterprises in Brazil'.

# Acknowledgements

This collection contains a number of papers which are published elsewhere, though some titles have been changed. I wish to thank the various copyright holders for permission to reprint:

Chapter 1: 'Is "Dependence" a Useful Concept in Analysing Underdevelopment?', *World Development*, vol. 3, nos. 11 and 12 (November–December 1975) pp. 799–810.

Chapter 2: 'Conflicts of Concepts: Welfare Economics and Developing Countries', *World Development*, vol. 4, no. 3 (March 1976) pp. 181–95.

Chapter 3: 'Less-Developed Countries and Private Foreign Investment: A Review Article', *World Development*, vol. 2, nos. 4 and 5 (April–May 1974) pp. 43–8.

Chapter 4: 'Private Foreign Investment and the Transfer of Technology in Food Processing', in C. Baron (ed.), *Technology, Employment and Basic Needs in Food Processing* (Oxford: Pergamon Press, 1979) ch. IV. It was originally prepared as a World Employment Programme Working Paper for the International Labour Office (Geneva, 1977).

Chapter 6: 'The Patent System and the Transfer of Technology to Less-Developed Countries', *Journal of World Trade Law*, vol. 10, no. 1 (January–February 1976) pp. 1–16.

Chapter 7: Prepared in 1978 as part of a larger study for the National Economic Development Office, London, and reprinted with NEDO's permission.

Chapter 8: 'Developing Countries as Exporters of Industrial Technology', *Research Policy*, vol. 9, no. 1 (Amsterdam: North-Holland Publishing Company, January 1980).

# Part One
# Some Conceptual Issues

# 1 Dependence and Underdevelopment[1]

## I INTRODUCTION

This essay was originally intended to produce a working definition of 'dependence'. It has ended up by being a critique of the concept of 'dependence' itself, at least as it is currently used in development economics. It is meant to be a sympathetic critique, since I subscribe to many of the fundamental tenets of the dependence school. I also hope that it is a constructive one, since it appears that the dependence literature has, at least in part, led to a concentration on the wrong problems and on unrealistic solutions, a serious defect which must be rectified if it is not to end up as yet another defunct branch of grand theorising.

'Dependence' as a particular explanation of underdevelopment is a relatively recent phenomenon. Its emergence as a distinct school can be traced to the writings of the *dependencia* economists from, or working on, Latin America, whose works began to appear in English around the mid-1960s.[2] This school began to have an impact on thinking on development elsewhere by the 1970s, and by now its terminology has become a part of the standard tools of development economists, mainly (but not exclusively) of left-wing persuasion.

As is only to be expected when a word in common use is given a special connotation and ascribed uncommon characteristics, some confusion has arisen over what 'dependence' means. In conventional economic parlance, a country may be described as being 'dependent' on foreign trade or foreign technology; or a process of great complexity may be said to involve greater 'interdependence' between different workers; or the world may be said to become more 'interdependent' because of increasing international trade and investment. In such usage, there is no hint of anything undesirable (on the contrary, most conventional economists would regard more interdependence as a good thing), nor is there any implication of a process of causation: dependence is defined

3

with reference to some particular objective economic fact, and says nothing, in a descriptive or causal sense, about the condition of the economy as a whole. In the usage of the *dependencia* school, on the other hand, 'dependence' is meant to describe certain characteristics (economic as well as social and political) of the economy *as a whole* and is intended to *trace certain processes which are causally linked to its underdevelopment* and which are *expected to adversely affect its development in the future.*

Even within the *dependencia* school, moreover, the word is given different meanings according to the user's beliefs about the particular historical processes which have caused underdevelopment and about the relative role of the various factors which are at present governing the future development of the poorer countries. In part this internal confusion is due to the school's mixed parentage. The dependence school in Latin America has evolved, on the one hand, from the structuralist tradition of Prebisch, Furtado and ECLA, and, on the other, from Marxist[3] and neo-Marxist[4] thinkers on imperialism—two very disparate modes of analysis with different tools, concepts and prognoses. *Dependencia* economists thus range from mildly socialistic nationalists like Furtado or Sunkel, via writers of increasing radicalism like dos Santos and Cardoso, to explicit revolutionaries like Frank. Many are in fact indistinguishable from straightforward Marxist analysts of imperialism and underdevelopment, and much of what is said below will apply equally to those Marxists who use 'dependence' in the same functional form as the *dependencia* school.

One sometimes gets the impression on reading the literature that 'dependence' is defined in a circular manner: less developed countries (LDCs) are poor because they are dependent, and any characteristics that they display signify dependence. In such tautologous definitions, 'dependence' tends to be identified with features of LDCs which the economist in question happens to particularly dislike, and ceases to offer an independent and verifiable explanation of the processes at work in the less developed world. A concept of 'dependence' which is to serve a useful analytical purpose must satisfy two criteria:

(1) It must lay down certain characteristics of dependent economies which are not found in non-dependent ones.

(2) These characteristics must be shown to affect adversely the course and pattern of development of the dependent countries.

If the first criterion is not satisfied, and crucial features of dependence are to be found in both dependent and non-dependent economies, obviously the whole conceptual scheme is defective. If the second is not satisfied, and peculiar features of dependence are not demonstrated to be causally related to the continuance of underdevelopment, the analytical purpose of the whole exercise is not served, and we end up with a catalogue of socio-economic 'indicators' which are singularly unhelpful for understanding economic backwardness.

In sections III and IV of this paper I shall consider various features of dependence which have been commonly advanced in the literature, and assess whether they satisfy these criteria of usefulness. I shall divide these features into those related to certain objective (but not necessarily quantifiable) characteristics of the dependent economy (the 'causes' of dependence), which I term 'static characteristics', and those related to their patterns of growth (the 'effects' of dependence), or 'dynamic characteristics'. Firstly, however, it is necessary to limit the subject matter in some ways; in section II, therefore, I describe certain features of the dependence model and the premises of the analysis.

## II  LAYING THE GROUNDWORK

Dependence literature is vast and sophisticated, and I cannot hope to survey it in any detail here. To keep the discussion to manageable proportions, therefore, I shall impose certain conditions. First, I shall use the term 'dependence' to refer to the *recent* experience of LDCs. While the concept is sometimes applied to the entire history of imperialism and the whole complex of relationships between the 'centre' and 'periphery', it is essentially directed at the post-colonial era when direct forms of colonial subjugation had ended and new forms of 'imperialism', by various means which ensure dependence rather than open domination, had supervened.[5] While I find myself in substantial agreement with various Marxist analyses of historical imperialism,[6] I find their use of the new dependency concepts somewhat less convincing, and this is the subject matter of this paper.

Secondly, as it is not my purpose here to question the *existence* of several features which are often ascribed to 'dependent' economies, but only to see whether these features add up to a *distinctive state* of 'dependence', I shall take for granted the following:

(1) Income distribution in most LDCs is highly skewed and in many (but not all) instances is getting worse with economic growth.
(2) The consumption patterns of the élite in the periphery (the LDCs)

are strongly influenced by tastes created in the centre (the highly developed countries).

(3) The technology utilised in the process of industrialisation is taken in a more or less unadapted form from the centre, either by means of direct investment by multinational companies (MNCs) or by means of licensing of local enterprises. This technology serves to perpetuate the inequitable distribution of income and to fulfil the consumption demands of the élites.

(4) There is usually a strong foreign economic presence in the shape of MNCs, foreign aid, foreign loans, and trade with the centre. The growth of industrialisation, whether import-substituting or export-promoting, does not usually reduce the reliance on foreign financing and technology, but tends to increase it; there is no indigenous technological advance of economic significance.

(5) Foreign influence is not confined to economic spheres, but extends to cultural, educational, legal and political spheres. No direct domination is necessary; it is sufficient to assume that the peripheries inherit and propagate systems used in the centre, and that their *ruling* élites—or the *hegemonic* class, if this is different from the ruling class, or even a weaker class (like the new industrialists) which is an *alliance* with the ruling class (say the landowners) but has different economic interests from it—perceive an identity of interest, at some level, with the economic interests of the rich capitalist countries.[7] This ensures that there exists what is termed a 'symbiotic' relationship between the dominant classes in the centre and the élites, or some part of the élites, in the peripheries. I do not need to employ a naïve version of 'conspiracy' theory. On the contrary, this relationship can be made extremely complex, and subject to tension and change; it is, however, essential to admit the existence of some internal forces which make for an increasingly capitalist mode of production and for a long-term integration with the world capitalist system.

These premises cover most of the factual statements about 'dependence' which exist in the literature.[8] I shall argue below that while there is a great deal of truth in them, they cannot be taken to constitute a category of 'dependence' which is analytically sound or useful.

Thirdly, it is necessary clearly to categorise the periphery or dependent countries separately from the centre or non-dependent ones. While no one has actually made such a list, the dependence literature seems to put *all non-socialist LDCs* (and this includes such avowedly 'socialist' countries as Egypt or India) *into the former class, and all the rich, highly industrialised countries into the latter.* There is a grey zone between the two, and we have to exercise some arbitrary judgement; we may put countries like Greece, Spain or Portugal into the periphery, and those like South Africa, Australia or New Zealand into the centre. Some dependence theorists may also like to include countries like Yugoslavia into the dependent category because of its increasing integration into the West European economic ambit; this does not affect our argument one way or the other.

## III STATIC CHARACTERISTICS

We may group the static characteristics of dependence into economic and non-economic: this is to some extent an arbitrary division if one believes in political economy rather than the orthodox limitations of 'proper' economics, but not one which does any harm in this context. Let us start with the *non-economic* characteristics of dependence.

A recent Marxist paper provides a clear statement of the socio-political aspects of dependence:

> [The] political structure of foreign rule still exists today though the accents are set differently, *and it still mirrors the profound penetration of the dependent areas by the outside centres.* This asymmetrical penetration of the dominating centres took place . . . in all the essential social fields. This was done by controlling the socialisation processes in the widest sense of the word (*cultural imperialism*); by controlling the media of communication (*communication imperialism*), as well as political, military and legal systems (*political imperialism*) . . . . A history of the *political* and *social* structures of the third world can be seen as a function of this external penetration.[9]

Similar views can be found in most dependence writings, and there is little doubt that as a description of the present condition of most LDCs they contain a great deal of validity. The evolving social, cultural and political systems of the poor capitalist nations *have* been strongly influenced by those of the central countries, and, strong nationalist sentiments notwithstanding, these influences are continuing to grow stronger.

Can this, however, be taken to mark a distinct state of 'dependence'? A moment's reflection will show that it cannot. All the developed countries in the capitalist world influence *each other* in cultural, educational and political spheres, just as much as they do the LDCs. This sort of influence has never been equal: some nations have always been dominant and others subservient, and history provides an ample record of changing patterns of dominance and the struggle to counter it. In the past two decades we have witnessed the rise of US influence in cultural, military and political affairs, and a chorus of protest from Europeans about each 'dominance'; we are now seeing a resurgence of European influence, but, again, some countries in Europe wield much greater power than others. There is certainly dominance and dependence, but it applies just as much to countries *within* the 'centre' as to countries outside it.[10]

Three objections can be made to such reasoning, in support of the view that 'dominance', in some particular sense, applies only to the centre – periphery relationship. First, it may be argued that the relationships between the developed countries at the centre are more *symmetrical* than those between developed and less developed ones, in that one rich capitalist country does not systematically dominate the other and there are more chances of a reversal of roles. Secondly, the hierarchical structure of power within the centre may be seen, not as an indication of fundamental dependence, but as a *necessary condition* for the preservation of a *mutually beneficial* (for the capitalist if not for the others) system, while the hierarchy between the centre and the periphery may be seen as one necessary to preserve a *basically exploitative* system. Thirdly, the cultural, legal and political systems of the developed countries may be thought of as being in essence *similar* and the product of *indigenous* development, even though they influence each other, while the transference of these systems to the LDCs may be regarded as being more alienating and therefore more distortive (and qualitatively different).

While there is some truth in these defences of the dependence school, which may lead us to say that certain countries (say, Brazil or Indonesia) are *more* dependent than others (say, Canada), they fail to provide a firm analytical basis on which we can distinguish dependent from non-dependent countries. Some countries within the centre (Denmark, Belgium or Switzerland) may *always* be in subordinate position in non-economic spheres *vis à vis* some larger capitalist countries (Germany or France), which may themselves be lower on the hierarchy than the 'hegemonic' power (the US). The condition of mutual benefit applies mainly to the *classes* which benefit from capitalism and so can be equally relevant to LDCs. Furthermore, the point about 'more alien' is a value judgement which does not take us very far. It is ultimately impossible to draw a line between dependence and non-dependence on these grounds without falling into the basic error of *defining* underdevelopment to constitute dependence (i.e., arguing that these features constitute dependence only when found in underdeveloped countries).

Thus, while not denying any of the factual statements about external influence and conditioning, we must deny that there is something peculiar about their occurrence in LDCs which can be said to constitute dependence. It seems to be much more sensible to think in terms of a pyramidal structure of socio-political dominance (a *scale* rather than a unique condition of dependence) in the capitalist world, with the top (hegemonic) position held by the most powerful capitalist country and the bottom by the smallest and poorest ones, and a more or less continuous range occupied by various developed and less-developed countries, with relative positions changing, between the two. It is not necessary to draw an arbitrary line at some level and classify the resulting groups as 'dependent' and 'non-dependent'; indeed, such a procedure may serve to divert attention from the real and immediate socio-political pressures upon particular LDCs, which may emanate from points along the scale quite unrelated to the simple centre–periphery schema. (Consider, for instance, the emerging role of Brazil in Latin America, or of Iran in the Persian Gulf.)

Let us now consider *economic* characteristics. The most commonly mentioned characteristics of dependence are: (i) a heavy penetration of foreign capital, (ii) the use of advanced, foreign, capital-intensive technologies in a relatively small industrial sector, (iii) specialisation in exports of primary commodities or labour-intensive manufactures, (iv) élite consumption patterns determined by those of the advanced countries, (v) 'unequal exchange', in various senses, and (vi) growing inequalities in income distribution, and rising unemployment ('marginalisation'), especially in urban areas.

As with non-economic characteristics, it is extremely difficult to *define* a state of dependence on this basis. While most LDCs may exhibit some or all of these features, some economies which are classified as non-dependent also show some characteristics of dependence, while some which are accepted to be dependent do not. Let us take them in turn.

(i) It is true that foreign capital is massively in evidence in many LDCs, and even where it is not (e.g., India) it may plausibly be argued that domestic capitalists are relying more and more on foreign capital and technology to support their expansion.[11] In fact, we may accept the general proposition that *all* countries, developed or otherwise, which remain within the capitalist ambit or which, like some Eastern European countries, come to demand capitalist patterns of consumption and technology, will be increasingly dominated by 'international capital' (i.e., MNCs, perhaps from a wider range of home countries, even including some LDCs, or with more dispersed ownership than at present). The dominance of foreign capital does not, however, provide a criterion of dependence: Canada and Belgium are more 'dependent' on foreign investments than are India or Pakistan, yet they are presumably not in the category of dependent countries. The relative economic dominance of MNCs does not seem to vary on a consistent basis between dependent and non-dependent countries: Europeans complain just as much about the 'American challenge' as do nationalists in LDCs, though perhaps with much less cause.

It may be argued that LDCs have to *pay much more heavily* for foreign investments (openly in the form of declared profits or in the form of royalties or transfer pricing), and this may signify dependence. I agree that the rate of profit is probably higher in many LDCs than in developed areas, and that this indicates greater market power on the part of MNCs operating there. However, in view of the fact that particular oligopolistic firms (like Xerox) earn extremely high profits in *all* areas of their operation, and that developed countries are just as liable to transfer-pricing practices (as with the UK and the Swiss pharmaceutical firm Hoffman La Roche), it again seems unlikely that this can serve as an analytical basis for determining dependence. The same reasoning applies to the dependence argument that foreign capital always 'takes out more than it puts in'. In particular circumstances—political 'unrest' or nationalist threats—MNCs certainly do use various means to ship enormous sums out of host LDCs. This should not, however, obscure the concomitant fact that in other circumstances—right-wing regimes, good market prospects and open door policies—foreign capital may flow in very rapidly and profits may be mostly reinvested. One of the most significant facts in this context is, as a leading business journal notes, that

US firms are losing their enthusiasm for investment in Europe. Its inflation, its political instability, its growing socialisation of the economy, its need to import raw materials: all are combining to make US companies look elsewhere for growth opportunities. . . . In the future, predicts John Ross, a Bank of America vice-president, US investors will increasingly favour the relatively rich and hospitable developing countries, mainly Brazil, Nigeria, Indonesia, Iran, Venezuela and Mexico.[12]

Thus, while it is of great importance to analyse the determinants and profitability of international capital flows, it is doubtful whether a general dependence approach can get us very far.

(ii) 'Dependent' economies are, usually rightly, said to suffer from the use of excessively capital-intensive technologies taken from the developed countries. The distortions that this practice creates, in terms of exacerbating a highly uneven distribution of income, 'marginalising' large sections of the population, and perpetuating the reliance on the import of foreign know-how, may be seen to provide a measure of dependence. We shall come to income distribution below; let us here consider 'technological dependence' alone.

There is no reason to doubt that LDCs as a group 'depend' for their industrial technology on advanced countries, in the sense simply of getting most of their technology from abroad. There is also no reason to question the argument that this technology is in some ways 'inappropriate' to the production and consumption needs of LDCs,[13] and that it leads to social ills, misdirected science and education policies, and to a self-perpetating structure of technological backwardness.

Do we then have a sound means of distinguishing dependent from non-dependent economies? Unfortunately not. A number of advanced countries 'depend' heavily on foreigners for their industrial technology, and this is one field in which the notion of any sort of 'independence' is growing rapidly obsolete. The proportion of patents taken out by foreign corporations as compared to local ones is almost as high, or higher, in Canada or Belgium as, say, in India or Brazil, and the extent of technological 'dependence' in Denmark is probably just as great as, say, in Colombia or Taiwan. We can quibble about the exact 'degree' of dependence, but it is, once more, a question of the *scale* and not the absolute presence or absence of dependence. As for 'appropriateness', there are two sets of problems:

(a) On the *production* side, there are two reasons why inappropriateness cannot be used as a criterion of dependence: first, there are several industries (mainly modern, technologically advanced ones, particularly those geared to export markets), where there is practically no scope for an intermediate technology, and where the most advanced technique may also be the most appropriate; and, secondly, the sort of technology chosen, while inappropriate with reference to some social optimum, may in fact be quite 'appropriate' to the income distribution and capitalist mode of production in existence in LDCs. The criticism should then be directed at the *mode of production* as such, and not the *distortion* created in it by relying on foreign technology. In fact, many of the points made by the dependence school are in fact attacks on the desirability of *capitalism* in LDCs rather than on their dependent status, and it is the basic argument of this paper that these attacks should be correctly formulated rather than aimed at a vague notion like dependence.

(b) On the *consumption* side, similarly, it is inadmissible to define dependence by judging the appropriateness of consumption patterns with reference to some social optimum derived from a different set of production relations (and income distribution). In any case, the fact that the tastes of élites are influenced from abroad and are 'alienated' from those of the masses is neither a new phenomenon characteristic of present-day LDCs, nor is it confined to dependent countries. The tastes of élites have always been in some sense alienated from those of the common people, and have always been heavily influenced by the dominant culture of the day. The achievements of modern media and travel do mean that the phenomenon is now more widespread, but in essence it simply reflects the existence of inequality and the dominance of particular material cultures. Again, the difference between developed and less-developed countries is one of degree—with the élite in the latter being rather smaller and somewhat more 'alienated'—and not one of kind.

(iii) It is often suggested that the peripheral economies are forced by the rules of international economic relationships (dictated by the centre) to specialise according to static comparative advantage in the export of primary products or simple manufactured goods. While it is true that many LDCs do conform to this pattern, and so continue to face stagnant export earnings often coupled with disruptive short-term fluctuations in prices, recent experience casts grave doubts on the *generality* of this hypothesis. A number of dependent economies have demonstrated an ability—backed perhaps by a heavy reliance on MNCs and on measures to integrate their economies closely with the world capitalist system—to break out of the constricting circle predicted by dependency and other theorists of 'export pessimism'. Certainly manufactured exports based on a labour-cost advantage have accounted for a large part (but not all) of this growth, but this can be interpreted as conformity with dynamic rather than static comparative advantage, and does not provide support for the dependence case. The interesting problems to investigate, then, are those concerning *why some* LDCs are able to successfully integrate themselves into a dynamic capitalist trade system and others are not, and what the *welfare implications* of following such an integrative policy are. A blanket concept of dependence applied to all LDCs is quite misleading.

(iv) The best statement of the consumption-distorted pattern of dependent development is by Furtado, who argues that:

> The existence of a ruling class tied with consumption patterns similar to those in countries where the level of capital accumulation was much higher and geared to a culture focusing on technical progress became the basic factor in the evolution of the peripheral countries.[14]

This is a structuralist rather than a Marxist view of the historical process of imperialism, in spite of the fact that Furtado conducts a great deal of his discussion in terms of 'social classes', 'surplus' and 'exploitation'. The influence of dependent consumption patterns is seen to persist today, and to determine the structure of production and distribution. Thus:

> It was the process of industrialisation, aimed at the substitution of imports, that reproduced the split in the structure of the productive apparatus, characterised by the coexistence of capital-intensive industries, catering to the modernised minority, with traditional activities (rural and urban) catering to the mass of the population and to foreign markets. . . . Furthermore, taking into account that dependence is permanently reinforced through the introduction of new products whose production requires the use of more sophisticated techniques and higher levels of capital accumulation, it becomes evident that industrialisation will only proceed if the rate of exploitation increases, that is, if income distribution keeps concentrating.[15]

Thus, the relationship between the classes, and the mode of production itself, are seen to depend on the pattern of consumption. Perhaps Marxist analysts would, as some have done with Frank's approach,[16] regard this as an undue concern with exchange relationships rather than with more fundamental relationships of production (which have their own dynamic process of income concentration); but this is not our concern here. We are mainly interested to see whether the particular importance of distorted consumption patterns can be taken to define a state of dependence.

We have already noted that differences in consumption patterns between different classes have *always* marked capitalist and pre-capitalist (and even some modern socialist) economies; the question is then whether this has a more decisive influence in creating a 'split' productive structure in LDCs today than it did in the case of non-dependent economies in their early stages of industrialisation. There are two ways of judging this: one, by simply looking at the relative industrial structures, and, the other, by comparing the results of this split in terms of successful and unsuccessful growth. The latter is considered in the following section. As for the former, it is certainly true that modern industry is more highly capital-intensive, and so the difference between it and the non-capitalist sector is greater, than was the case in the early stages of the Industrial Revolution. This is, however, simply a *description* of one facet of economic backwardness—obviously, the more primitive the economy, the greater the leap required to reach modern technology—and cannot be used as an *analytical* category without falling back on tautologous definitions (i.e., underdevelopment equals dependence). Furthermore, it is not clear that the dividing line between dependent and non-dependent economies can be drawn on this basis: Italian agriculture may in parts be extremely primitive and Taiwanese agriculture may be relatively advanced; or the relative differences between the modern and traditional sectors may be much greater between different regions of the same country (say, Brazil) than between dependent and non-dependent countries. There is bound to be considerable 'disarticulation' of the productive structure of very backward economies in the process of capitalist development, and it is doubtful that the extent of such disarticulation can provide a clear means of demarcating dependence within the capitalist universe.

(v) There may be different meanings attached to 'unequal exchange'. In one particular Marxist interpretation it is the consequence of having unequal wage rates in different areas which produce the same commodity, with the same technique, at equal rates of profit.[17] In this version, one can get unequal exchange between two regions of a country or between two countries within the centre, but it may be argued that its impact is greater when applied to the centre–periphery configuration. In a static sense it is again impossible to draw a dividing line between dependent and non-dependent *economies* (rather than regions) on the basis of this criterion: not only would we find a gradation of wage rates which would have to be cut across arbitrarily to define dependence, but also the *ceteris paribus* assumptions about identical techniques and productivities would be extremely difficult to retain. In a dynamic sense, we may judge the existence of unequal exchange by its effect of perpetuating underdevelopment. This is considered below.

Unequal exchange may also be interpreted to mean that 'exporters in industrialised countries possess more monopoly power than the exporters of underdeveloped countries',[18] leading to unfavourable terms of trade for the latter. This is very much a matter for case-by-case analysis, and the oil industry shows that one cannot make general statements about dependence on this basis.[19] All theories based on inequalities of bargaining or market power need to be qualified rather carefully, and it is far from obvious that the lines drawn on this basis correspond to the line between developed and less developed countries.

(vi) The phenomenon of increasing inequalities in income and the growing 'marginalisation' of large numbers of people in many less developed countries, which we freely admit to be the case, may be taken to signify dependence. We must note, however, that empirical evidence[20] does not support the view that worsening inequality is true of *all* dependent economies; we must also remember that it typified the early stages of capitalist growth in the developed countries. There are, moreover, 'marginalised' classes in the richest of the developed capitalist countries, the United States, and it may be argued that 'centre and periphery do not coincide with developed and underdeveloped countries respectively, as in the Prebisch model. On the contrary, the dynamic core of the capitalist economy overlaps national economies, has become transnational; and the peripheries, while remaining national, also appear both in developed and underdeveloped economies'.[21]

It must be stressed that I am *not* denying the existence, nor the reprehensibleness, of growing inequality and mass unemployment in several LDCs; and I am not defending the process of capitalist growth. What I am trying to deny is the analytical usefulness of lumping different types and stages of the capitalist development process in the various less developed economies under *one* category of 'dependence'. If one wants to preserve the capitalist system but promote equality, a particular sort of analysis is called for (which may well show that at certain stages the two are incompatible), while if one wants to attack the capitalist system as such, regardless of its income distribution effects, a different sort of analysis is required. Neither is, however, furthered by dependency theories.

To sum up this section, therefore, it appears that the dependence school is trying to pick off some salient features of modern capitalism as it affects some LDCs and put them into a distinct category of 'dependence'. While it has certainly made important and substantial contributions to the understanding of particular phenomena and of individual LDCs, its attempts to form a general category do not seem to have been successful. On static criteria, it would perhaps be more sensible to proceed in terms of a 'scale' of dependence than a discrete class of dependent countries. Much of the appeal of the school would no doubt be lost if this were done, but there is little long term purpose in basing appeal on false distinctions.


## IV   DYNAMIC CHARACTERISTICS

It may be argued that while in terms of static characteristics it is analytically impossible to draw a clear line between dependent and non-dependent economies, and that in all these characteristics the difference is a matter of degree rather than of kind, in the dynamic terms of their effects on growth the *cumulative result may be distinctive*. We can, therefore, look for distinguishing characteristics of a dependent *process* of growth. Unfortunately, although all dependence theorists agree that economic growth in the less developed countries is in various ways conditioned by external forces reacting on internal structures, there seems to be considerable difference of opinion on what exactly the dynamics of dependence are. We may, at the risk of some over-simplification, distinguish between analyses of the *possibility* of dependent growth and of the *pattern* of dependent growth.

POSSIBILITY OF GROWTH

One of the main points of agreement between a number of dependence theorists and neo-Marxist writers on development, and also one of the major points of departure from classical Marxist writings on impe-rialism, is the contention that dependence blocks or inhibits the economic growth of the capitalist developing countries. While Marx and Engels believed that in the final stages of capitalism the 'bourgeois mode of production' would spread to the backward nations, and Lenin at times, and Luxemburg explicitly, argued that capitalism would spread industrialisation to the LDCs, much of neo-Marxist theorising, starting from Baran and most forcefully propagated by Frank, has been concerned to show that the historical process of capitalist growth is not repeatable and that dependency is incompatible with development.[22]

The dependence view of growth possibilities may be subdivided into three categories: (i) the strong position (André Gunder Frank) that dependence leads to *immiserisation*; (ii) the medium position (early Furtado, Sunkel and dos Santos) that it runs into market constriction and *stagnation*; and (iii) the mild position (Cardoso) that some growth is possible but always in a *subservient* or '*marginalised*' role.

(i) *Immiserisation.* The dynamics of dependence are seen here to be a continuation of the forms of 'primitive' exploitation which marked the earlier stages of imperialism; they lead, in Frank's famous and oft-criticised phrase, to the 'development of underdevelopment'. It is not necessary for us to go into the complex reasoning and historical precedent which support this argument;[23] if we can simply show that there is no *general* case to be made that all dependent economies are growing poorer, then we have established our point about the in-adequacy of the dependency concept. And we do not have to look very far. A glance at any set of national income statistics will show that a number of dependent countries, in Latin America and elsewhere, *have* produced impressive and sustained performances in terms of real *per capita* incomes in the recent past, and there is little reason to believe that this is going to come to a sudden stop.

The immiserisation case may, however, be put slightly differently: dependence may be seen to lead to the growing poverty of the *mass* of the population. As we have noted with reference to inequality and marginalisation, this is certainly the case with a large number of LDCs, but, as before, we cannot accept it as a general and universal criterion of dependency. Not only does it ignore the evidence of some dependent countries which have raised the living standards of their poorest sections, as well as of marginalisation in some non-dependent econ-omies, it also defines as dependence something which may be an *inevitable concomitant of certain forms or stages of capitalist growth, regardless of whether or not it was externally conditioned.* If this is admitted, then there remains very little in the phenomenon of de-pendence which provides strong grounds for believing that early capitalist growth is now unrepeatable.

(ii) *Market constriction.* The same criticisms may be made of the school which argues that dependent, import-substitution industrialisation inevitably runs into bottlenecks created by growing income inequality and a concentration on the domestic market. While import substitution as an exclusive strategy may obviously face this problem, there is nothing in dependent status which necessitates such an exclusive concentration on domestic demand. Developing countries can, and, as Sunkel in his later writings and Furtado argue, do turn to international capitalist markets for their continued expansion, and in this sort of 'dependence' they are no different from any capitalist country, rich or poor, which has its fortunes tied to the development of the whole system. Some dependent economies can manage the integration better than others, and the reasons for this are a major area for political-economic investigation, but there is no common dynamic element in their experience which we can put down to dependence (as distinct simply from their underdevelopment).

(iii) *Subservience*. It is difficult to interpret the empirical content of the 'marginalised' role that dependent but growing economies are assigned. One meaning may be 'unequal exchange' (in the second sense, see above), in that LDCs pay more for their trade and foreign investments than developed countries do and so are able to grow less fast than otherwise. Another may be that the surplus available for productive investment is smaller than otherwise because of the very existence of foreign investments and of wasteful forms of élite consumption. A third may be that dependent economies are receiving less investment and trade over time, and that their exports are doomed to stagnation. A fourth may be that their technological dependence renders them liable to monopolistic practices and to increasingly inappropriate forms of industrialisation. In so far as these are merely amalgams of arguments dealt with in the previous section, we need not repeat them here. We may merely reiterate that while all, or some, of these may well be true of some dependent countries, they are not true of all, and more important, they may be equally true of a number of non-dependent countries. In so far as they are meant to suggest that dependent economies are failing over time to improve their position in the international capitalist framework, we can only point to ample evidence to the contrary for the few LDCs that are succeeding.[24]

PATTERN OF GROWTH

Some dependence theorists, like Sunkel, do not make explicit prognostications about the possibility of dependent growth, but concern themselves with the form that it takes. Thus, they point to several undesirable consequences, which we have already discussed, such as inequality, wasteful consumption, lack of domestic technological innovation, subjection to international fluctuations, and the like, as the distinctive features of the process of dependent development. In showing this concern, they differ from the orthodox Marxist analysts of development who do not make value judgements about the conditions accompanying capitalist accumulation and reproduction, but are interested primarily in the viability of the capitalist system in developing countries (though the line between normative and positive analysis is increasingly difficult to draw in writings in this area).

The attention drawn to the undesirable concomitants of dependent growth has been one of the most valuable contributions of the dependence school, particularly since it has shown that many of these features are *direct effects* of the sort of development undertaken and not simply accidental aberrations. This being granted, however, we are forced to argue that these are features of *capitalist* growth in general—in certain stages and in certain circumstances—and are not confined to the present condition of the less developed countries. Certainly there are 'costs' associated with capitalist forms of industrialisation, and it is arguable that there are other forms which are more humane and also more efficient; certainly there are some cases in which capitalist growth can work much more successfully than in others; and certainly this sort of growth has certain constraints and faces immense conditioning pressures from other capitalist economies. But if one is trying to analyse these questions, the concept of dependence, *as an analytical category*, is not only unhelpful but misleading. The reasons for this have all been given above and need not be discussed again.

## V CONCLUSIONS

We conclude, therefore, that the concept of dependence as applied to less-developed countries is impossible to define and cannot be shown to be causally related to a continuance of underdevelopment. It is usually given an *arbitrarily selective definition which picks certain features of a much broader phenomenon of international capitalist development*, and its selectivity only serves to misdirect analysis and research in this area. The desire to promote attacks on the capitalist mode of production causes some dependence and neo-Marxist analysts to concentrate on the appealing but mistaken argument that it can never lead to a repetition of the experience of the developed capitalist countries, when in fact they should be drawing attention to the intrinsic costs of the capitalist system as such, and to its continuously evolving dynamics. The fact that it leads to uneven development and often to great suffering on the part of the great masses of the population in LDCs should not obscure the fact that it has so far proved to be a viable system *on its own terms*. This raises two sorts of implications for thinkers of the dependency school.

First, for those who, like Warren, believe that capitalist industrialisation must be undergone and the full productive powers of society realised *before* a move is made towards socialism, research and policy recommendations should be concentrated on the conditions within LDCs which prevent a full integration with the capitalist system.

Secondly, for those who believe that a completely different path is feasible for achieving 'true' development, attention should not focus on how the capitalist system is not working in LDCs but on what needs to be done even if it *is* working in terms of breaking out of the international capitalist mould. To underplay the effectiveness of the capitalist system is surely to underestimate its strength and to attack it on its least vulnerable points.

Our argument, finally, must not be taken to denigrate the real contributions and the intellectual sophistication of the dependency theorists. There are many indications that the earlier patterns of dependency analysis are being dropped, to be replaced by more appropriate and rigorous political–economic research.[25] This should not, however, hold us back from questioning the older concepts which are still gaining widespread acceptance in the literature. The 'dependence' model must be severely qualified if it is to remain in use in the study of underdeveloped countries.

NOTES

1. I would like to thank Massimo di Matteo, Ruman Faruqi, Keith Griffin, Deepak Nayyar, Peter O'Brien, Samir Radwan and Paul Streeten for their interest and comments.

2. Mainly, Frank (1967) and (1969), Sunkel (1969–70) and (1973), Furtado (1970) and dos Santos (1970). For a brief review of the literature see O'Brien (1975), and for an exposition of 'dependence'-type theories, but using the approach of the 'structuralists', see Griffin (1969) and Furtado (1964).

3. See Barratt Brown (1974) for a recent survey of the classical and modern theories, and Booth (1975) and O'Brien (1975) for discussions of the antecedents of Latin American *dependencia* theories.

4. Such as Baran (1957), Baran and Sweezy (1966), Magdoff (1969) and various articles appearing in *Monthly Review*. Also see Amin (1974), Foster-Carter (1974), Laclau (1971), Sutcliffe (1972) and Warren (1973) for discussion and critique of modern dependence-type Marxist theories.

5. Sutcliffe (1972, p. 172) divides Marxist views on imperialism into three stages: (1) Marx and Engels on imperialism as plunder and use of peripheral markets; (2) Lenin and others on growth of monopoly and extraction of raw materials from the peripheries; and (3) recent analyses of the 'more complex, post-colonial dependency' of the periphery. It is in this last sense that we use the term 'dependence'.

6. See, for instance, Barrat Brown (1974) for a general introduction and survey, Frank (1967) and (1969), and Furtado (1970) on Latin America, and a particularly stimulating article by Bagchi (1972) on India.

7. On the various possible configurations of power within the capitalist state, see the excellent theoretical analysis by Poulantzas (1972), especially ch.

III, pt 4; for an application of Marxist theories of the state, with special reference to the role of MNCs, to Pakistan and Bangladesh see Alavi (1972).

8. While most dependence theorists would accept these premises, some Marxists like Warren (1973) may not agree with some of them, particularly the ones concerning continued reliance on foreign technology and conflict/alliance between the local bourgeoisie and foreign interests.

9. Senghaas (1974, pp. 162–3). Emphasis in the original text. Also see Sunkel (1969–70) for a brief analysis of the historical evolution of cultural dependence in Latin America, and Amin (1974) for a more extended general discussion.

10. While this aspect of international capitalism is relatively neglected by dependence economists, Marxists working on developed countries have been greatly concerned with it. See, for instance, Mandel (1970), Poulantzas (1974) and Rowthorn (1971), for different interpretations of recent changes in the distribution of power in the developed capitalist world.

11. See Patnaik (1972) on the Indian case.

12. Howe (1975, p. 47). This is supported by figures given in the *IMF Survey*, 26 May 1975 (p. 152), which show that foreign manufacturing affiliates of US MNCs plan to expand their investments by only 10 per cent in developed countries, and by 39 per cent in developing countries. Most of this increase is directed at Brazil, though the rate of growth (from a much lower level) is considerably higher in the Middle East.

13. See Stewart (1974).

14. Furtado (1973, pp. 3–4).

15. Ibid., pp. 10–11.

16. Laclau (1971). For a discussion, see Booth (1975).

17. See Emmanuel (1972) and Kay (1975). The same result can, of course, be derived from a non-Marxist classical (e.g., a Sraffa-type) framework.

18. Sutcliffe (1972, p. 188).

19. Vernon (1975) criticises dependence theories on this ground.

20. Chenery *et al.* (1974).

21. Sunkel (1974, p. 2). Needless to say, this seems to be a modification of Sunkel's earlier analysis of dependence.

22. See Barrat Brown (1974) and Booth (1975). Szymanski (1974) provides a useful comparison and empirical testing of the classical and modern theories, while Warren (1973) provides a stimulating antidote to the modern view.

23. See the various works by Frank and critiques by Laclau (1971) Barrat Brown (1974) and Booth (1975).

24. See Warren (1973).

25. Booth (1975) mentions an unpublished paper by Frank where he admits the need to modify the earlier dependence model.

REFERENCES

Alavi, H. (1972), 'The State in Post-colonial Societies: Pakistan and Bangladesh', *New Left Review* (July–August 1972) pp. 59–82.
Amin, S. (1974), *Accumulation on a World Scale* (New York: Monthly Review Press, 1974).

Bagchi, A. K. (1972), 'Some International Foundations of Capitalist Growth and Underdevelopment', *Economic and Political Weekly* (August 1972) pp. 1559–70.

Baran, P. A. (1957), *The Political Economy of Growth* (New York: Monthly Review Press, 1957).

Baran, P. A., and Sweezy, P. (1966), *Monopoly Capital* (New York: Monthly Review Press, 1966).

Barrat Brown, M. (1974), *The Economics of Imperialism* (Harmondsworth: Penguin, 1974).

Booth, D. (1975), 'André Gunder Frank: an Introduction and Appreciation', in I. Oxaal *et al* (eds), *Beyond the Sociology of Development* (London: Routledge & Kegan Paul, 1957).

Cardoso, F. H. (1972), 'Dependency and Development in Latin America', *New Left Review* (July–August 1972) pp. 83–95.

Chenery, H. B. *et al.* (1974), *Redistribution with Growth* (London: Oxford University Press, 1974).

dos Santos, T. (1970), 'The Structure of Dependence', *American Economic Review, Papers & Proceedings*, pp. 231–6.

Emmanuel, A. (1972), *Unequal Exchange* (London: New Left Books, 1972).

Foster-Carter, A. (1974), 'Neo-Marxist Approaches to Development and Underdevelopment', in E. de Kadt and G. Williams (eds), *Sociology and Development* (London: Tavistock Publications, 1974).

Frank, A. G. (1967), *Capitalism and Underdevelopment in Latin America* (New York: Monthly Review Press, 1967).

Frank, A. G. (1969), *Latin America: Underdevelopment or Revolution* (New York: Monthly Review Press, 1969).

Frank, A. G. (1972), *Lumpenbourgeoisie and Lumpendevelopment* (New York: Monthly Review Press, 1972).

Furtado, C. (1964), *Development and Underdevelopment* (Berkeley: University of California Press, 1964).

Furtado, C. (1970), *Economie Development of Latin America* (London: Cambridge University Press, 1970).

Furtado, C. (1973), 'Underdevelopment and Dependence: the Fundamental Connections', paper presented to the Faculty Seminar on Latin American Studies, Cambridge University, November 22 (mimeo).

Griffin, K. B. (1969), *Underdevelopment in Spanish America* (London: Allen & Unwin, 1969).

Howe, R. (1975), 'US Investment in Europe: the Glow Wears Off', *Vision* (January 1975) pp. 47–9.

Kay, G. (1975), *Development and Underdevelopment: A Marxist Analysis* (London: Macmillan, 1975).

Laclau, E. (1971), 'Feudalism and Capitalism in Latin America', *New Left Review* (May–June, 1971).

Magdoff, H. (1969), *The Age of Imperialism* (New York: Monthly Review Press, 1969).

Mandel, E. (1970), *Europe vs. America: Contradictions of Capitalism* (London: New Left Books, 1970).

O'Brien, P. (1975), 'A Critique of Latin American Theories of Dependency', in

I. Oxaal *et al* (ed), *Beyond the Sociology of Development* (London: Routledge & Kegan Paul, 1975).

Patnaik, P. (1972), 'Imperialism and Growth of Indian Capitalism', in R. Owen and B. Sutcliffe (eds), *Studies in the Theory of Imperialism* (London: Longman, 1972).

Poulantzas, N. (1972), *Political Power and Social Classes* (London: New Left Books, 1972).

Poulantzas, N. (1974), 'Internationalisation of Capitalist Relations and the Nation State', *Economy and Society* (May 1974) pp. 145–79.

Rowthorn, R. (1971), 'Imperialism in the Seventies—Unity or Rivalry?', *New Left Review* (September 1971) pp. 31–54.

Senghaas, D. (1974), 'Peace Research and the Third World', *Bulletin of Peace Proposals* (1974) pp. 158–72.

Stewart, F. (1974), 'Technology and Employment in LDCs', *World Development* (March 1974) pp. 17–46.

Sunkel, O. (1969–70), 'National Development Policy and External Dependence in Latin America', *Journal of Development Studies* (1969–70) pp. 23–48.

Sunkel, O. (1973), 'Transnational Capital and National Disintegration in Latin America', *Social and Economic Studies* (March 1973) pp. 132–76.

Sunkel, O. (1974), 'External Economic Relations and the ' Process of Development: suggestions for an alternative analytical framework', IDS Discussion Paper No. 51 (mimeo).

Sutcliffe, B. (1972), 'Imperialism and Industrialisation in the Third World', in R. Owen and B. Sutcliffe (eds), *Studies in the Theory of Imperialism* (London: Longman, 1972).

Szymanski, A. (1974), 'Marxist Theory and International Capital Flows', *Review of Radical Political Economics* (Fall 1974) pp. 20–40.

Vernon, R. (1975), 'Multinational Enterprises in Developing Countries: issues in dependency and interdependence', in D. E. Apter and L. Goodman (eds), *The Multinational Corporation as an Instrument of Development—Political Considerations* (New Haven: Yale University Press, 1975).

Warren, B. (1973), 'Imperialism and Capitalist Industrialization', *New Left Review* (September–October 1973) pp. 3–44.

# 2 Welfare Economics and Development Problems[1]

## I INTRODUCTION

The relevance of theoretical welfare economics to the general field of 'development economics' has never been very clear. With recent extensions of welfare theory into highly abstract and formal models of interdependent utility, social choice, public goods and the like, moreover, the relationship between it and the *ad hoc* and loosely defined art of analysing the problems of LDCs has begun to seem even more tenuous. It may, indeed, appear that there is very little overlap between the two: with a few exceptions, like parts of trade theory or social cost-benefit analysis, there is practically no aspect of development economics which draws upon the existing body of welfare theory.

Appearances can, however, be misleading. The ordinary practice of development economics, relying as it does on large doses of casual empiricism, fairly 'unrigorous' theorising and an eclectic approach to related social sciences, can certainly dispense with the bulk of 'high' welfare theory. However, the fundamental concepts of welfare economics, defined broadly, provide, not only the tools with which any branch of applied economics and economic policy must work, but also the meaning of the language used, the value judgements adhered to, the questions asked, and the methods used for interpreting the answers found. In short, welfare economics furnishes the *paradigm* within which conventional development economics operates.

Given the overwhelming dominance of the neo-classical (especially the Paretian) school in the development of welfare theory, the paradigm used by the majority of development economists has embodied the ideological premises, value judgements and factual assumptions of this particular school.[2] There has in recent years been increasing criticism of and concern with the validity and ethical acceptability of many of these premises and assumptions. In some cases, as with the growing school of 'radicals', this has led to an explicit rejection of the conventional

24

paradigm. In others, the paradigm has been retained, but with more or less substantial modification of its elements. This has led to great internal stresses, as some exceptions to its rules have turned out to be more weighty than the rules themselves, and as the search for morally acceptably solutions to the problems of LDCs has come up against insuperable barriers posed by the paradigm itself.

This paper seeks to clarify some of these problems and contradictions faced by development economics founded on the neo-classical paradigm (henceforth referred to for brevity as the 'conventional' school). No solutions are proposed here; indeed, it is very doubtful whether solutions are possible within the conventional framework. Nor are alternative approaches discussed directly. My purpose here is simply to show how some of the important issues confronting development economics today cannot be dealt with by the tools of conventional welfare economics because the answers conflict with its basic ('domain') assumptions.

In section II I shall present a schematic outline of the structure underlying conventional welfare economics, pointing out its various premises and assumptions but not discussing its actual mechanics or conclusions. In section III I shall illustrate some problems arising from the application of this structure to development issues. I shall concentrate on a few aspects which have concerned me in my work, but the nature of the problem is quite general. In section IV I shall present my conclusions.

## II  STRUCTURE OF THE NEO-CLASSICAL WELFARE PARADIGM

It may be debated whether there is a 'paradigm' of neo-classical welfare economics in the sense in which Kuhn applies the concept of paradigms to scientific research. It is, in fact, uncertain if the social sciences in general have paradigms at all, or if they operate in a 'pre-paradigm' situation.[3] Be that as it may, it is certainly the case that they work with a certain 'vision' of society, and with certain ethical and factual assumptions of how people behave, or ought to behave, which taken together constitute a structure that is used, and is necessary, for analysis and research. Neo-classical economics does use a 'paradigm' in this sense, as indeed does any coherent school of thought in social science; just how valid and useful a paradigm it is has become a matter of increasing controversy in recent years, but the existence of a paradigm in some sense is hardly in doubt.

It is common in economics to draw a sharp distinction between its positive and normative branches, and to treat the former as more 'neutral', 'objective' and 'scientific' than the latter. If this is simply taken to mean a difference of *degree*, in that positive economics makes fewer value judgements or has less direct relevance to policy, then it is probably quite true. Or if it is meant to apply to certain parts of positive economics which deal solely with technical features of production, and do not depend on a particularly neo-classical paradigm (like operations research or input–output analysis), it is certainly the case that such economics is more 'objective' in some sense than welfare economics. The bulk of positive economics is not, however, an undertaking of this sort. It purports to explain the functioning of actual economies, and necessarily has a 'vision' of them which involves accepting certain premises, values and legitimate fields of enquiry.[4] To this extent, the positive and normative aspects of economics share common foundations, however abstract the form in which positive analysis is posed. This is not a criticism of the objectivity or validity of any particular school of economics: all economics, and all social sciences in general, must function in some such framework, and *cannot* be 'pure' in the sense of operating outside a particular vision. Development economics, in particular, has never had any of the pretensions to 'purity' that high economic theory has had. Being a primarily applied and policy-orientated subject, it has intermingled 'ought' and 'is' rather freely, without devoting too much thought to the premises on which its analyses and precriptions were based.

As far as welfare economics is concerned, the earlier efforts to show it to be value-free and non-ideological seem to have been generally abandoned,[5] and these fundamental issues, with a few exceptions,[6] having been shelved, recent developments have tended to take the existence of a silent consensus as implicit proof of the validity of the conventional paradigm. This is unfortunate, since 'consensus does not denote neutrality in welfare economics matters', and

the practitioners of the Paretian dogma are now so confident in their approach, so enraptured by the formal elegance and mathematical rigour of their exercises and so contemptuous of their less highly formalised and less elegant competitors that they incline increasingly to the *passing off of their normative policy judgements as positive contributions.* The policy-makers are expected, by those who perpetrate this misdemeanour, to regard the mechanics of the welfare exercise with the awe accorded by the early Church of Rome to the contents of a Papal Bull, though, perhaps thankfully, in practice they are justifiably suspicious of *economic analysis that appears to offer clear-out solutions to complex politico-economic problems.*[7]

In describing the structure of the conventional welfare economics (and here I include the liberal as well as the Paretian schools), it will be useful to distinguish between three elements which constitute its basis. These may be termed the 'ideological base', the 'individualistic premises' and the 'state-power premises'. The *ideological base* is conceived here quite narrowly, not as comprising all value or moral judgements or the whole paradigm of neo-classical economics, but as *that premise which is essential to make any system of welfare economics compatible with a capitalist mode of production.* For the sake of simplifying the exposition, I shall contrast two idealised modes of production, capitalist and socialist, and accord to them alternative ideologies regarding the socio-economic organisation of society. Since conventional welfare economics has evolved largely in a capitalist framework—and the fact that socialist economists have contributed to certain aspects of the development of welfare theory, especially as regards planning methods, does not affect the validity of this statement[8]—it has, by a Schumpeterian 'pre-analytic cognitive act', attributed certain characteristics to a capitalist society which can enable it to conceptualise and legitimise its 'welfare'. Being ideological in this sense, this premise cannot hold for a socialist conception of welfare. Being 'vision', it can neither be proved nor disproved.

The ideological base may be combined with a number of different specifications of welfare within capitalist societies. The *individualistic* form is only one, though it is practically the only one in use. It contains a mixture of normative (or ethical) and factual assumptions, the former, like 'vision', being susceptible neither of proof nor disproof, the latter being in principle open to empirical validation, but often defined in a circular manner, and sometimes embodying concealed normative assumptions. The same is true of the *state-power* premise, which embodies a particular conception of the role of the state in a capitalist society (and is based on the same 'vision' as the basic economic approach). Taken together, this combination of ideology, value judgements and factual assumptions comprises the paradigm in which welfare economics functions.

Before discussing these elements of the paradigm, it may be worth noting that their function is not only a positive one of providing a structure for grouping facts and concepts together in a meaningful manner and providing hypotheses for testing, but also a persuasive and negative one. The persuasive function obviously arises from the legitimising vision of capitalist society and from the use of ethical premises to persuade people what is 'good' in economic terms and what 'ought' to be done. The negative function is that of drawing lines of demarcation between the proper subject of economics and that of other related fields such as ethics, philosophy, sociology, politics, history and so on. It is necessary to draw such lines in order to advance a subject at all, but the precise way in which this is done strongly affects its content, formulation and findings. I shall remark on this below; let us now consider the three elements.

A  THE IDEOLOGICAL BASE

The fundamental assumption about capitalist society which enables conventional welfare economics to talk in terms of the 'welfare of society' is that of *fundamental harmony of interest between all members of such a society*. It is only this assumption which can enable one to conceptualize an unambiguous definition of the welfare of society *as a whole*, and to reconcile this with the individual welfares of all the persons in it. If there were a fundamental disharmony of interest, it would become nonsensical to speak of the welfare of society *as a whole*, and welfare would *have necessarily to be defined in terms of one group or the other*. In more specific terms, this assumption denies the existence of disharmony between *social classes*, based on the division between those who, in capitalist society, own the means of production and those who do not.[9]

For welfare economics this premise opens the way to easy transitions from social to individual welfare and vice versa. Thus, while a comparison and summation of individual welfares may prove very difficult – except in very special cases (e.g. Paretian conditions for unambiguous rises in 'welfare'), or by imposing some particular ordering rule (e.g. a hierarchy of 'liberal' values as proposed by Rowley and Peacock), or a 'social' welfare function[10] – it is always implicitly accepted that there *is* such a thing as social welfare made up of basically harmonious individual welfares. For positive economics, the harmony premise dispenses with the need for any sort of class analysis (it simply assumes away, rather than disproves, any possibility of class 'exploitation'), and, backed by the formidable *apparat* of logical positivism,[11] enables the analysis of society to proceed in terms which we know as neo-classical economics.

What sort of 'harmony' is required of the ideological base? Clearly, 'disharmony' in the sense of competition between firms or individuals is not ruled out; on the contrary, it is the very essence of the neo-classical system. Nor is 'disharmony' arising from imperfect competition or in the minor sense of personal envy, hate or other forms of 'interdependence' in individual utility functions, ruled out.[12] These do not affect the presumption of the fundamental harmony of the capitalist mode of production and distribution, since they do not call into question the legitimacy of the socio-economic structure or of any of the categories of payments to the factors of production.

A *fundamental* disharmony can arise only if this legitimacy is challenged. The best-known challenges to the neo-classical theory of distribution have come from the neo-Ricardians and from the Marxists,[13] the approaches of both schools being essentially antithetical to the economic theories of the neo-classicists. In terms of welfare economics, however, there is an essential conceptual distinction to be drawn between these two schools. This distinction tends to be forgotten because of the fact (much dwelt on by some neo-classicals, but which is, as John Vaizey notes, only 'contingent'[14]) that many neo-Ricardians happen to be socialist, and because of the ease with which some of their tools can be adapted for use for Marxist analysis.[15] Both approaches reject the neo-classical theory of distribution (the determination of profit in terms of the productivity of capital and its legitimacy as a reward for waiting), and both accept the role of the 'class struggle' and socio-political forces in deciding the distribution of income. However, while the neo-Ricardian approach accepts a particular sort of disharmony in distribution, it does not postulate a fundamental disharmony in *production* relations, and it does not question the legitimacy of the capitalist system as such. In other words, an economist could easily accept that the distribution of income is determined by a bargaining process unrelated to marginal productivity, and at the same time believe that the capitalist mode of production is essentially harmonious and legitimate. Indeed, many classical economists (including Ricardo) accepted this view of distribution and based their economic theories on (a potentially revolutionary) labour theory of value, but also believed in the sanctity of private property and the virtues of free enterprise—a combination of beliefs which got them into various contradictions.[16] It is, therefore, possible to *conceive* of a welfare theory in a capitalist system which follows from neo-Ricardian premises, and the fact that all 'class struggle' type of analyses have been taken to be Marxist should not obscure this.

A fundamental disharmony of interest *intrinsic to the capitalist mode of production* can only arise on Marxist assumptions of exploitation and oppression of one class by another.[17] Given such disharmony, it becomes nonsensical to speak of the welfare of a capitalist society *as a whole* (except perhaps in the convoluted sense of its approach to socialism, i.e., the closer the society to the destruction of the capitalist mode of production, probably by revolution, the greater its welfare). This approach need not deny the historical role of the capitalist class as the agent of accumulation, only that the society itself has a basic harmony of interests. As soon as one posits an alternative (socialist) society where accumulation can also proceed, but under non-exploitative circumstances, the first system can no longer be legitimised.

The harmony-of-interest assumption is basic to any welfare economics in the conventional sense. The lines that it draws are not so much between economics and other social sciences but *within* each of these sciences. It is not, for instance, the case that if we turn to sociology we would find a full discussion of the existence or absence of class harmony; even in sociology, we would find that there would be different paradigms with different basic 'visions' of conflict in society.[18] There is no empirical method for choosing scientifically between the visions; the *same* social reality can be examined through either.

## B  INDIVIDUALISM

There is, as we noted above, a mixture of normative and factual assumptions contained in the 'individualistic premise'. The straight normative one is that it is *individual utility* (or preference, or whatever suitable term is chosen) which should be maximised. This is unexceptionable as it stands, and may be used as an ethical premise in capitalist or socialist societies. Before it is used in a capitalist society, however, it is obvious that the ideological premise must be accepted. Only if there is a harmony of interest among all members of society, and social classes are not the relevant agents for economic analysis, can one proceed to think of maximising individual welfares (or, if one is a liberal, of maximising individual liberties) as the sole condition for maximising social welfare.

The factual assumptions concerning the individual are that he is the *best judge* of his own welfare (though this could also be put normatively, that he should be left free to decide his own welfare), that he acts (or

should act) to *maximise it*, and that the *determinants* of his welfare—
preferences as regards consumption, saving, work and leisure—*are given*
(which again can be put normatively that (a) these preferences should
not be interfered with, and (b) the scope of economics should not extend
beyond given preferences to see how they are formed). There are several
criticisms of these positive–normative assumptions about the individual: his preferences may not be revealed in his behaviour, they may be
interdependent with others' preferences or 'unconnected',[19] based on
imperfect knowledge, perhaps harmful to himself or others, and they
may be conditioned by various market, social and other forces. Some of
these criticisms are more damaging than others, but the one I want to
concentrate on is the last one, which concerns the conditioning and
formation of preferences.

It is hardly open to doubt that preferences are not only affected by
commercial efforts in a narrow sense but are in general moulded by the
individual's social, cultural, educational, political and religious *milieu*,[20]
much of which is an *intrinsic part of the economic structure* of capitalism
(being based on the structure of class and income distribution). The
refusal of conventional welfare economists to go into these factors,[21] by
drawing a strong line between the 'proper' scope of economic enquiry
and that of psychology, sociology, politics or history, and taking
preferences as autonomous and given, reveals not so much an amazing
naïvity about human beings on their part as an *implicit approval of the
system of preference formation in capitalist societies*. This is why the
attacks of critics such as Gintis have so little cutting edge. Though they
may accept that minor distortions are caused, say, by promotional
activities in 'imperfect' markets, conventional welfare economists (and
here I would include institutionalists like Galbraith) *cannot* go on to
question the inherent features of capitalist society (which radical critics
do) that produce the 'capitalist man': to do so would be to question the
system itself. The implicit argument of these economists seems to be that
*every* society imposes its own basic conditioning, and a capitalist system
produces better (more 'liberal', 'free', etc.) people *because* it is (ideologi-
cally) a better system. We are then back to the 'vision', and beyond the
reach of argument.

C STATE POWER

The role of the state is fundamental to welfare economics, not just
because many 'welfare' services have to be provided publicly but
because, aiming at policy formulation, welfare economists must address

their work directly to the state. There must, therefore, be a theory of the state in a capitalist society explicitly or implicitly contained in welfare theory. This theory is, in fact, mostly implicit and fairly simple, with the usual mixture of positive and normative elements. The state is *neutral* between different groups in society (or should be); *it knows what the national interest is* and *tries to achieve it* (or should do); and it has *a harmony of interest with other states* in economic terms (which is simply the international extension of the domestic harmony-of-interest premise).

It is clear that the neutrality and national-interest attributes of the state must be based upon the ideological assumption. If there is no basic conflict of interest in society, and there are no classes in the Marxist sense, the economic structure cannot influence the distribution and exercise of political power, and the government must (despite occasional aberrations) ˙remain the repository of the national interest.[22] This idealised picture of political power enables economists to draw another line between economics and related social sciences, and to proceed to recommend 'sound' economic policies on political matters (like income distribution) and to analyse such matters on 'purely economic' grounds.[23] It provides the basis for the kind of pure economics which has taken precedence over political economy, and accounts for some of the grossest mistakes perpetrated by modern economics.

Needless to say, an alternative view of state power, as an expression of the *economic* structure of class relations,[24] throws the whole purpose of welfare economics, as normally understood, totally out of gear. It erases the line drawn between economics and politics; it makes the traditional concept of 'social welfare' meaningless; it makes the welfare evaluation of public policies a very different matter from the normal cost-benefit procedure based on an ideal competitive model; and it renders the role of the economist as a 'policy maker in the social interest' much more limited, if not totally absurd. This is, of course, a strong interpretation of the alternative view of the state. Even a mild interpretation, however, which admits of a positive and continuous overlap of the economic and political élites and of some possibilities for conflict of interest, casts grave doubt on the normal forms of analysis and prescription in economics.

These three elements of the conventional paradigm interact with and reinforce each other, so that it is practically impossible to seriously criticise one without attacking the whole structure: such is the nature of paradigms that they are generally immune to disproof and marginal changes, and must be accepted or superseded *in toto*. However, even an acceptance of the paradigm does not, at least in the social sciences, exclude the possibility of internal conflict and stress, and in the next section I hope to show, with reference to a few selected issues, how these have arisen in the application of the paradigm to the developing countries.

The structure of the paradigm outlined above itself provides the bulk of the material needed to 'prove' the main neo-classical theorems in the normative and positive branches of economics. It only needs the addition of some specific assumptions, about the shape of preference schedules, cost curves, technology, competition and information, in order to derive conditions for optimality, equilibrium, and so on, at several levels of rigour and sophistication. There are, certainly, major gaps—especially with respect to the welfare aspects of income distribution (of which, more below)—but the general effect of the application of the paradigm is (regardless of the unreality of many of its assumptions) to create a presumption in favour of free competition, *laissez faire*, political conservatism and the promotion of capitalistic enterprise. Of course, exceptions are sometimes admitted to this presumption: agricultural land reform may, for instance, be strongly advocated (with appropriate caveats about effects on efficiency) in certain circumstances; this sort of 'radicalism' does not, however, detract from the general ethos in favour of untrammelled private enterprise in the industrial and commercial sectors of the economy. In any case, it should be remembered that an attack on the land-owning oligarchy is often a part of the ideological equipment of a rising industrial bourgeoisie, especially when that oligarchy turns out to be anti-industry and strongly entrenched in power.

## III THE PARADIGM AND SOME WELFARE ISSUES IN LDCs

The issues concerning the welfare of LDCs which we shall discuss here concern (1) the use of market prices in assessing welfare, (2) some applications of the concept of 'efficiency', and (3) some aspects of international economics. The discussion is not intended to be comprehensive but merely to illustrate how much of the recent (and *not* explicitly 'radical') writing in development economics, in seeking to find more satisfactory answers to development problems than the early orthodoxy, but remaining within the conventional paradigm, finds itself using conceptual tools which are inadequate (and, at times, is frustrated by the limits of the paradigm from evolving more adequate tools), or else reaches conclusions which appear acceptable but which cast doubt on the validity of the paradigm itself.

Until fairly recently, the only measure used by most economists to measure 'development' (and so economic welfare) in LDCs was the value of *per capita* GNP at market prices. (This argument also applies to measuring 'social' costs and benefits generally). It should be clear that, in the sort of conceptual framework outlined above, with universal harmony and the individual pursuit of welfare, values expressed at market prices are the *only possible measure* of economic welfare. There are, however, two major qualifications admitted by conventional economics. First, income distribution may not be optimal with reference to some ideal standard; and, second, actual prices may be distorted by market 'imperfections' and, more importantly, by government interventions in the market mechanism.[25]

The admission of these problems has led, especially (in the field of 'development economics') in the last few years, to important attempts by neo-classical economists to adjust for price 'distortions' or 'socially undesirable' income distributions, while keeping intact the basic yardstick of the conventional paradigm. Let us consider these efforts in turn.

*Price distortions.* In the neo-classical system, welfare is maximised (given the income distribution) in a régime of free competition with perfect information and with no monopoly or monopsony elements in the market and no distortionary taxes or subsidies imposed by the government. In the messy real-life world of LDCs, where distortions of all sorts exist, from large elements of monopoly power and highly imperfect information to pervasive government interventions, the neo-classical solution has been to use a simulated model of free market prices as the measure of welfare, the method most commonly used being to employ 'shadow prices' given by prices reigning in the world market.[26]

There is an initial objection, a relatively minor one, to relying on world market (or 'border') prices as an approximation to the 'free market' prices postulated in neo-classical theory: the world market itself is highly oligopolistic in its production, technology and information structure, and so is extremely 'imperfect'. In theory, therefore, it should not provide 'shadow prices' approximating to a neo-classical optimum. To this it may be answered that world market imperfections are simply a constraint which LDCs can do little about—just one of the many facts which make this a 'second best' world—and they should maximise their welfare within its limits. While theoretically unsatisfactory, this answer does make practical sense: world prices can provide, at the very least, a standard against which domestic efforts can be judged. They will do for day-to-day purposes, *if all the other implicit value judgements are accepted.*

It is these other judgements which cause trouble. The nature, composition and prices of commodities in the world market overwhelmingly reflect the tastes and incomes of the highly developed countries as well as the technological and marketing practices of the multinationals which dominate production there. By taking the relative values of different commodities yielded by world markets as providing socially optimal values for LDCs, it is being implicitly assumed that the expression of 'preferences' in the market of the dominant socio-economic bloc (the rich countries) is ethically acceptable in another (the poor ones). Since 'preferences' are the primary and unquestionable data of conventional economics, such an assumption is, of course, inevitable; however, in practice two sorts of problems arise when the 'social' value of commodities in poor countries is considered.

(a) Many people, including many neo-classical economists, would admit that there was nothing sacrosanct or socially optimal about the world market valuation of, say, a Cadillac or a Dior dress relative to a quantity of food grain, when the context was an extremely poor economy with widespread malnutrition. How would neo-classical welfare economics resolve the valuation problem in such a setting? Two answers are possible. First, the moral unacceptability of world market valuations may be taken to reflect the maldistribution of income in the poor country, and the recommendation would be that the government should simply impose a more 'appropriate' distribution (and let people get on with expressing and fulfilling their preferences). Let us leave distribution problems until later. Second, income distribution may be taken as given, and it may be proposed that the government should impose 'appropriate' taxes and subsidies on the purchase of the relevant commodities so as to enforce a socially more desirable structure of consumption, an illiberal but practical makeshift solution.

The welfare solution in both cases is to remove the problem of making ethical judgements (about 'appropriate' distributions or consumption patterns) from the 'economic' to the 'social' or 'political' spheres, where a supposedly neutral and objective government undertakes this task on some 'non-economic' criteria. The paradigm defines the *economic* problem of valuation in such a way that the economist can say nothing about the social desirability of different 'characteristics' of commodities.[27] Yet it is clear that many economists do wish to pass judgements on this score, and they may argue[28] that several 'characteristics' of products offered in world markets—determined by the product-differentiation and marketing practices of large oligopolistic companies selling to rich markets rather than by any rational consideration of fulfilling the most urgent needs of poor countries—are costly, inappropriate and unnecessary in LDCs. Assume, for example, that there is a need for long-distance motorised transport in a poor country. The world market would provide thousands of models of cars, buses, motorcycles, and so on (each with different 'characteristics' with respect to power, trimmings, colour, extras, all changing every few years). The social cost of providing the whole range would be considerably higher than that of providing one or two basic, simple vehicles which fulfilled the *need*, defined in some sensible way, for moving people from one point to another.[29]

Neo-classical economics finds it very difficult to accomodate such 'sensible' definitions of what products should be, though individual economists on occasion admit the need (on the part of the 'neutral' government) to exercise some discrimination and control. Obviously, when welfare has been defined as fulfilling individual preferences expressed in the market, and the economist has, by the limits of the paradigm, been *barred* from passing any judgement about the social value of those preferences, a 'sensible' evaluation of products is *only possible if one steps outside the paradigm*. Neo-classical economics has always admitted some exceptions of this sort, under the guise of 'merit wants', but these have been exceptions to a basically sound rule. If it is argued, and this certainly would be my argument, that *the judgement of 'need' has to be passed on every commodity*, the rule itself collapses, and a non-individualistic concept of welfare has to be introduced.

(b) A further, but related, problem arises from the fact that there is no way in which conventional welfare economics can distinguish needs which are *created*, by commercial pressures or by the exposure of LDCs to the consumption patterns of developed countries, from those which are 'natural'. In many ways such a distinction is, as neo-classicists never tire of pointing out, analytically untenable; however, it is generally accepted that new wants *are* created by advertising and demonstration, even though the line between these and others is impossible to draw. One of the tenets of the 'dependence' school of development economists is that some of the major problems with the pattern of growth now taking place in LDCs are created by the 'alienated' consumption patterns of their élite.[30] Again, neo-classical economists may well admit (as the exception) the desirability of controlling 'ostentatious' consumption and restraining 'harmful' advertising. But how does one draw the line between permissible and ostentatious or unnecessary consumption, or between 'good' and 'bad' advertising, when demonstration, ostentation and need-creation are the rule rather than exceptions, without over-stepping the bounds of the neo-classical paradigm? Even a mild admission to the effect that the sort of conditioning which pervades a society is undesirable damages the liberal basis of economics and also damages (though it cannot destroy) the 'vision' of capitalist society as a Good Thing in principle.

The usual escape-route of conventional economists is to 'leave it all to the government'. If the government can decide in the national interest what needs are to be fulfilled, in what manner and in what order, the neo-classical paradigm (though very strained as to its liberal and Paretian ethics) can survive with a few modifications. But the assumption that the government is the proper guardian of the national interest is, of course, *just* an assumption. It has little grounding in fact. Any realistic study of the political system, especially in LDCs, shows how the government represents *particular* interests—whether of class or groups depends on the political paradigm adopted—and how its power is used to preserve particular structures of élite *dominance* and *privilege* (though different sections of the élite constantly struggle for supremacy). This is why recommendations that governments should alter the élites' consumption patterns have so little impact in an élitist political framework: most such welfare prescriptions are simply a waste of time.

Here is a real dilemma. To quote Frances Stewart, the ordinary procedure of cost—benefit analysis (this applies to all welfare economics),

in so far as it implies that social welfare maximisation or national welfare maximisation is meaningful (and also possible) in conflict societies, is highly misleading, and sometimes dangerously so, since it dresses up one set of activities—those of taking the objectives of one section of society, normally those represented by the Government, and showing how they can be more efficiently fulfilled—as another, that of maximising the benefits to society. The former being a meaningful (and possible), but for many an undesirable objective: the latter being meaningless and therefore impossible, though desirable.[31]

It is possible to argue that the economist should then either confine his recommendations to what is feasible within a framework of conflict and domination or else recommend what he thinks best for society in the hope that it will persuade the élite to compromise their real interest. This is fair enough, but it is a far cry from the normal conception of what welfare economics is about. In fact, I would submit that the implicit acceptance of conflict, especially *class* conflict, challenges the ideological basis of the conventional paradigm, which is fundamentally dependent upon the harmony-of-interest assumption, and so renders the whole structure suspect. Furthermore, if it cannot be *implicitly* taken for granted that there is some non-economic mechanism which always tends to operate towards restoring the ethical validity of the free-market system (via harmony of interest and governments representing the national interest), the practical role of the traditional welfare economist becomes far more restricted, if not totally redundant.

In sum, therefore, the method by which 'social' valuations can be derived from market prices in conventional welfare economics is highly unsatisfactory. Not only does the discipline not provide any means of distinguishing between commodities which fulfil social needs from those which do not, or between social costs which are necessary from those which are unnecessary (see below under 'efficiency'), it also merely assumes a vital fact which needs to be investigated, whether or not the recipient and executor of the prescriptions of welfare economics is 'neutral' and 'objective'. The basic structure of the welfare paradigm itself prevents these problems from being resolved.

*Income distribution.* One of the major blind spots of conventional welfare economics is its treatment of income distribution. While distribution was the main issue which occupied classical and Marxist economists, the use of the particular combinations of assumptions described above caused modern welfare economics to be 'concerned with precisely that set of questions which avoid judgements on income distribution altogether'.[32] The use of the same set of assumptions in positive economics produced sophisticated and complex theories of distribution which say almost nothing about the actual distribution of income in real societies or about how the structures of wealth and power interact with one another over time. While critics of the neo-classical approach may not have yet produced comprehensive alternative theories which would fit the complexities of modern industrial societies, it is at least arguable that they are asking the more relevant questions and so are more likely to find the right answers.

There is practically nothing in existence by way of a theoretical explanation of income distribution (excluding abstract growth models applicable to any society) in LDCs; but recent evidence that distribution is very unequal, and in a number of the poorest countries getting considerably worse,[33] has stimulated a great deal of interest in the subject and provoked a spate of recommendations on how this could be remedied. This is, of course, eminently laudable. Most people now agree that more equality would be a good thing, and that the increasing poverty of the poorest sections of the population is a bad thing.[34] But *how much equality*? And *how is it to be achieved*? Here again problems arise with the neo-classical welfare paradigm.[35]

The initial barriers to saying anything definite about the degree of equality to be achieved arise from the harmony-of-interest and individualistic (especially Paretian) assumptions. If there *is* harmony of interest, there is a presumption (which then has to be refuted, rather like the presumption of innocence in English law) that nothing much is really wrong with the way the capitalist system functions. If distribution *is* taken to be undesirable, the presumption is that there is nothing inherent in the economic structure (the capitalist mode of production) which, at that particular level of economic development, causes income distribution to take that form. The exact degree of equality then to be achieved by redistribution is presumed not to be the concern of the economist ('leave it to the government') since the paradigm provides no means of comparing the welfare levels of different distributions. With the addition of a few behavioural assumptions, however, the paradigm does provide a strong *a priori* case that redistribution can have adverse effects on GNP growth by affecting various incentives to save and work.

Before even looking at any evidence for any particular developing country, therefore, certain lines of analysis are already determined by the paradigm. Thus, the *causes* of inequality are not to be traced to anything inherent to the mode of production, but simply to be left at other symptoms of inequality, such as the lack of 'assets' (means of production), education, opportunities, etc. on the part of the under-privileged classes.[36] It is not to be asked whether the lack of 'assets' and other privileges is itself a result of the working of the social–political–economic process, because this would imply a disharmony of interest. Then, the *aim* of policy is not to be to achieve 'equality', because this has no particular value in the paradigm, but to achieve 'more' equality, a vague but appealing prescription which can be fulfilled without drastically upsetting the existing distribution of property and power.[37] And the *means* of implementing this prescription is to make marginal changes in the other symptoms of inequality within the limits set by the adverse effects on growth within the capitalist mode of production.[38] The basically uncompromising demand for equality is, therefore, greatly diluted by the paradigm by its superficial analysis of the causes of inequality, its inability to attach 'economic' value to any given form of income distribution, and its basic 'vision' of harmony.

The discovery that there is a U-shaped relationship between inequality and levels of *per capita* GNP, with inequality rising with growth from very low levels and falling at higher levels, lends a comforting backdrop to this sort of *a priori* reasoning. Obviously, if 'more' equality is achieved automatically with higher incomes, no strong measures for reform are really called for, certainly nothing which challenges the legitimacy of capitalist forms of ownership. This backdrop serves to obscure moral misgivings about the goodness of income distribution in existing rich capitalist societies and also to gloss over the long and arduous struggles which have taken place historically in order to get even that far.

As for policy measures, we are back at the 'leave it to the government' problem. While recent discussions of the subject have given up the earlier naïve assumption that appropriate taxes and subsidies could very simply solve the maldistribution problem, and have incorporated some awareness of 'constraints' set by political factors, they have not been able to surmount the barrier between economics and politics set up by the conventional paradigm, and are unable to come to grips with a theory of the state which incorporates both. Thus, reams are written about detailed plans by which governments can achieve 'more' equality, and a small rider is added that political 'constraints' may prevent these plans from being realised, and which renders the whole analysis largely superfluous. The World Bank/IDS book again provides a clear illustration. What is the point of recommending welfare indices with distributional weights, backed by a host of redistribution strategies, when, as Bell notes in an unusually frank chapter on 'The Political Framework', the chances of success are very small?

There are a number of régimes for which the strategy proposed in this volume is 'out of court'. Some are dominated by entrenched élites who will relinquish nothing to the underprivileged except under duress of armed force. Others have attacked successfully the causes of poverty by means far more direct and radical than those discussed here. Yet that still leaves a considerable range of societies for which the strategy is at least plausible, even though in some of them the likelihood that it will be adopted with any vigour is remote. In such cases, the key factor is the emergence of a coalition of interests able to grasp power which sees some advantage in implementing a redistributive strategy, despite the fact that some sections of it stand to lose thereby.[39]

Surely the proper subject for study should then be the determinants of the political–economic conditions which have *caused* changes in distribution and not the symptoms (better 'asset' distribution or more services for the poor) which have accompanied them. Yet this cannot be undertaken within the conventional paradigm, which dooms its analyses of such topics to practical sterility or irrelevance. A more realistic approach, on the other hand, condemns the paradigm.

B   EFFICIENCY

There are only two aspects of the conventional notion of 'efficiency' that I wish to discuss here. The first concerns the concept of 'efficient production' in LDCs as judged by the market-orientated criteria of neo-classical welfare economics, and harks back at the discussion above of 'real' and 'artificial' needs. One of the basic theses of the neo-classical paradigm is that 'any work receiving a market remuneration is productive work, and, if the market is competitive, the remuneration will be proportional to the productivity at the margin. No economically significant distinction can be drawn between a machine operative and a salesman, between an engineer and an advertising employee.'[40] There is, and the former discussion should have clarified why, no room here for a classical–Marxist distinction between productive and unproductive labour in positive terms, or between need-fulfilling and need-creating work in welfare terms. Yet there are many instances in LDCs where we might feel it incumbent upon us to make such a distinction, between efficient work which fulfils real needs and inefficient (or undesirable) work which distorts them: we might, in other words, wish to redefine 'efficiency' with reference to welfare criteria not tied to market success in a capitalist mode of production. This is ruled out by the limitations and assumptions of the paradigm, which then renders a discussion of some important facets of, say, multinational activity in LDCs very difficult and often incoherent.

The second notion of 'efficiency' concerns the application of appro-priate technology. It is freely admitted by conventional writings on LDCs that the technology used in manufacturing industry, while it may be 'efficient' in an engineering sense, is not 'efficient' economically because it is excessively capital-intensive for the needs and endowments of LDCs. The general recommendation is that factor prices should be corrected and subsidies provided for the market to come up with a suitable intermediate technology. Some recent writing goes much further.[41] It questions the neo-classical assumption of smooth and continuous production functions, and argues that, given various rigidities, the nature of the technology employed cannot be changed without changing the sorts of (inappropriate) goods which are produced. It also argues that many factor-price 'distortions' which lead to the wrong choice of technology are in fact created by political pressures by local and foreign élites, and that science and research policies in LDCs, which may be expected to produce alternative technologies, are themselves subject to the same structural distortions which prevent the adoption of appropriate technology by industrialists.[42]

These new analyses have large elements of truth in them, and it is clear that they contravene the orthodox paradigm in many ways: they challenge the rationality of consumers' preferences and the neutrality of governments, and implicitly they also reject the harmony-of-interest assumption. However, by starting from within this paradigm they are unable to analyse whether the development of the capitalist mode of production *itself* determines the sort of technology which is adopted in all the areas (developed or underdeveloped) of its operation. If it is the case that the most 'efficient' technology in the advanced countries is also the most 'efficient' one for most (perhaps not all) industries in poor countries because it helps in establishing the supremacy of the capitalist mode of production, forging links with the leading capitalist enterprises and markets, and securing the hegemony of one class over another, then it is somewhat misguided to argue for reforms within the existing structure to solve this 'problem'.[43] The 'problem' can only be solved by breaking out of the structure itself—a conclusion reached by many of the economists cited, but in a far more roundabout fashion.

C INTERNATIONAL ASPECTS

A brief consideration of some aspects of the conventional welfare paradigm as it affects international economic relations will serve to round off this discussion. In the field of trade theory the usual assumptions of the paradigm are (implicitly) supplemented by the assumption of harmony of interest between nations, and the familiar theorems of comparative advantage, benefits from trade and investment, etc. follow automatically. There are, however, four sorts of disharmony which can occur in international economic relations, some of which damage the conventional paradigm while others can be accomodated with some qualifications to the standard theories.

First, there may be disharmony between the *governments* of two countries, simply in the sense that one wishes to dominate or influence the other for economic or other benefits. The most obvious case is, of course, historical imperialism, any analysis of which immediately threatens the ideological basis of conventional economics. Aid is a more recent example. The self-seeking and political ('imperialistic') use of aid policies by major donors is hardly a fact which arouses much scepticism now,[44] and this casts some doubt on the harmony and neutrality assumptions. However, one can, if one believed in the paradigm strongly enough, regard this sort of non-economic influence as legitimate, or simply irrelevant to the 'economic' issues involved.

Second, there may be disharmony between nations as regards the *distribution of benefits* arising from trade and investment. A great deal of trade takes place under conditions where the bargaining strength of the trading partners is of decisive importance in determining the allocation of benefits; the convenient fiction of a competitive market price simply does not hold. This is obviously true of trade in many primary commodities where vertically integrated multinationals can set world prices themselves: in these days of the 'New International Order' one can hardly doubt the strength of feeling on the part of LDCs that they have been hard done by on this account. It is also true of many manufactured commodities where trade is heavily dominated by multinationals. Not only do they preponderate in the production and selling of these commodities on world markets, a substantial part of trade actually takes place *within* the firms themselves, with benefits being allocated on principles which have little to do with received trade theory.[45] Similarly for international sales of technology, or skills, or marketing advantages: there are clear conflicts where the impersonal laws of competitive markets, and the welfare formulae derived therefrom, have little significance.

These are, it must be noted, more criticisms of the particular way in which trade theory has abstracted from reality than of the neo-classical paradigm as such. In so far as it is simply a problem of introducing such imperfections as *bargaining* into the picture, no serious hindrance is created to the continued use of neo-classical premises. To launch a *real* attack on these premises would require that the critique of conventional competitive assumptions be reinforced by a demonstration that trade and investment, consistently and over a long period, result in a *one-sided* exchange, with the developed world (or multinationals) *consistently exploiting* the LDCs.[46] Many neo-Marxist economists have in fact argued this, without making much of a dent on the main body of traditional trade theory; even without using Marxist concepts, however, it is arguable that the balance of power is such that the imperfect working of market forces may lead to some countries (or firms) possessing inherent and long-run superiority over others.[47] A fairly mild admission to this effect may have serious implications for welfare theory related to trade, but it is doubtful if such an admission would be made.

Third, there may be disharmony between nations as regards the *distribution of production*. Critics of some static versions of comparative cost theory have long argued that the application of this theory to LDCs condemns them to a backward and stagnant production structure. Moreover, a glance at the history of LDCs shows that in many cases this structure was directly or indirectly imposed by imperial policy. The first is not a serious criticism of neo-classical trade theory; the second is, but may be countered on the ground that 'things ain't what they used to be'. Thus, today, the growth of multinationals, the transfer of technology and the enlargement of world markets (unfortunately held back by protectionist measures) have created proper conditions for international specialisation based on dynamic comparative advantage: such a neo-classical argument has considerable weight and validity, at least within its capitalist framework. There is, in my view, no sound basis for attacking this argument *as such*, relying on the existence of disharmony between countries.[48] The only sustainable critique can come from a questioning of the premises on grounds indicated in earlier sections, i.e. the implicit definition of welfare, the defence of individual preferences, government neutrality and the like, and *not on grounds of country-wide conflict*. In other words, trade theory may be criticised, not for promoting policies which *hold back a capitalist form of development* (which many opponents accuse it of doing), but precisely *for advocating such a course*.

Fourth, there may be disharmony *between classes* in the traditional Marxist sense. How this affects trade theory as a distinct branch of economics is not at all clear, beyond the sorts of points which have already been made in the previous sections. In general, trade and investment may be regarded as the most important means of spreading the capitalist mode of production internationally, and any welfare theory which purports to to show that they are promoting the well-being of LDCs may be exposed to the same criticisms as are directed at the mode of production itself. And, in so far as the neo-classical paradigm is found wanting on this count, the trade theory built upon it will be found similarly wanting. Many critics of conventional trade theory weaken rather than strengthen their case by attacking it on other grounds (such as bargaining or location of production).


IV  CONCLUSIONS

This paper has tried to outline the main assumptions and judgements that underlie conventional welfare economics, and to show how its application to the situation of LDCs results in difficulties and contradictions. There is little doubt that these difficulties are felt, in a more or less acute form, by many economists who work on development, and that the structure of the welfare paradigm itself serves to perpetuate the problems or direct the search for solutions along unsuitable lines. A resolution of the conceptual conflict can be brought nearer by using a paradigm based on classical or Marxian lines of 'political economy'. This alternative paradigm has not been directly discussed here, and, in particular, the differences between Marxian and non-Marxian political economy have not been analysed: my aim has been much more limited, to show how conceptual frameworks are rooted deeply in unquestioned, and in some ways unquestionable, premises, and cannot be adapted to changing needs and values except by fundamental reappraisal. It is evident that such a reappraisal is imperative in development economics.


NOTES

1. I am grateful to Peter Balacs, Giorgio Gagliani, Keith Griffin, Paul Streeten and Rosemary Thorp for comments and discussions.
2. For a clear and concise exposition of the value judgements of conventional welfare economics (but not its ideological basis) see Rowley and Peacock (1975), who provide an excellent critique of Paretian welfare theory from a liberal standpoint (which is itself subject to some of the problems discussed here).
3. See Kuhn (1962) and Foster-Carter (1976).
4. Schumpeter (1954) sees this 'vision' as a 'pre-analytic cognitive act' which necessarily precedes any scientific analysis, though he argues that such 'ideological' factors have played a small role in much of recent economic thinking. This is strongly challenged by Dobb (1973) and Meek (1967). For a devastating critique of the philosophical methods used to justify the neutrality and scientific nature of neo-classical economics, see Hollis and Nell (1975).
5. One of the best works on the subject of values and ideology in economics is still Myrdal's book, first published in German in 1932 and much later in English (in 1953), on what he terms 'the political element' in economic theory.

Also see Dobb (1973), Lange (1963), Nath (1969), Robinson (1962) and Streeten (1963).

6. As with Rowley and Peacock (1975), mentioned above, from the liberal point of view.

7. Ibid., pp. 1 and 22–3. Emphasis added.

8. Lange is one of the major contributors, and while admiring the contribution to 'praxiology' of bourgeois economics, he clearly perceives (and severely criticises) its ideological justification of capitalism. See Lange (1963) vol. I.

9. This ideological assumption is also at the base of the great bulk of political, sociological, ethical and historical thinking, where problems of the sort discussed here also arise.

10. This itself leads to severe difficulties of how such 'functions' are to be formulated from individualistic premises, the best known being the Arrow General Impossibility theorem. There is now a large and highly sophisticated literature on the problems of collective choice, the relevance of which to economic practice is not very clear; for a concise and lucid discussion, however, see Sen (1970). In development economics a less demanding rule is often imposed by judging 'welfare' with reference to 'objective functions' set by the government or by economic planners. This is based on a strong interpretation of the state-power assumption discussed below and is in direct conflict with the strict Paretian and liberal views of welfare.

11. The logical positivist approach, though obviously not necessary to support a methodology which takes the legitimacy of capitalism for granted, has in fact been used as the main philosophical tool for rejecting analyses of society based on class. As an epistemological theory, however, it suffers from crippling drawbacks, as Hollis and Nell (1975) argue at great length; in particular, its analytic–synthetic distinction is shown to be fatal, and a rationalist approach is proposed in its stead.

12. This sort of 'interdependence' has long been ignored in conventional welfare economics, but it can be taken into account (albeit uneasily) by sufficient mathematical manipulation of conventional welfare concepts. See references in ch. 3 of Rowley and Peacock (1975) and Becker (1974).

13. There is a vast literature on the subject which cannot be referred to here, but see the last chapter of Dobb (1973) and an extremely useful article by Rowthorn (1974) for a summary view.

14. Vaizey (1975) p. 12.

15. Sraffa's commodity production model is very similar to Marx's own schema (see Meek (1967), essay 10) and can be used fruitfully to extend Marxist analysis (the most recent example being Bose (1975)).

16. Analysed with wit and penetration by Myrdal (1953). See also Bose (1975), ch. 3, and Rowthorn (1974). The Hollis and Nell book, unfortunately, talks in terms of 'classical–Marxian economics' and does not bring out the real distinction between these two schools.

17. The distinction between 'oppression', which is the prevention of a particular class from the direction of its own affairs, and 'exploitation', which is the appropriation of surplus value arising from the coercive nature of capitalist production, is important, but we shall not dwell on it further here. For a brief exposition see Henry (1975).

18. See, for instance, the survey and critique of class theories by Giddens (1973) and Poulantzas (1975).

19. On 'unconnected' preferences and the problems raised by particular types of interdependent preferences, see Sen (1973).

20. For a strong statement of this line of attack on welfare economics, see Gintis (1972).

21. Liberals appear to be more realistic in this respect than Paretians, according to the case presented by Rowley and Peacock (1975). They accept that preferences are changeable and that existing preferences are not the ultimate data for economic analysis; in fact, they envisage 'exercising all reasonable means of persuasion available . . . short of coercion, to alter the preferences of those who would encourage illiberal policies' (p. 97). Like Paretians, however, liberals take for granted the overall ideological conditioning of capitalist societies.

22. Modern liberals differ from the Paretians again, by admitting the possibilities of influence, coercion, propaganda and bribery (based on Breton (1974)). They also differ from Paretians in giving the *minimum possible* economic role to the state, while the Paretians are quite willing to have state intervention under specified conditions (see Rowley and Peacock).

23. The role of *ceteris paribus* clauses is crucial. It enables economists to dismiss political problems by assuming that there is an ideal role for the state towards which it will *naturally* tend over time, and so allows them to treat even the most glaring misuses of state power as temporary deviations. See also footnote 9.

24. Marxist theories of the state are still relatively undeveloped, but see Poulantzas (1973) and (1975) for a general theoretical discussion, and Alavi (1972) and Leys (1975) for the application of class theories to state power in less developed countries.

25. There are other problems, concerning comparisons for *per capita* incomes between countries, the value of 'non-quantifiables' like environment etc., and the correct accounting of transactions taking place in non-monetized subsistence sectors in LDCs but these are not germane to the present argument and will be ignored here.

26. This is the method proposed by Little and Mirrlees (1974).

27. Lancaster (1966) introduced the concept of 'characteristics' of products into demand theory, but stayed firmly within the bounds of that theory by taking preferences as the ultimate data and refusing to pass any normative judgement on the characteristics themselves.

28. As Stewart (1974) has done persuasively.

29. The phenomenon of over-specified, over-differentiated and over-promoted products is, of course, not restricted to such marginal needs in LDCs as cars or stereo sets; it applies equally to such essentials as food products (see Horst (1974)) and medicines (Lall (1974)).

30. See, for instance dos Santos (1970). The distortion is not just one which offends a moral judgement about ostentatious and luxury consumption in very poor countries; it may also have damaging effects on health and physical welfare. For instance, the promotion campaigns of baby food manufacturers in LDCs has affected poor, illiterate mothers in such a way that 'unknown thousands of babies were being fed over-diluted milk from unsterilized bottles

and were therefore exposed to disease and malnutrition'. *The New Internationalist* (1975).

31. Stewart (1975) pp. 36–7.

32. Sen (1973a) p. 6. The early Utilitarians were seriously concerned with distribution, but Myrdal (1953) describes how their radical conclusions were sterilised by later liberals.

33. Adelman and Morris (1973) and Chenery *et al.* (1974).

34. This should not obscure the fact that in the early days of development economics, for example Lewis (1954), increases in inequality were recommended, with some protestations of regret, of course, in order to increase growth.

35. For an illustration, see Chenery *et al.* (1974).

36. 'Although definitive statistical analyses are lacking, it is quite plausible to associate much of the variation in income at the lower levels with a lack of human skills, as well as lack of ownership of physical capital and access to complementary assets and other inputs'. Ibid., p. 44.

37. 'The preceding section suggests that the objective of distributive justice is more usefully conceived of as accelerating the development of the poorer groups in society rather than in terms of relative shares of income'. Ibid., p. 45.

38. ' . . . in areas such as land ownership and security to tenure, some degree of asset redistribution is an essential part of any program to make the rural poor more productive. . . . Beyond this essential minimum, a vigorous policy of investment reallocation in a rapidly growing economy may well be a more effective way of increasing the productive capacity of the poor than redistribution from the existing stock of assets, which is likely to have a high cost in social and political disruption'. Ibid., p. 49.

39. Ibid., p. 71–2.

40. Hollis and Nell (1975) p. 215.

41. See Helleiner (1975), Morawetz (1974) and Stewart (1974).

42. Cooper (1974).

43. This is not contradicted by the fact that certain countries can fit into the international capitalist structure by specialising in the production of labour-intensive goods. On the contrary, such a development is an intrinsic part of the uneven spread of the capitalist mode of production, and in no way impedes its development. A real challenge is mounted only if the new 'appropriate' technology effectively upsets the structure of class relations of the expanding capitalist mode.

44. See Hayter (1971).

45. See Lall (1973).

46. It may also be done by adopting a non-neoclassical (Ricardian or Marxist) framework where it can be shown that under certain conditions, even given perfect competition in product markets, there occurs 'unequal exchange' between developed and developing countries. (See Emmanuel (1972).) As this involves explicitly using a non-conventional paradigm, however, I have not discussed it any further.

47. This is argued with respect to technology by Griffin (1974).

48. Though many 'dependence' economists have done so, their case is not very convincing. See chapter 1.

REFERENCES

Adelman, I., and Morris, C. T. (1973), *Economic Growth and Social Equity in Developing Countries* (Stanford: Stanford University Press).
Alavi, H. (1972), 'The State in Post-colonial Societies: Pakistan and Bangladesh', *New Left Review* (July–August) pp. 59–82.
Becker, G. (1974), 'A Theory of Social Interactions', *Journal of Political Economy* (November–December) pp. 1063–94.
Bose, A. (1975), *Marxian and Post-Marxian Political Economy* (Harmondsworth: Penguin).
Breton, A. (1974), *The Economic Theory of Representative Government* (London: Macmillan).
Chenery, H. B., Ahluwalia, M. S., Bell, C. L. G., Duloy, J. H. and Jolly, R. (1974), *Redistribution with Growth* (London: Oxford University Press).
Cooper, C. (1974), 'Science Policy and Technological Change in Underdeveloped Economies', *World Development* (March) pp. 55–64.
Dobb, M. (1973), *Theories of Value and Distribution since Adam Smith: Ideology and Economic Theory* (London: Cambridge University Press).
Dos Santos, T. (1970), 'The Structure of Dependence', *Am. Econ. Rev. Papers & Proc.,* pp. 231–36.
Emmanuel, A. (1972), *Unequal Exchange* (London: New Left Books).
Foster-Carter, A. (1976), 'From Rostow to Gunder Frank', *World Development* pp. 167–80.
Giddens, A. (1973), *The Class Structure of the Advanced Societies* (London: Hutchinson).
Gintis, H. (1972), 'A Radical Analysis of Welfare Economics and Individual Development', *Quarterly Journal of Economics.,* pp. 572–99.
Griffin, K. (1974), 'The International Transmission of Inequality', *World Development* (March) pp. 3–16.
Hayter, T. (1971), *Aid as Imperialism* (Harmondsworth: Penguin).
Helleiner, G. (1975) 'The Role of Multinational Corporations in the Less Developed Countries' Trade in Technology', *World Development* (April) pp. 161–90.
Henry, J. F. (1975), 'Productive Labour, Exploitation and Oppression—a Perspective', *Australian Economic Papers* (June) pp. 35–40.
Hollis, M. and Nell, E. (1975), *Rational Economic Man: A Philosophical Critique of Neo-Classical Economics* (London: Cambridge University Press).
Horst, T. (1974), *At Home Abroad: A Study of the Domestic and Foreign Operations of the American Food-Processing Industry* (Cambridge, Mass.: Ballinger Publishing Company).
Kuhn, T. S. (1962), *The Structure of Scientific Revolutions* (Chicago: University of Chicago Press).
Lall, S. (1973), 'Transfer Pricing by Multinational Manufacturing Firms'. *Oxford Bulletin of Economics and Statistics* (August) pp. 173–95.
Lall, S. (1974), 'The International Pharmaceutical Industry and Less-Developed Countries, with Special Reference to India', *Oxford Bulletin of Economics & Statistics* (August) pp. 143–72.
Lancaster, K. J. (1966), 'A New Approach to Consumer Theory', *Journal of Political Economy.* (April) pp. 132–57.

Lange, O. (1963), *Political Economy*, vol. I (Oxford: Pergamon Press).

Lewis, W. A. (1954), 'Economic Development with Unlimited Supplies of Labour', *Manchester School*, pp. 139–91.

Leys, C. (1975), *Underdevelopment in Kenya: The Political Economy of Neo-Colonialism* (London: Heinemann).

Little, I. M. D. and Mirrlees, J. A. (1974), *Project Appraisal and Planning for Developing Countries* (London: Heinemann).

Meek, R. L. B. (1967), *Economics and Ideology and Other Essays: Studies in the Development of Economic Thought* (London: Chapman & Hall).

Morawetz, D. (1974), 'Employment Implications of Industrialisation in Developing Countries: a Survey', *Economic Journal* (September) pp. 491–542.

Myrdal, G. (1953), *The Political Element in the Development of Economic Theory* (London: Routledge & Kegan Paul). Translated from the 1932 German edition by P. P. Streeten.

Nath, S. K. (1969), *A Reappraisal of Welfare Economics* (London: Routledge & Kegan Paul).

*New Internationalist, The* (1975), 'Kicking the Bottle', (March) pp. 13–15.

Poulantzas, N. (1973), *Political Power & Social Classes* (London: New Left Books).

Poulantzas, N. (1975), *Classes in Contemporary Capitalism* (London: New Left Books).

Robinson, J. (1962), *Economic Philosophy* (London: C. A. Watts).

Rowley, C. K. and Peacock, A. T. (1975), *Welfare Economics: a Liberal Restatement* (London: Martin Robertson).

Rowthorn, B. (1974), 'Neo-classicism, Neo-Ricardianism and Marxism' *New Left Review* (July–August) pp. 63–87.

Schumpeter, J. A. (1954), *History of Economic Analysis* (London: Allen & Unwin).

Sen, A. K. (1970), *Collective Choice and Social Welfare* (San Francisco: Holden-Day).

Sen, A. K. (1973), 'Behaviour and the Concept of Preference', *Economica*, pp. 241–59.

Sen, A. K. (1973a), *On Economic Inequality* (Oxford: Clarendon Press).

Stewart, F. (1974), 'Technology & Employment in LDCs', *World Development* (March) pp. 17–46.

Stewart, F. (1975), 'A Note on Social Cost-benefit Analysis and Class Conflict in LDCs', *World Development* (January) pp. 31–9.

Streeten, P. P. (1963), 'Values, Facts and the Compensation Principle', in E. von Beckerath and H. Giersch (eds), *Probleme der Normativen Ökonomik und der Wirtschaftspolitischen Beratung* (Berlin: Verlag von Duncker and Humbolt) pp. 164–79.

Vaizey, J. (1975), 'In Defence of General Economics', *Australian Economic Papers* (June) pp. 1–13.

# Part Two
# International Investment

# 3 Developing Countries and Foreign Investment[1]

I

This paper is partly a review of an important new work by Professor G. L. Reuber and associates on the economics of private foreign manufacturing investment in less-developed countries (LDCs),[2] and partly an attempt to examine some of the larger issues facing the study of such investment. Reuber's book is an interesting and provocative one, and in this essay I shall concentrate on the first 250 pages which contain the analytical sections, and which constitute a vigorous defence of foreign investment in LDCs. The book also contains five appendices on its structure and distribution, the characteristics of selected projects, the interview procedure and the sources and definitions of the data. The analysis is based on published and unpublished information as well as on direct interviews with about 80 investing firms, and claims to be a major contribution to our knowledge in this field.

*Private Foreign Investment in Development* is the first work which deals exclusively with the general problem of foreign investment in LDCs, and, as such, is destined to become a standard text in the field. The argument and methodology of the book seem academic and thorough, and its tone appears to be neutral and objective. The authors have, however, a large axe to grind: they are concerned to establish the benefits of foreign investment for LDCs, and to prove their case they summarily dismiss many valid criticisms of foreign investment; their conclusions are, moreover, derived from a set of value judgements which are not explicitly defined and which may be regarded as unacceptable by many groups affected by foreign investment.

A review of this book may, therefore, serve as an appropriate place to discuss some of the basic values underlying the study of foreign investment. Section II uses a simple taxonomy to highlight some of the important elements on which different approaches to foreign investment are based; Section III evaluates Reuber's work in terms of this taxonomy and in terms of his treatment of some specific issues related to foreign investment.


## II


The analysis of the phenomenon of private foreign investment, and of its recent manifestation in the form of the multinational enterprise (MNE), has been undertaken by schools which represent every shade of political and economic belief. There is at present hardly any subject in economics which arouses so much controversy and such a variety of interpretation, the differences arising not so much from disagreements about the data (though these are also present) as from disagreements about fundamental values and definitions in the context of economic and political development. The approaches to foreign direct investment may, at the risk of some oversimplification, be grouped into six categories, three for it and three against:

### A  PRO-FOREIGN INVESTMENT

(i) At the extreme right of the spectrum lies the *business-school* approach. The essential characteristics of this approach are an implicit belief in the moral and practical virtues of the free enterprise system; an acceptance of the existing distribution of income within and between countries; a disregard for the over-all economic, political and social effects of an extension of the system to other countries; and, consequent on the above, prescriptions for government policy that centre on the well-being of business enterprises as opposed to all other groups, and call for an environment of stability and non-interference conducive to 'good business'. Business-school analysts not only provide firms with guides to greater efficiency, but also serve to rationalise and defend their evolving structure or practices to the outside world. There is an enormous collection of this sort of literature, ranging from purely organisational analysis to recommendations on how to counter expropriation, how best to use 'financial tools' to minimise tax burdens,[3] and how to plan the most profitable ownership strategies.

(ii) A more academic line of analysis which closely resembles the previous one but which explicitly formulates the economic theory involved may be termed the 'traditional economic' approach. While this is not at all concerned with the organisational and motivational analysis of foreign investors, the assumptions on which it is based lead to very similar prescriptions of *laissez-faire* and maximisation of foreign capital flows.[4] These assumptions are the essential ones of the bulk of Western normative economics, and cannot be properly discussed here; however, the ones most relevant to foreign investment in LDCs are as follows:

(*a*) Foreign investment constitutes a net addition to investible resources in host countries, and as such raises their rates of growth. This is based on a further set of assumptions about the competitive nature of product and factor markets, mobility of factors between occupations, incremental capital – output ratios, use of capacity, and so on—in short, all the standard premises of 'growth model' economics (usually with 'externalities' assumed absent).

(*b*) The pattern of growth which results is desirable. This presumes a host of specific conditions and values which underlie welfare economics, mainly that the market is the best determinant of economic and social welfare—thus, the distribution of income reflected in the market is desirable, or, more subtly, not the concern of economists at all, and that the preferences revealed are independently formed and true indicators of 'welfare'. In the particular case of foreign investment in LDCs, the implications are that the products introduced and marketed, the tastes created, and the needs met, all benefit the countries, as long as the ventures earn profits.[5]

(*c*) The freeing of international trade and capital flows is conducive both to total world welfare and to the welfare of each individual country—another fundamental tenet, this time of trade theory. The assumptions required for this are similar to those mentioned above; in the case of LDCs the desirability of foreign investment is increased because of its integrative effect on host economies. The operation of foreign firms, especially of modern multinational firms, knits countries closer into the web of international commerce, both by (virtical and horizontal) economic integration and by the transmission of tastes, designs, ideas, and technology.

(*d*) Foreign investment also brings benefits which are not recognised in the orthodox literature, but which are central to much of the recent work on the subject. These concern the introduction of new technology, better management and organisation, superior marketing and some-times cheaper finance. The beneficial nature of these contributions is generally taken for granted, though clearly the economic rationale is derived directly from (*b*) above, i.e., it must be 'good' if it is profitable, even though the circumstances are very different from the perfectly competitive situation envisaged by the early welfare economists. The new schools of technology- and management-oriented analysts, whose roots lie partly in business schools, assume essentially that the free enterprise system as it operates in the leading capitalist countries represents the best from of economic and social organisation, and that its wholesale extension, including the forms of technology produced, the differentiation of products, the methods of advertising and selling, and the philosophy of corporate operation, to LDCs is *per se* desirable.

What has been termed the 'traditional economic' approach therefore embraces vast tracts of received economic wisdom as well as accretions of hard-headed business pragmatism. Since the free enterprise system is assumed to be the most efficient means of promoting well-being, the policies which are prescribed for LDCs naturally entail minimisation of controls, interference and public ownership. The recent proponents of this approach include Kindleberger (1969) and Vernon (1971), though sometimes exhibit features of (iii) below.

(iii) There are some analysts concerned with the oligopolistic, predatory and concentrated nature of MNEs who, while holding a basic belief in the desirability of foreign investment, recommend controls and official regulation; this may be called the *neo-traditionalist approach*. Its proponents believe in the good, old-fashioned virtues of early capitalism and are worried by the giantism and power of the present MNE; they are more realistic than the real traditionalists in that they realize better the extent of change and the problems created, but they share the same fundamental economic values and believe in the same framework of analysis. The distinguishing characteristic of this approach is a free admission of the potential for a divergence of intrests between foreign investors and host countries; the remedies range from setting up multinational political units to cope with MNEs (Goldberg and Kindleberger, 1970) and implementing various national measures (Behrman, 1970) to drastic reversals of policy to attack 'bigness' and restore competition (Bannock, 1971). In general, the proponents of this school take the MNE as the more powerful and lasting—and often more desirable—entity than the nation-state, and see the latter evolving to catch up with the former rather than any tendency in the reverse direction.

B   ANTI-FOREIGN INVESTMENT

(i) A shift of emphasis from the virtues of international capitalism (in some form) to those of nationally owned development leads to the *'nationalist' approach*. In this approach, the standpoint is usually that of the less-developed host country rather than of the investing firm or the capital-exporting country: the change is significant, because the basic virtues of the international free market system are brought into question and its various implicit values criticised. The main arguments of this approach can be summarised as follows:

(*a*) There may be various external effects of foreign investment which damage host economies, such as the suppression of domestic entrepreneurship, the effects on the economy of the importation of unsuitable technology and of unsuitable products, the extension of oligopolistic practices such as unnecessary product differentiation, heavy advertising, or excessive profit-taking, and the worsening of income distribution by a self-perpetuating process which simultaneously reinforces high-income *élites* and provides them with expensive consumer goods. In a nutshell, the market no longer provides an infallible guide to national welfare.

(*b*) The cost of private foreign investment may be too high as compared to the next best alternative, even in the absence of external effects, because the foreign investor is able to extract monopoly profits or use superior bargaining power to gain concessions, or because there are costs inherent in the mode of operation, such as the introduction of unsuitable products or technology, or the misuse of transfer pricing and other tools to remit hidden profits, or the imposition of export restrictions and unfair marketing practices.

(*c*) The degree of integration with the international trading system implicit in allowing MNEs to enter an economy may not be acceptable, either because LDCs may consider free (or freer) trade more damaging than beneficial to their economic growth, or because the pattern of production and distribution entailed by such integration may be regarded as undesirable.[6]

It should be noted that the nationalist school says little about the internal strategy of development (whether it should be socialist or capitalist). Its main emphasis is on minimising the cost and extent of foreign investment while extracting to the full its more suitable elements, especially technology, and it is assumed that the domestic industrialist class is capable of undertaking and sustaining a desirable pattern of growth and distribution. This leads to policy recommendations stressing stringent regulation of foreign investments, case-by-case bargaining, shopping around for better deals, and exchange of information between LDCs; some examples of this sort of approach are Streeten (1973), Streeten and Lall (1973), Vaitsos (1970).

(ii) The *'dependence' approach*, which has its origins in Latin

America, incorporates most of the features of the nationalist school, but stresses the broader ramifications of the whole capitalist development process of which foreign investment is one element. It analyses the social, political and economic consequences of the penetration of capitalist institutions and methods into LDCs, and concludes that the inherently dependent status of these countries can never permit real development. The greatest contribution of the dependence school is its broad perspective and its analysis of the internal politcal/economic forces which reinforce the historical dominance of the central capitalist countries. The remedies are seen, consequently, in sweeping changes in both external relations and internal power structures; in a very mild form, however, the prescriptions are not very different from those of the nationalists, while in an extreme one they come close to the Marxist school.

The conventional economic framework cannot accommodate the dependence approach: no amount of discussion of 'externalities' and 'utility from nationalism' can capture its full implications. Though some dependence-school economists tend at times to give the impression that they are only employing orthodox economic tools, their most interesting reasoning, about the very *nature* of 'genuine development' and its contrast with dependent development, lies outside the scope of such tools. The dependence school still has to formulate its analytical apparatus fully, but as it stands it does afford a novel standpoint to the subject, not quite Marxist and not simply nationalistic; Dos Santos (1970), Sunkel (1969–70), and Hymer (1972) may serve as good examples.

(iii) *The Marxist approach* to foreign investment is conducted more explicitly in terms of class conflict: modern Marxists (such as Baran, 1957) employ the concept of 'economic surplus', which in this context is extracted from LDCs by foreign investors. Where the dependence school talks of the dangers of dependence, this approach talks of 'neo-imperialism' and 'exploitation'; the analysis lies further outside the scope of conventional economics, and *all* the values of the capitalist system are under attack. The dependence school is concerned with *national* development, in which the final class structure is left ambiguous, while the Marxist school is concerned with socialist development, in which the final class structure is clearly defined, and it is one which is not attainable within the framework of the existing system of ownership within LDCs or within that of integration with the international capitalist system. The remedy is, therefore, seen as internal revolution and complete rejection of foreign capital. Recent Marxist analysts, such as Magdoff (1969) and Sweezy and Magdoff (1972), have advanced the theory of imperialism to take account of the emergence of MNEs and their effects on LDCs; in the particular context of LDCs, the work of Frank (1972) and Weisskopf (1972) has great value.

The six approaches sketched out above each embody a different interpretation of economic reality, a different emphasis on certain aspects of that reality, and a different concept of the value and meaning of changes in it. Even given the basic premise that everyone wants to promote the well-being of LDCs and some measure of agreement on the hard data (investment flows, value of output, employment, growth rates, and the like), there is bound to remain a fundamental divergence in views about the desirability and contribution of foreign investment to LDCs. There cannot, in other words, be a 'value-free' or 'objective' assessment of foreign investment[7]—hardly an original or startling fact, but one which is often forgotten or hidden in the polemics that rage round the subject.

If there *cannot* be an objective assessment, and no concensus on any particular system of values is likely to emerge, how then should one set about discussing the problem? There are two possibilities: first, the values on which the analysis is based can simply be taken for granted as *a priori* postulates; or, second, they may be defined, rationalised and stated explicitly. In the first case, though the conclusions may be derived by legitimate logical steps from the premises and appear perfectly rational and acceptable to those who share those premises, the *real* argument is concealed and the debate cannot really begin. In the second, it can at least be seen *where* the disagreement lies, which does not by any means provide a solution but does represent some progress, if only in an intellectual or moral sphere.

Both pro- and anti-foreign investment schools have examples of the concealed premises approach. The former, however, has used it far more because the values on which it is based are in the established tradition of Western economics. This does not make it any the less objectionable, because alternative systems *have been* proposed and tried, and because an unalloyed transfer of that system to less-developed nations, where the assumptions are not really valid and whose aspirations are not really taken into account, leads both to morally unjustifiable conclusions as well as to practical problems of hostility and incomprehension.[8] Ultimately, therefore, the practice of economics in LDCs cannot remain simply an 'economic' exercise but must step into the realm of politics; it would be self-deception to pretend otherwise.

The general observations may be useful in understanding the nature of the present controversy about foreign investment in LDCs; they are also helpful in reviewing the book at hand, to which we now turn.


## III

This section is a critical evaluation of *Private Foreign Investment in Development*. Though it concentrates on the negative aspects of the book, mainly in order to redress its bias in favour of foreign investment, it is not intended to denigrate many of its positive qualities. The book contains a number of valuable facts about foreign investment in LDCs, and its analysis is clear and logical; it offers a welcome antidote to various vague and emotive debates on the subject, and opens up many possibilities for useful research. This being admitted, let us consider the other side.

*Private Foreign Investment in Development* stands firmly with one foot planted in approach A(i) (business school) and the other in approach A(ii) (traditional economic). Its business-school orientation derives from the fact that its original research is based almost entirely on interviews with and data given by the *parent companies* of firms investing in LDCs; there is no attempt to discover and present the viewpoints of host governments, locally-owned enterprises or even the local subsidiaries of foreign firms. Thus, a discussion of the motivation of the investors figures rather prominently, and the emphasis throughout is on their preferences, practices and aversions, as though these were more real and important than those of LDCs. The 'traditional economic' approach is more pervasive; Reuber tends to be even more 'traditional' than other present representatives of this school, and the basic assumption is that foreign investment provides a net increase in capital formation, raises output and employment, and is therefore beneficial, except for a strong qualification in cases where the investment is highly protected (for which the blame is put squarely on the host government's shoulders) and results in very low or negative value-added at international prices.

The 'traditional economic' beliefs are so firmly held that the entire structure of the reasoning and policy conclusions follow from them as self-evident propositions. The data adduced neither prove nor disprove the social desirability of foreign investment, since no attempt is made at a social benefit–cost analysis (despite strong recommendations that LDCs apply such techniques to foreign investment projects).[9] The argument basically proceeds by starting from a competitive model (with market prices measuring social values) and allowing for distortions (which are mostly the fault of government policies) in the form of tariffs, taxes and controls; foreign investors are seen as neutral providers of capital, expertise and technology, superior in all these to local alternatives; putting the two together, it follows that foreign investment is necessarily beneficial unless the host government has adopted incorrect policies.[10] Some harmful effects of foreign investment are discussed but are not taken very seriously; we return to these below, but Reuber's general case could really have been made much more briefly and without appeal to the rather spurious support provided by his data.

Criticisms of this sort of reasoning at the most general level have already been mentioned in the previous section. To what extent do market prices, corrected for the sort of 'distortion' mentioned above, measure *welfare* in LDCs? Is growth in *per capita* GNP at these prices really what LDCs should be striving for? If the pattern of consumption, technology, distribution of power and wealth are at all important, how much relevance does conventional welfare economics have? If the dependence school has a valid point to make, does it make sense to leave their reasoning completely out of account, simply because it is not 'purely economic'? An aspect of Reuber's which may be found especially unsatisfactory is the direct link assumed between the firm's profitability and the host country's welfare: is a less developed country's welfare really increased by 'market development' (high pressure sales tactics), product differentiation, oligopolistic market structures, transmission of certain types of technology which displace labour or lead only to frequent model changes? One could go on and on, but the basis of disagreement is clear, and concerns the values involved as well as the concealed premises of the analysis. Let us now briefly consider a few specific aspects of Reuber's treatment of foreign investment.

(*a*) *Foreign investor–host government relationships.* It follows logically from the framework of Reuber's analysis that government policies should aim at removing tariff, tax and direct control 'distortions' in LDCs, at encouraging the inflow of foreign capital, and at minimising specific controls on foreign investors. Over the long run the ideal situation would presumably be a fully integrated international production structure dominated by MNEs, with few or no government controls or national restrictions. A number of objections can be raised to this 'ideal' and to its policy implications. First, the conflict of interests between MNEs and LDCs may be much more serious than Reuber makes out. He avoids mentioning not only the extensive literature on the MNE state conflict (such as Behrman (1970), or Menderhausen (1969)), but also the ITT–Chile fiasco, or the excellent political-economic study of India by Kidron (1965) (though India is one of the LDCs covered by Reuber). He argues that foreign investors do not constitute a particularly strong pressure group, but ignores historical evidence from Latin America and the dependency and Marxist schools' literature on this. Second, though the possibility of bargaining with MNEs is mentioned at several points, Reuber in fact ignores this when considering policy. Proponents of the nationalist school argue, with reason, that strong controls are needed on every aspect of foreign investors' activities because of their oligopolistic powers, ability to transfer profits undetected, and numerous other damaging effects; and, given the distribution of power and resources, it is possible for host countries to get a much better deal from them by tough bargaining than by doing nothing.[11] Third, by dismissing the desirability of control and bargaining Reuber also ignores any consideration of how an LDC's bargaining power can be improved, by means of collecting information, international co-operation, shopping around, and so on. This is a serious fault of the book, because it is here that LDCs' governments look most for guidance at the operational level.

(*b*) *Transfer-pricing and export restrictions.* These constitute serious practical problems in the operation of foreign enterprises. As far as export restrictions are concerned, Reuber brushes off the problem by saying, 'Little evidence of such restrictions was uncovered in our survey' (p. 163), and does not mention several studies in existence which have found such evidence (UNCTAD, various) in a number of countries; when favourable effects are concerned, of course, he quotes widely from the literature.[12] Similarly with transfer-pricing, Vernon is quoted as saying that there does not appear to be a 'systematic bias in favour of assigning the largest profits to the parent';[13] Vernon's statement is based on reports given by the MNEs themselves, and, moreover, is quite consistent with the proposition that LDCs as a whole lose via transfer pricing to developed countries (see Lall (1973), and Vaitsos (1970)).[14] When he argues that there is not enough evidence, it may be answered that while it *is* very difficult to get evidence on transfer-prices and their appropriateness, the few investigations which have taken place have *all* shown that transfer-prices are used against LDCs. (UNCTAD (1971b).)

(*c*) *Technology.* Reuber draws a peculiar distinction between 'techniques', which are easily available internationally, and 'technology,' which is new and under the control of MNEs; he then pays little attention to the former, which in fact comprises a major part of the technology (in the sense of productive knowledge) needed by LDCs, and argues that foreign investment is the best way to transfer the latter. Whether or not direct investment is preferable to licensing for LDCs is not proved; it is assumed on *a priori* grounds that the former is cheaper (mainly because MNEs prefer it). The *real* costs of technology transferred by direct investment, comprising a substantial element of profits and not only royalties and fees, are not compared to the costs of licensing. As for the problem of the appropriateness of the techniques transferred, the possibility of intermediate technology is summarily dismissed, and it is argued that the technology transferred by MNEs 'seems as appropriate to the factor endowments found in LDCs as the transfers made through other channels', which begs the question of the real alternatives.[15] As with the general recommendations on government regulation, the potential for bargaining is minimised; this again is a pity, because the highly imperfect nature of the technology market and the weak position of LDCs in fact calls for a much more active role on part of their governments (see Streeten (1972b)).

(*d*) *Costs of foreign investment.*[16] The net economic costs of foreign investment may be calculated by comparing it with the costs of the next best alternative. Reuber tends generally to assume that in the absence of foreign investment the project would not be undertaken at all, or, at least, much less efficiently; again, he simply *assumes* superior management and organisation on part of foreign firms on the basis of the fact that they find it easy to compete, ignoring their numerous oligopolistic advantages which may be much more significant in this respect. The fact that many projects actually run by foreigners could be just as well, if not bettter, run by local enterprises, the basis of the so-called 'Streeten dilemma',[17] is dismissed as resting on 'special and highly implausible assumptions' (p. 38). In fact, an empirical survey of a number of countries and foreign firms leads one to believe that there is nothing special or highly implausible about this (Streeten and Lall (1973)); undoubtedly a number of foreign enterprises could not be fully locally replaced, but, equally undoubtedly, a number could. An aspect of the financial cost of foreign investment which is not properly treated is that of local gearing. On page 213, Reuber misrepresents the case of critics who argue that foreign investors put in relatively little capital of their own but gear themselves highly on local borrowing. He puts the argument (source unspecified) as relating to locally reinvested profits, while in fact that area of concern is local *borrowing*; he then proceeds to knock down the straw man. It may be of interest to note that for a sample of 56 firms in Colombia, foreign loans provided only 38 per cent of total loans, and that gearing, especially based on borrowing from local banks, had a significant correlation with profitability.[18] The higher the extent of local gearing, the higher, of course, is the profitability of the foreign capital invested; and investigations have shown that foreign investors try to gear themselves as highly as possible in their host countries.

Perhaps enough has been said to vindicate the criticisms voiced at the start of the paper. Further objections may be raised on a score of other issues, but this is not the appropriate venue for a lengthy discussion of the complicated problems. Reuber's analysis is interesting and consistent—once the general premises are accepted—but it cannot claim to have contributed greatly to our understanding of the phenomenon to which it is addressed. No new analytical tools are forged, and most of the sample data adduced add little to the force of the argument. Large sections serve simply to review the literature in a highly selective fashion; the policy prescriptions are, at best, inadequate and, at worst, very misleading.

NOTES

1. I would like to thank Deepak Nayyar and Paul Streeten for their comments and suggestions.

2. Grant L. Reuber, with H. Crookel, M. Emerson, G. Gallais-Hammonno, *Private Foreign Investment in Development* (Oxford: Clarendon Press, 1973). (Prepared under the auspices of the OECD Development Centre, Paris.)

3. A recent work which aptly illustrates these characteristics is by Robbins and Stobaugh (1973), who build a sophisticated model of how MNEs can greatly raise their profits by a better use of transfer-prices and other financial channels. The fact that the loss from such 'revenue shifting' will be borne by host governments, and certainly by most host LDCs, is not considered relevant to the 'optimum strategy' proposed; even the use of technical euphemisms (in quotation marks) is intended to raise possibly objectionable practices to the status of efficient—and therefore desirable—business tactics.

4. With minor exceptions for the imposition of 'optimum' tariffs and taxes on flows of commodities and capital.

5. This would be qualified to 'earned profits in an internationally competitive framework' if protection were introduced.

6. See, for instance, Stewart (1973) for a discussion of the undesirable effects of free trade on LDCs' technology and consumption patterns.

7. The place of value judgements in economics has been treated at great length in Myrdal (1968), especially in the Prologue and appendices 2 and 3.

8. ' . . . studies of the problems of underdeveloped countries are now undertaken, not with a view to the universal and timeless values that are our legacy from the Enlightenment, but with a view to the fortuitous and narrow political or, narrower still, military-strategic interest of one state or bloc of

states. . . . Sometimes this intention is stated, though not in the form of a reasoned presentation of specific value premises logically related to the definition of the concepts used. More often it remains implicit in the approach. This type of reasoning must often make the public and scholars in the underdeveloped countries irritated, as they naturally want their problems analysed from the point of view of their own interests and valuations.' Myrdal, ibid., pp. 8–10.

9. For an application and discussion of the limitations of such methods in the context of foreign manufacturing investment in LDCs see Lall and Mayhew (1973) and Streeten and Lall (1973).

10. For instance, in discussing the distributive effects of foreign investment, Reuber states: 'The broad distributive effects of private foreign investment seem reasonably clear, assuming government policy to be the same after foreign investment occurs as before. In the long run, after all general equilibrium effects have worked themselves out, one may expect capital inflows to lower the real incomes of local capitalists and to raise the real income of labour and other complementary factors. Moreover, by enhancing the supply of capital available to the country and thereby reducing capital costs from what they would otherwise be, investment in industries and localities with less favourable access to capital markets becomes economically feasible. In addition, by keeping capital costs down foreign capital inflows make feasible more long term projects . . . for which capital service changes . . . are an important cost' (p. 218). This paragraph graphically illustrates the model underlying the whole study; the reader may judge for himself its relevance to LDCs.

11. Reuber refers to local control as being 'under the thumb of local governments and bureaucrats' (p. 215).

12. For Canada, for instance, Safarian is often mentioned, while the Canadian government's massive, and often critical study (1972), and Levitt (1970), are completely ignored. Safarian is, as is to be expected, a solid 'traditional economist'.

13. Vernon (1970) p. 139.

14. Even the US Tariff Commission's massive study (1973), which supports MNEs, says on page 133, 'The chief strategy of tax minimization by multinational companies is manipulation of transfer prices.' Robbins and Stobaugh (1973) conclude, 'we foresee continued opportunity for MNEs to make extensive use of revenue-shifting tools, especially transfer pricing' (p. 186): and they are business-school economists proper.

15. See Griffin (1974), who makes a fascinating case that the whole process of the international transmission of technology worsens inequality between nations.

16. By costs I mean the cost to the host economy of having foreign investment rather than costs of production.

17. See chapter 11 of Streeten (1972a) where the implicit assumption of the sort Reuber makes is attacked.

18. Lall and Mayhew (1973). A similar investigation of 21 firms in India and 9 in Iran with foreign majority equity holdings showed that foreign long-term borrowing comprised 28 per cent and 12 per cent respectively of total long-term borrowing (Lall and Elek, 1971).

REFERENCES

Bannock, G. (1971), *The Juggernauts: The Age of the Big Corporation* (London: Weidenfeld & Nicolson).
Baran, P. A. (1957), *The Political Economy of Growth* (New York: Monthly Review Press).
Behrman, J. N. (1970), *National Interests and Multinational Enterprise: Tensions Among the North-Atlantic Countries* (Englewood Cliffs: Prentice Hall).
dos Santos, T. (1970), 'The Structure of Dependence', *American Economic Review*, Papers and Proceedings, 1970, pp. 231-6.
Frank, A. G. (1972), *Lumpenbourgeoisie and Lumpendevelopment* (New York: Monthly Review Press).
Goldberg, P. M. and Kindleberger, C. P. (1970), 'Towards a GATT for Investment: A Proposal for Supervision of the International Corporation', *Law and Policy in International Business*, Summer, pp. 295-325.
Griffin, K. B. (1974), 'The International Transmission of Inequality', *World Development* (March).
Hymer, S. (1972), 'The Multinational Corporation and the Law of Uneven Development', in J. N. Bhagwati (ed.), *Economics and the World Order* (New York: Macmillan) pp. 113-40.
Kidron, M. (1965), *Foreign Investments in India* (London: Oxford University Press).
Kindleberger, C. P. (1969), *American Business Abroad* (New Haven, Yale University Press).
Lall, S. and Elek, A. (1971), *Balance-of-Payments and Income Effects of Private Foreign Investment in Manufacturing: Case Studies of India and Iran*, Geneva, UNCTAD, November, TD/B/C 3(V)/Misc. 1.
Lall, S., and Mayhew, K. (1973), *Balance-of-Payments and Income Effects of Private Foreign Investment in Manufacturing: Case Studies of Colombia and Malaysia*, Geneva, UNCTAD, July, TD/B/C 3(VI)/Misc. 1.
Lall, S. (1973), 'Transfer-pricing by Multinational Manufacturing Firms', *Oxford Bulletin of Economics and Statistics*, August, pp. 173-95.
Levitt, K. (1970), *Silent Surrender* (Toronto: Macmillan).
Magdoff, H. (1969), *The Age of Imperialism* (New York: Monthly Review Press).
Menderhausen, H. (1969), 'Transnational Society versus State Sovereignty', *Kyklos*, pp. 251-75.
Myrdal, G. (1968), *Asian Drama* (Harmondsworth: Penguin Press).
Robbins, S. M., and Stobaugh, R. B. (1973), *Money in the Multinational Enterprise* (New York: Basic Books).
Safarian, A. E. (1969), *The Performance of Foreign Owned Firms in Canada* (Montreal: Canadian-American Committee).
Stewart, F. (1973), 'Trade and Technology', in P. P. Streeten (ed.), *Trade Strategies for Development* (London: Macmillan) pp. 231-63.
Streeten, P. P. (1972a), *The Frontiers of Development Studies* (London: Macmillan).
Streeten, P. P. (1972b), 'Technological Gaps between Rich and Poor Countries', *Scottish Journal of Political Economy*, November, pp. 213-30.
Streeten, P. P., and Lall, S. (1973), *Summary of Methods and Findings of Study of*

*Private Foreign Manufacturing Investment in Six Developing Countries*, Geneva, UNCTAD, May, in 3 parts:

(i) *Methodology Used in Studies on Private Foreign Investment in Selected Developing Countries*, TD/B/C 3(VI)/Misc. 6.

(ii) *Some Reflections on Government Policies Concerning Private Foreign Investment*, TD/B/C 3(VI)/Misc. 7.

(iii) *Main Findings of a Study of Private Foreign Investment in Selected Developing Countries*, TD/B/C 3/111.

Streeten, P. P. (1973), 'The Multinational Enterprise and the Theory of Development Policy', *World Development*, October, pp. 1–14.

Sunkel, O. (1969–70), 'National Development Policy and External Dependence in Latin America', *Journal of Development Studies*, pp. 23–48.

Sweezy, P. M., and Magdoff, H. (1972), *The Dynamics of US Capitalism* (New York: Monthly Review Press).

UNCTAD (1971a), *Restrictive Business Practices* (Geneva) TD/122 and Supp. 1.

UNCTAD (1971b), *Policies Relating to Technology in the Countries of the Andean Pact: Their Foundations* (Santiago) TD/107.

UNCTAD (1971c), *Restrictions on Exports in Foreign Collaboration Agreements in India* (New York) TD/B/389.

UNCTAD (1972), *Restrictions on Exports in Foreign Collaboration Agreements in the Republic of the Philippines* (New York) TD/B/388.

UNCTAD (1973), *Restrictive Business Practices in Relation to Trade and Development of Developing Countries* (Geneva) TD/B/C 2/119.

US Tariff Commission (1973), *Implications of Multinational Firms for World Trade and Investment and for US Trade and Labour* (Washington, DC: US Senate).

Vaitsos, C. V. (1970), 'Transfer of Resources and Preservation of Monopoly Rents' (mimeo), Harvard Development Advisory Service.

Vernon, R. (1971), *Sovereignty at Bay: The Multinational Spread of US Enterprises* (New York: Basic Books).

Weisskopf, T. E. (1972), 'Capitalism, Underdevelopment and the Future of the Poor Countries', in J. N. Bhagwati (ed.), *Economics and the World Order* (New York: Macmillan) pp. 43–77.

# 4 Food Transnationals and Developing Countries[1]

## 1 INTRODUCTION

This chapter draws upon the existing literature and data on the role of transnational corporations (TNCs) and of foreign investment generally in food processing in developing countries, to discuss the main issues which arise for these countries in terms of the transfer of technology by foreign firms. We shall undertake an examination of the extent and nature of foreign investment in this industry, using data published by the two leading investor countries (the United States and the United Kingdom), on the large firms which dominate it internationally and by the leading food processing transnational, Unilever. This examination will, it is hoped, permit us a clearer understanding of the effects that the transfer of foreign technology and the entry of large transnational firms might have on various aspects of economic life in developing host countries.

The data at hand are far from satisfactory. The virtual absence of comprehensive published studies on this subject, compounded by capital exporting countries apart from the United States and the United Kingdom, and the lack of relevant data in host countries, makes analysis very difficult. The conglomerate and diversified nature of the TNCs concerned and the highly diverse nature of the industry itself, raise problems of specification and inference. The differences in levels of income and industrialisation, policies towards foreign investment and consumption patterns among developing countries render generalisations rather risky. Even if all the facts were available, their interpretation in terms of the welfare of host economies would be contentious and value-laden. Thus the reader should be warned at the outset to be aware of the delicacy of the ground on which we tread.

We shall proceed as follows: section II describes the extent and distribution of foreign investment in food processing by the United

States and the United Kingdom; section III deals with the dominant TNCs, discussing the characteristics of their home economies which give rise to them and the main features of their expansion abroad; section IV describes the overseas operations of Unilever, relying on the firm's published annual reports and some unpublished studies of its operations in three developing countries; section V analyses the implications for developing host countries of the transfer of technology and direct investment by foreign firms; and section VI summarises the main conclusions.

## II  FOREIGN INVESTMENT IN FOOD PROCESSING BY THE UNITED STATES AND THE UNITED KINGDOM

The United States and the United Kingdom account for most direct foreign investment in food processing. The next section shows that firms from these two countries hold about 80 per cent of the assets of the leading transnationals in this industry and, although data are not available on the activities of small investors, there is little reason to believe that the picture is very different for foreign investment as a whole. Fortunately, these two countries regularly publish data on the value, distribution and earnings of their investments abroad; the United States also publishes figures on sales of its overseas affiliates and on the extent of intra-firm trade.

### THE UNITED STATES

Let us start with the United States figures. Table 4.1 shows the growth of the sales of United States subsidiaries over 1957–75 by geographical area, while Table 4.2 shows the distribution of assets held by foreign majority-owned affiliates in the industry at the end of 1975 and compares it with the distribution for all manufacturing industry.

Table 4.1 indicates that although the distribution of sales over the past 18 years has remained relatively stable in broad terms, and the share of developing countries has dropped by less than 1 percentage point, that of Asia has expanded at the cost of Latin America's. However, Latin America continues to account for about 90 per cent of sales in the developing world, and within this region Mexico (28 per cent of sales in the developing world), Brazil (19 per cent), Argentina (11 per cent) and Venezuela (16 per cent) dominate the scene. The first two, Mexico and Brazil, account by themselves for nearly half the total of United States

TABLE 4.1   US foreign affiliates in food processing: sales abroad in 1957 and 1975

| Area | 1957 Sales ($ millions) | 1957 Distribution (%) | 1975 Sales ($ millions) | 1975 Distribution (%) | % Growth (1957–75) |
|---|---|---|---|---|---|
| Canada | 928 | 37.8 | 4,475 | 24.5 | 9.1 |
| Europe | 734 | 29.9 | 8,068 | 44.1 | 14.2 |
| Japan | 2 | 0.1 | 241 | 1.3 | 30.4 |
| Other developed* | 147 | 6.0 | 1,023 | 5.6 | 11.3 |
| Total developed | 1,811 | 73.7 | 13,807 | 75.5 | 11.9 |
| Latin America | 612 | 24.9 | 4,013 | 22.0 | 11.0 |
| Asia | 16 | 0.7 | 421 | 2.3 | 19.9 |
| Africa | 2 | 0.1 | 36 | 0.2 | 17.4 |
| Total developing | 630 | 25.7 | 4,470 | 24.5 | 11.5 |
| Total | 2,457 | 100 | 18,277 | 100 | 11.8 |

NOTE
* Australia, New Zealand and South Africa.
SOURCES
US Department of Commerce (1975) and Chung (1977).

TNC sales in developing countries, and we shall consider their situation in more detail below.

The developing world as a whole accounts for less than 20 per cent of total foreign assets in food processing (and in manufacturing generally), and for about 25 per cent of foreign affiliate sales. The general pattern of investment in food processing closely resembles that of total manufacturing.

Food processing is not a dynamic sector in United States foreign investment. Despite the impressive increases recorded in the last column of Table 4.1, a comparison with the growth of sales of manufacturing affiliates as a whole shows that its importance is declining. In 1966, food processing affiliates accounted for 12 per cent of total manufacturing affiliate sales; by 1975 this had slipped to 9.5 per cent. This is not, surprisingly, due to lower returns on food processing investments, as Table 4.3 shows.

TABLE 4.2  Assets of US majority-owned affiliates in manufacturing and food processing, end 1975

|  | All manufacturing | | Food processing | | % of all manufac-turing |
|---|---|---|---|---|---|
|  | Assets | Distri-bution | Assets | Distri-bution | |
| Canada | 14,718 | 26.3 | 1,364 | 28.9 | 9.3 |
| Europe | 26,136 | 46.6 | 2,023 | 42.9 | 7.7 |
| Other | 4,747 | 8.5 | 426 | 9.0 | 9.7 |
| Total developed | 45,601 | 81.4 | 3,813 | 80.9 | 8.4 |
| Latin America | 8,555 | 15.3 | 725 | 15.4 | 8.5 |
| Africa and Middle East | 395 | 0.6 | 34 | 0.6 | 8.6 |
| Asia | 1,489 | 2.7 | 144 | 3.1 | 9.7 |
| Total de-veloping | 10,438 | 18.6 | 903 | 19.1 | 9.6 |
| Total | 56,039 | 100.0 | 4,716 | 100.0 | 8.4 |

SOURCE
Friedlin and Whichard (1976).

TABLE 4.3  Earnings of food processing and total manufacturing affiliates of US firms

|  | 1974 | | 1975 | |
|---|---|---|---|---|
|  | Earnings | % of Assets | Earnings | % of Assets |
| Food: | | | | |
| Developed | 462 | 13.1 | 454 | 11.9 |
| Developing | 118 | 14.2 | 135 | 15.0 |
| Total | 580 | 13.3 | 589 | 12.5 |
| All manufacturing: | | | | |
| Developed | 5,596 | 13.3 | 4,916 | 10.8 |
| Developing | 1,178 | 12.8 | 1,316 | 12.6 |
| Total | 6,774 | 13.2 | 6,232 | 11.1 |

SOURCE
Friedlin and Whichard (1976).

In the last two years, earnings on food processing investments were, in all cases except one, higher than those on manufacturing investments as a whole. More interestingly, earnings on food investments in developing countries were significantly higher than those in developed ones in both years; for all manufacturing, this was true only in 1975. However, figures for earnings in these years of recession cannot be taken as necessarily representative of long-term trends; such trends may show a relatively low return for food processing.

Most sales by food subsidiaries were in the domestic markets of the host countries. In 1975 some 91 per cent of sales in developed countries and 92 per cent in LDCs were local, as compared to 77 per cent for manufacturing affiliates as a whole. Of the remainder, 15 per cent was exported to the United States and 85 per cent elsewhere. This rather low figure for exports to the home country (1 per cent of total sales in food as compared to 6 per cent for all manufacturing) in an industry based on processing a primary product like food may at first sight seem surprising. However, this may occur for two main reasons: first, much of food imported into the United States may be in an unprocessed form (like tropical fruit), and so does not show up in the trade of manufacturing affiliates; second, the United States is a food surplus country (unlike the United Kingdom or Japan) and its foreign food investment aims to sell high-income products developed for home markets rather than to exploiting foreign resources for consumption at home. Domike (1976, pp. 38–9) remarks on this characteristic of United States food firms, and the contrasts with Japanese firms which operate abroad mainly to serve their home markets.

Let us now consider the situation in Mexico and Brazil, the largest bases of United States food manufacturing in the developing world. A recent study by Newfarmer and Mueller (1975), which draws on data provided by some of the largest United States TNCs to the United States Senate, provides interesting data on these countries. The share of all foreign firms in value added in this sector in *Mexico* came to 3.4 per cent in 1962 and 6.1 per cent in 1970: the share of United States TNCs alone came to 3.2 per cent and 5.6 per cent respectively. The food sector did not, in relation to manufacturing as a whole, seem to be particularly important for foreign investors: the comparable shares in value added for all manufacturing came to 17.6 per cent (8.1 per cent for United States TNCs) in 1962 and 22.7 per cent (12.4 per cent) in 1970. However, the rate at which United States TNCs expanded their assets in the period 1960–72 in the food industry (834 per cent) exceeded the rate for all manufacturing (557 per cent). Clearly, the food sector is one in which, because of its relatively simple and unchanging technology, local firms have traditionally played a dominant role. With industrialisation and the rise in incomes however, the role of TNCs, with highly differentiated and sophisticated products, has become more significant, and they seem to predominate in those categories of food products for which advertising is important.[2] We may note in this context that the levels of industrial concentration in Mexico and Brazil are generally quite high, higher than similar levels in the United States. In eight sub-sectors of food processing in Mexico, for instance, the four-firm concentration ratio (the share of the leading four firms in total industry sales) ranged between 60 and 100 per cent, with a mean of 78 per cent, in 1972; the only exception was 'oils', at 30 per cent (see Connor and Mueller (1977)). Given the tendency towards increasing concentration in food processing in the advanced countries (see below), we may expect industries in developing countries to become even more concentrated as they mature, with TNCs taking the dominant positions in several sub-sectors.

The chief mode of entry of United States firms into the Mexican food industry was the establishment of new factories: this was, as in other manufacturing industries, the most direct way of introducing new products and new methods of production. Acquisitions of Mexican enterprises did, nevertheless, provide 24 per cent of the growth of United States assets in 1960–72, as compared to 20 per cent for manufacturing as a whole. This relatively greater propensity to acquire local firms in food processing may be attributed to the 'low' technology of large parts of the industry:[3] thus, some existing firms may possess marketing and distribution systems to which the addition of foreign brand names and promotion can do wonders in terms of profitability, without greatly changing the product range of the existing production facilities.

In terms of earnings, United States food firms were less profitable than manufacturing TNCs as a whole, using a narrow definition of profits (after-tax profits on equity), but significantly more profitable on a broader definition (including technical payments in profits). The difference between the two definitions for 1972 (9.1 per cent and 19.6 per cent for food, and 11.1 per cent and 16.2 per cent for all manufacturing) is so striking, especially for food firms, that we are led to wonder whether 'technical payments' were in fact the legitimate price paid for imported technology (a dubious proposition in a low technology sector like food) and trademarks, or whether they were simply profit remittances disguised to minimise the foreign enterprises' tax burdens. We remarked earlier that intra-firm trade is relatively small in food processing. This reduces the scope of transfer pricing on intra-firm commodity trade, and may lead TNCs to concentrate profit-shifting strategies on payments for technology: a substantial part of technical payments may, in other words, be profit remittances.

In *Brazil* the share of United States TNCs in total sales of food products came to 8 per cent in 1966 and 3 per cent in 1970, as compared to 13 per cent and 20 per cent respectively for all manufacturing. United States firms owned 30 per cent of total assets in food products in 1969, with other foreign firms accounting for another 26 per cent, as compared to 17 per cent and 25 per cent for all manufacturing, and 14 per cent and 21 per cent for all sectors together. In contrast to Mexico, United States firms lost their share of the food product market in 1966–70, despite a faster growth of assets in food over 1960–72 than in all manufacturing. Such an experience was rare, since in nearly all other industries (except for rubber) the United States' share increased in this period. Newfarmer and Mueller estimate that the share of non-United States TNCs rose faster for manufacturing industry as a whole than that of United States TNCs, and remark that 'Denationalisation—as measured by the level of MNC penetration among the largest manufacturing enterprises and by the extent of foreign ownership of industrial assets—is substantial [in Brazil] . . . both the pace and degree of denationalisation are notably greater than in Mexico and very high' (see Newfarmer and Mueller (1975), p. 114).

The role of acquisitions in the growth of United States assets was also different from that in Mexico. In Brazil, acquisitions accounted for only 11 per cent during 1960–72 (compared to 24 per cent in Mexico), while they accounted for 24 per cent in all manufacturing (20 per cent in Mexico). Whether this was due to government policy, the lack of suitable candidates for acquisition, or an unknown bias in the sample is impossible to say.

The rate of return on food investments in Brazil came to 20.7 per cent in 1960, 11.6 per cent in 1966 and 16.1 per cent in 1972, compared to 10.4 per cent, 14.6 per cent and 14.4 per cent respectively for all manufacturing. Brazilian affiliates thus gave a much better performance, as (somewhat) narrowly defined, than those in Mexico; and in contrast to the latter, they also generally performed better than in manufacturing as a whole. The addition of technical payments does not affect returns in Brazil very greatly. In 1966 the rate rose to 14.9 per cent (by 28 per cent) and in 1972 to 16.3 per cent (by 1 per cent) for food, and to 16.4 per cent (by 12 per cent) and 15.3 per cent (by 6 per cent) for all manufacturing. Clearly, the tax (or other) advantages of channelling profits through this route were less than in Mexico. Taking the broad definition of earnings Mexican affiliates showed a better record than Brazilian ones.

THE UNITED KINGDOM

Data provided by the British Government on overseas investments are not as copious as those published by the United States, but suffice to give a clear picture of their distribution and profitability. Table 4.4 gives the

TABLE 4.4    Book value of net assets abroad (UK) at end-1974 (£ million)

| | Food, drink and tobacco | | All manufacturing | | FDT Assets as a % of all manufacturing |
|---|---|---|---|---|---|
| | Assets | Distribution (%) | Assets | Distribution (%) | |
| W. Europe | 468.1 | 30.2 | 1,698.0 | 28.2 | 27.6 |
| of which,  EEC | 404.3 | 26.0 | 1,462.2 | 24.3 | 27.7 |
|   EFTA | 35.5 | 2.3 | 101.3 | 1.7 | 35.0 |
|   Other | 28.3 | 1.8 | 102.8 | 1.7 | 27.5 |
| N. America | 413.9 | 26.7 | 1,338.2 | 22.2 | 30.9 |
| Other developed | 309.0 | 19.9 | 1,955.4 | 32.5 | 15.8 |
|   Total developed | 1,191.0 | 76.7 | 4,982.6 | 82.8 | 23.9 |
| Africa | 93.9 | 6.0 | 288.8 | 4.8 | 32.5 |
| Asia | 105.8 | 6.8 | 366.5 | 6.1 | 28.9 |
| S. America + Caribbean | 160.9 | 10.4 | 365.2 | 6.1 | 44.1 |
| Total developing | 361.5 | 23.3 | 1,025.6 | 17.1 | 35.2 |
| Total | 1,552.5 | 100 | 6,017.2 | 100 | 25.8 |

SOURCE
United Kingdom, Department of Industry (1976).

geographical distribution of net assets owned abroad in 1974 by United Kingdom firms, and Table 4.5 shows their earnings. It should be noted that the figures include tobacco investments.

The distribution of United Kingdom investment between the developed and developing regions is similar to that of the United States. For food processing, the share of LDCs comes to 23 per cent for the United Kingdom and 19 per cent for the United States; for manufacturing as a whole, the figures are 17 per cent and 19 per cent respectively. Within the developing world, however, there are marked differences, due mainly to the historical patterns of investment of the two countries.

TABLE 4.5   UK earnings on overseas assets in food, drinks and tobacco, 1974

| | Total | W.*<br>Europe | America | Other<br>dev. | Total<br>dev. | Africa | Asia | America | Total<br>LDC |
|---|---|---|---|---|---|---|---|---|---|
| Earnings (£m) | 215.7 | 56.8 | 71.9 | 26.2 | 154.9 | 10.7 | 18.7 | 31.4 | 60.8 |
| % of net assets | 13.9 | 12.1† | 17.4 | 8.5 | 13.0 | 11.4 | 17.7 | 19.7 | 16.8 |

NOTES
* See Table 4.4
† The rates for EFTA and EEC separately are 20.0 and 11.7 respectively.
SOURCE
United Kingdom, Department of Industry (1976).

The United Kingdom owns a much smaller proportion of its developing country assets in Latin America (45 per cent) than the United States (82 per cent), and a relatively larger proportion in Africa (26 per cent as compared to 4 per cent) and Asia (29 per cent as compared to 14 per cent).

The United Kingdom has invested more in food processing abroad relative to total manufacturing than the United States. This may partly be due to the inclusion of tobacco in the United Kingdom figures, but in the main it probably reflects a different sectoral pattern of foreign investment by the two, with the United States more highly concentrated in high technology sectors than the United Kingdom (see Buckley and Casson (1976) especially Chapter 1). If we convert United Kingdom figures into dollars at the 1974 exchange rate ($2.3 to £1) and compare them to US figures for end 1974, we find that United Kingdom assets in food came to 82 per cent of United States assets for the industry as a whole, 78 per cent in the developed and slightly more (by 0.2 per cent) in LDCs. However, this comparison must be viewed with caution because the data coverage for the two countries is different: the United Kingdom figures include all investments abroad, while the United States figures pertain only to majority-owned affiliates. On an equivalent basis, United States assets abroad would probably exceed United Kingdom assets in food processing by a much large amount.

As with United States investments, United Kingdom food processing firms abroad earn higher profits in developing than in developed areas. While the over-all rates of return and rates in developed areas are remarkably similar for both countries, the United Kingdom seems to show, at least in 1974, a better performance in LDCs than the United States. As for manufacturing investment as a whole, United Kingdom affiliates earn 12.6 per cent in all areas, 11.9 per cent in developed and 16.0 per cent in developing countries. United States affiliates showed better returns over-all in that year and in the developed world, but their performance in developing countries (12.8 per cent) was much worse. A longer run of figures would however be needed before any conclusions can be drawn from such comparisons.

There are no data available on the extent of intra-firm trade by United Kingdom food TNCs (although some are provided by Unilever, as indicated in section IV). While figures on the nature of exporting firms show that as much as 96 per cent of food exports from the United Kingdom came from firms with some foreign affiliation (parents or subsidiaries),[4] as compared to about 51 per cent for the United States,[5] nothing can be inferred from this about *intra-firm* trade.

## III   THE LEADING FOOD TRANSNATIONAL CORPORATIONS

WHO ARE THEY?

There are several problems in drawing up a list of firms with transnational operations in food processing. While a perusal of lists of leading firms such as published by *Fortune, Vision, The Times* and other journals immediately yields a list of names of well-known TNCs, and *Fortune* provides the two-digit industrial group of each firm, there remain some difficulties. There are four specific gaps in our knowledge: first, on firms with diversified activities (very common in this context), which are classified under an industry different from food but which may be active transnationals in food processing; second, on food firms which are acquired by conglomerates and, again, are not shown as distinct entities; third, on the transnational nature of the activities of food firms (this is a particular problem with new firms, say from Japan); and fourth, on food processing activity as opposed to food distribution or other food-related activity.

As there is no easy way to fill these gaps, we have to proceed with our survey despite them. The list shown in Table 4.6, drawn from the latest available figures in *Fortune*, includes most of the large firms active in the food group. A few have been excluded: the brewers and distillers of alcoholic beverages (soft drinks are included); one or two conglomerate firms on which no information exists as regards food processing; and one or two Japanese firms which are unlikely to be transnational. This still leaves some dubious choices in our list, but by and large it may be taken as reasonably accurate. We have restricted our list to the top 60 firms for manageability, but a more extensive list could be drawn up from available data.[6] The main line of business of the selected firms is also shown. Since there was no way of separating the non-food from the food activities of these firms, all the figures refer to their *total* operations: the exaggeration of *food* activities in these figures should be borne in mind. A number of smaller active TNCs from the United States, like Libby, McNeill and Libby, Green Giant, Gerber, Wrigley and so on, have been left out of the list, but since the purpose of the exercise is to illustrate broad magnitudes, perhaps this is not a great loss.

Tables 4.7 and 4.8 summarise the data on the 60 leading transnational corporations according to nationality. The former shows that the United States accounts for about 60 per cent of the total sales of these firms and the United Kingdom for another 26 per cent: between them,

TABLE 4.6  Leading 60 food TNCs ranked by sales: data for 1976* ($ million)

| Firm | Activity | Nation-ality | Sales | Assets | Net Income | Net Income as % Assets | Employ-ment ('000s) |
|---|---|---|---|---|---|---|---|
| 1. Unilever | a | UK/Neth. | 15,762.2 | 7,793.8 | 517.6 | 6.6 | 317 |
| 2. Nestlé | a | Switz. | 7,627.9 | 5,706.9 | 348.9 | 6.1 | 137 |
| 3. Proctor & Gamble | b | US | 6,512.7 | 4,103.0 | 401.1 | 9.8 | 52 |
| 4. Esmark | c | US | 5,300.6 | 1,757.5 | 82.6 | 4.6 | 47 |
| 5. Kraft | a | US | 4,976.6 | 1,821.9 | 135.7 | 7.4 | 47 |
| 6. Beatrice | a | US | 4,690.6 | 1,844.4 | 153.1 | 8.3 | 67 |
| 7. LTV | c | US | 4,496.9 | 2,134.9 | 30.7 | 1.4 | 57 |
| 8. General Foods | a | US | 3,978.3 | 2,012.9 | 150.4 | 7.1 | 47 |
| 9. Greyhound | c | US | 3,727.3 | 1,472.6 | 77.1 | 5.2 | 52 |
| 10. Ralston Purina | b | US | 3,393.8 | 1,556.3 | 125.9 | 8.0 | 59 |
| 11. Borden | a | US | 3,381.1 | 1,808.5 | 112.8 | 6.2 | 40 |
| 12. Imperial Group | b | UK | 3,321.6 | 2,577.8 | 147.7 | 5.7 | 97 |
| 13. Coca Cola | a | US | 3,032.8 | 1,903.1 | 285.0 | 14.9 | 33 |
| 14. Taiyo Fishery | a | Jap. | 2,993.6 | 1,362.4 | 2.6 | 0.1 | 21 |
| 15. George Weston | a | UK | 2,826.9 | 1,098.0 | 51.9 | 4.7 | 105 |
| 16. Pepsico | a | US | 2,727.5 | 1,541.7 | 136.0 | 8.8 | 54 |
| 17. Consolidated Foods | a | US | 2,726.5 | 1,146.5 | 89.5 | 7.8 | 77 |
| 18. CPC Internat. | a | US | 2,695.8 | 1,459.3 | 122.0 | 8.0 | 43 |
| 19. General Mills | a | US | 2,645.0 | 1,328.2 | 100.5 | 7.5 | 52 |
| 20. Tate & Lyle | a | UK | 2,558.7 | 879.7 | 50.6 | 5.7 | 16 |
| 21. BSN–Gervais Danone | a | Fr. | 2,463.1 | 938.2 | 9.7 | 1.0 | 62 |
| 22. United Brands | a | US | 2,276.6 | 1,085.3 | 16.3 | 1.5 | 48 |
| 23. Carnation | a | US | 2,167.0 | 1,079.2 | 104.4 | 9.6 | 22 |

TABLE 4.6  (continued)

| Firm | Activity | Nationality | Sales | Assets | Net Income | Net Income as % Assets | Employment ('000s) |
|---|---|---|---|---|---|---|---|
| 24. Nabisco | a | US | 2,027.3 | 1,058.5 | 77.0 | 7.2 | 48 |
| 25. Heinz | a | US | 1,882.4 | 1,168.2 | 74.0 | 6.3 | 33 |
| 26. Central Soya | a | US | 1,836.8 | 431.8 | 37.7 | 8.7 | 9 |
| 27. Standard Brands | a | US | 1,810.0 | 991.9 | 67.6 | 6.8 | 21 |
| 28. CSR | a | Austral. | 1,806.3 | 1,348.9 | 52.6 | 3.8 | 11 |
| 29. RHM | b | UK | 1,780.2 | 834.2 | 36.4 | 4.3 | 58 |
| 30. Norton Simon | b | US | 1,683.8 | 1,418.9 | 92.4 | 6.5 | 26 |
| 31. Campbell | a | US | 1,634.8 | 924.3 | 101.0 | 10.9 | 33 |
| 32. Unigate | a | UK | 1,619.2 | 614.1 | 24.7 | 4.0 | 37 |
| 33. Quaker Oats | a | US | 1,473.1 | 854.9 | 53.1 | 6.2 | 24 |
| 34. Del Monte | a | US | 1,430.4 | 796.5 | 53.2 | 6.7 | 34 |
| 35. Pillsbury | a | US | 1,421.9 | 881.7 | 41.6 | 4.7 | 38 |
| 36. Cadbury Schweppes | a | UK | 1,420.9 | 916.3 | 27.8 | 3.0 | 46 |
| 37. Kellogg | a | US | 1,385.4 | 765.5 | 130.4 | 17.0 | 20 |
| 38. J. Lyons | a | UK | 1,382.2 | 914.9 | 13.3 | 1.5 | 45 |
| 39. Brooke Bond Liebig | a | UK | 1,179.1 | 507.0 | 22.8 | 5.7 | 72 |
| 40. Oscar Meyer | a | US | 1,133.1 | 349.9 | 33.4 | 9.5 | 13 |
| 41. Spillers | a | UK | 1,128.0 | 484.3 | 12.1 | 2.5 | 30 |
| 42. Amstar | a | US | 1,118.5 | 483.2 | 43.4 | 9.0 | 8 |
| 43. Pet | a | US | 1,010.6 | 475.1 | 23.8 | 5.0 | 17 |
| 44. Ajinomoto | a | Jap. | 961.8 | 666.5 | 15.7 | 2.4 | 6 |
| 45. United Biscuits | a | UK | 940.6 | 429.6 | 28.1 | 6.5 | 36 |
| 46. Castle & Cooke | a | US | 905.0 | 724.8 | 37.9 | 5.2 | 25 |

| | | | | | | | |
|---|---|---|---|---|---|---|---|
| 47. Gold Kist | US | a | 892.9 | 345.1 | n.a. | n.a. | 7 |
| 48. Reckitt & Colman | UK | c | 874.3 | 544.1 | 52.9 | 9.7 | 26 |
| 49. Beghin-Say | Fr. | a | 834.3 | 824.2 | 13.4 | 1.6 | 10 |
| 50. Glaxo | UK | c | 819.6 | 733.6 | 69.1 | 9.4 | 31 |
| 51. Internat. Multi-foods | US | a | 800.8 | 300.3 | 16.4 | 5.5 | 7 |
| 52. Kane–Miller | US | b | 799.9 | 203.2 | 7.0 | 3.4 | 6 |
| 53. Anderson–Clayton | US | b | 759.3 | 435.1 | 35.6 | 8.2 | 8 |
| 54. Nippon Suisan Kaisha | Jap. | a | 740.8 | 467.4 | 6.1 | 1.3 | 10 |
| 55. Meiji Milk Pro. | Jap. | a | 736.6 | 294.7 | 4.0 | 1.4 | 6 |
| 56. Koninklyke Wassenen | Neth. | a | 720.5 | 255.1 | 5.7 | 2.2 | 3 |
| 57. Campbell Taggart | US | b | 697.8 | 278.8 | 21.3 | 7.6 | 18 |
| 58. Rowntree Mackintosh | UK | a | 694.9 | 357.3 | 30.7 | 8.6 | 30 |
| 59. FMC | UK | a | 681.3 | 106.8 | 0.9 | 0.8 | 9 |
| 60. Jacobs | Switz. | a | 656.9 | 303.8 | 20.5 | 6.7 | 4 |
| Total | | | 139,968.9 | 71,902.6 | 4,641.6 | 6.4 | 2,417 |

SOURCE
*Fortune* (1977a), (1977b).

NOTE
* Main activity as shown by Domike (1976): (a) food, (b) food related, and (c) non-food.

TABLE 4.7   60 Leading TNCs grouped by nationality

| Nation-ality | | Sales (£m.) | (%) | Assets (£m.) | (%) | Income (£m.) | (%) | Employment (000s) | (%) |
|---|---|---|---|---|---|---|---|---|---|
| US | (35) | 83,432.9 | (59.6) | 40,943.0 | (56.9) | 3,069.8 | (66.1) | 1,192 | (49.3) |
| UK | (15) | 36,969.7 | (26.4) | 18,791.5 | (26.1) | 1,092.6 | (23.5) | 955 | (39.5) |
| Other | (10) | 19,546.3 | (13.9) | 12,168.1 | (16.9) | 479.2 | (10.3) | 270 | (11.1) |
| Total | (60) | 139,968.9 | (100) | 71,902.6 | (100) | 4,641.6 | (100) | 2,417 | (100) |

NOTES
(1) Unilever is counted as a UK firm here.
(2) Income for firm no. 47 not available.
SOURCE:
Table 6

TABLE 4.8   Performance of 60 leading TNCs

| Nationality | Income/ Assets | Assets/ Sales | Income/ Sales | Sales/ Employment | Assets/ Employment | Income/ Employment |
|---|---|---|---|---|---|---|
| US | 7.6 | 49.0 | 3.6 | 70.0 | 34.3 | 2.6 |
| UK | 5.8 | 50.8 | 3.0 | 38.7 | 19.7 | 1.1 |
| Other | 3.9 | 62.2 | 2.4 | 72.4 | 72.4 | 1.8 |
| Total | 6.4 | 51.3 | 3.3 | 57.9 | 29.7 | 1.9 |

NOTE
As for Table 4.7.
SOURCE
Table 4.6.

they account for over 85 per cent of the group's sales. This dominance is even more pronounced for earnings, reaching 90 per cent of the total. As noted earlier, there is no reason to believe that this national pattern would change if a larger number of firms is included in the sample: a casual examination of the *Fortune* list of smaller firms shows a large number of American and British firms in this sector. The pattern of concentration within the largest 60 (the top 13 firms account for 50 per cent of total sales of the sample) implies, moreover, that bringing in small firms would not affect the over-all picture very greatly.

The tables show some interesting differences in performance between the different groups according to origin. Bearing in mind the usual caveats on generalising from small samples and short periods, it appears that United States firms operate more efficiently than others in terms of earnings on assets and sales per unit of capital employed. British firms use the least capital per employee, perhaps signifying a specialisation in more traditional areas of food processing. The 'other' firms, and among these particularly the Japanese, are relatively low profit-earners and also very capital-intensive (according to assets/sales as well as assets/employee).

We do not have comprehensive data on the foreign operations of the leading food firms, but scattered pieces of evidence are available. The record of Unilever is reviewed later. Nestlé's sales by region, taken from its 1974 Annual Report, shows that 50 per cent went to Europe, 34 per cent to North and South America, 2 per cent to Oceania, 5 per cent to Africa and 9 per cent to Asia. A United Nations study shows that, in 1971, 98 per cent of Nestlé's sales were outside its home country (see United Nations (1973), Table 3). Table 4.9 shows the available information for 1970–1 on some other companies.

Most of these large firms are highly diversified in their operations, both within the sub-sectors of the food industry and outside it. Data collected by Domike (1976, p. 13) show that in 1963 large United States food firms had more than three non-food lines each on average and that in 1969 the 69 largest food processors derived 24 per cent of their sales revenue from non-food activity. Since the tendency has been towards increasing diversification and conglomeration of large firms in the industry, we may safely assume that this percentage is considerably higher today. We shall return to this point again.

Table 4.10 shows the diversity of food interests of the leading 170 food firms in the world as calculated by Domike. It is not possible to say how diversified the *foreign* operations of these firms are. It is likely that in rich and developed markets they are fairly diverse, while in poor markets they are more restricted: this, at least, is what available information on Unilever shows. The diversity of operations per firm clearly declines with the size of the firm, except at the very lowest end, where it rises slightly.

This ends our description of the large food processors. Let us now consider the main characteristics of the industry in developed countries and the strategies of growth of these firms.

STRUCTURE OF THE FOOD PROCESSING INDUSTRY IN DEVELOPED COUNTRIES

The structure of the food industry has been studied most intensively in the United States, particularly by the Federal Trade Commission (FTC).[7] Several studies have traced the evolution of concentration there

TABLE 4.9  Share of foreign assets or earnings for some food TNCs and number of foreign subsidiaries (1970–1)

| | Share of foreign assets | Share of foreign earnings | Subsidiaries (no.) | | Share of foreign assets | Share of foreign earnings | Subsidiaries (no.) |
|---|---|---|---|---|---|---|---|
| General Foods* | 21 | — | 15 | Carnation* | 19 | — | — |
| Borden* | 12 | 13 | — | General Mills* | 10 | — | — |
| Beatrice* | 16 | 5 | 13 | Nabisco* | — | — | 16 |
| Ralston Purina* | — | — | 26 | Standard Brands* | 23 | — | 26 |
| Coca Cola* | 30 | — | 11 | Campbell* | 10 | — | 7 |
| Consolidated Foods* | 5 | — | 10 | Heinz* | 10 | 8 | — |
| Asstd. British Foods† | — | 34 | — | Del Monte* | 18 | — | — |
| FMC* | — | — | 19 | Gerber* | 12 | — | — |
| Taiyo Fishery (Jap.) | — | — | 25 | Kellogg* | 23 | — | — |
| Pepsico* | 19 | — | 25 | Quaker* | 13 | — | — |
| Imperial Group† | — | — | 13 | Wrigley* | 25 | — | — |
| | | | | Green Giant* | 5 | — | — |

NOTES
* US ownership.
† UK ownership.
SOURCES
United Nations (1973), Table 3; Horst (1974), p. 102; Foster (1977).

TABLE 4.10 Diversity of food industry operations of largest food firms*

| Firm size annual sales ($ billions) | No. of Firms | Meat | Dairy | Fish | Fruits/ veg. | Grains | Oils | Sugar | Bev- erages | Spices | Total | Per firm |
|---|---|---|---|---|---|---|---|---|---|---|---|---|
| Over 5 | 6 | 4 | 5 | 4 | 4 | 4 | 2 | 0 | 4 | 2 | 29 | 4.8 |
| 3–5 | 17 | 7 | 9 | 5 | 1 | 7 | 5 | 5 | 3 | 0 | 42 | 2.5 |
| 2–3 | 21 | 4 | 7 | 5 | 8 | 10 | 4 | 9 | 2 | 2 | 51 | 2.4 |
| 1.5–2 | 21 | 5 | 4 | 1 | 5 | 12 | 2 | 7 | 2 | 1 | 39 | 1.9 |
| 1.0–1.5 | 33 | 3 | 4 | 1 | 7 | 13 | 0 | 6 | 2 | 1 | 37 | 1.1 |
| 0.75–1.0 | 25 | 6 | 3 | 0 | 2 | 7 | 1 | 3 | 1 | 2 | 25 | 1.0 |
| 0.5–0.75 | 47 | 11 | 8 | 3 | 5 | 16 | 3 | 9 | 3 | 2 | 60 | 1.3 |
| Total | 170 | 40 | 40 | 19 | 32 | 69 | 17 | 39 | 17 | 10 | 283 | 1.7 |

NOTE
* Data for 24 firms believed to be incomplete.
SOURCE
Domike (13, p. 18)

and tried to analyse its causes and effects in terms of industrial organisation theory. A recent study of the United Kingdom food industry,[8] sponsored by the European Community, traces the evolution of concentration in different sectors, but does not attempt to statistically test for its causes or its effects. We shall concentrate our discussion on the United States, but some figures and findings for the United Kingdom will also be mentioned.

*United States*

Because the United States is the home of most of the largest TNCs in this industry, and since it points the way, in several senses, along which other economies, developed and developing, will travel, it is useful to look at its experience in some detail. The two main features of the evolution of its industrial structure—and they are not of course peculiar to the food processing industry—are the *growing concentration of production* in practically all sub-sectors except for meat packaging (which has special legal constraints), and the increasingly *diversified and conglomerate nature* of many of the leading food processing firms. Data collected by the FTC (1966a) show that in 1958 nearly 80 per cent of food processing value added originated in industries classified as 'oligopolistic' according to Bain's criteria, and some 20–25 per cent in industries classified as 'very highly concentrated' oligopolies. If we look at the position of the leading manufacturers, we find that the 100 largest firms increased their share of assets to 60 per cent and of profits to 67 per cent over the period 1954–63. Thus

> although food manufacturing supports in excess of 30,000 companies, only a very few account for other than a small share of production and sales. In 1963 just 50 companies accounted for three-eighths of total food industry value added; they controlled half of total food industry assets and earned over 60 per cent of total food industry profits. Even more important is the fact that these 50 largest firms controlled 70 per cent of the leading four positions of the individual product industries included within the food group . . . Over-all concentration has increased at a fast pace since 1950. Concentration of both value added and assets has increased about 1 per cent per year. Concentration of profits has increased even faster—15 per cent in the last seven years.[9]

The process of concentration has been accompanied by increased diversification and conglomeration. 'Between 1954 and 1963 the largest companies increased the number of industries in which they participated by two-thirds, a rate of increase between two and three times greater than that of lower ranking companies of the 200 largest' (USFTC (1969), p. 59). Horst has analysed the characteristics of the firms which tended to diversify and found that the main ones were the slower rate of growth and lower rate of profit in the sub-sectors out of which firms were diversifying: food companies spread into other industries (but mainly into other branches of food processing) to escape the constraints of their original specialisation (see Horst (1974), pp. 60–4). Most of the diversification took place by means of mergers and takeovers of existing firms rather than by internal growth; in fact, nearly 90 per cent of the new industries entered by the 25 largest food firms between 1950–66 were entered by merger. 'The acquired companies, in addition to being leading producers in individual product industries, usually held product differentiation advantages. Many had been innovators of new products and most exhibited favourable growth potential.'[10] Naturally, most takeover activity has been concentrated in the largest firms; in fact, 'mergers were the cause of a net increase in concentration of approximately 25 per cent'.[11]

Most of the merger movement has historically been 'horizontal' (i.e. the takeover of competing firms), but this has been on the decline because of the threat of official anti-trust action. Part has been 'vertical', with firms moving into can and label production, and sometimes into closer links with the production of the primary food materials or with retail distribution. However, backward integration by food retailers has been more extensive than forward integration by food manufacturers, at least until 1966.[12] The growing ability of the retail trade to compete, using their own 'private' brands, with large food producers with 'national' brands, has led them to enter production directly. The FTC finds evidence that retailers have tended to enter the *more* concentrated processing sectors rather than the less-concentrated ones (with apparently lower barriers to entry), and explains this as follows: ' . . . concentrated food manufacturing industries tend to have higher profits and larger marketing margins due to heavy promotional expenses than do less concentrated industries. Hence, these findings support the hypothesis that large retailers integrate into food manufacturing so as to share in these oligopolies and/or to enhance their own profits by eliminating the high costs of achieving product differentiation.' In fact, as we shall see later, Horst finds that retailers' competition in the United States has been a significant restraint on food manufacturers' profits.

Backward integration into agricultural activities has been more common in the United States than elsewhere. It is estimated that, in

1970, 31 per cent of all United States' livestock was produced under contract and 5 per cent directly by the food firms, and 10 per cent of crops were grown under contract and 5 per cent directly by processors.[13] Given the magnitude of United States agricultural production, these are very large amounts in absolute terms. The practice has also spread in developing countries, and will be touched upon again when we come to discuss the effects of TNCs in these countries.

Part of the merger movement has also been into (or from) unrelated industries—the truly 'conglomerate' merger. Although this was relatively uncommon before 1966, when the FTC study was prepared, there are good reasons to believe that it has speeded up considerably since. Horst also remarks on the extension of diversification activity by food firms across national boundaries. The tough US controls within the United States on horizontal mergers may well have caused US TNCs to seek to acquire potential competitors abroad.

*United Kingdom*

The food industry in the United Kingdom seems to be more highly concentrated than in the United States, France or West Germany.[14] Data for 1971 in the *Census of Production* show that five-firm concentration ratios for value added in 13 groups of food processing and soft drinks averaged 61 per cent (unweighted); in 8 of these 13 groups it was over 50 per cent and in all but one it was over 40 per cent. The largest 15 firms in the industry as a whole accounted for 47 per cent of gross output and 44 per cent of value added (in 1963 they had accounted for 39 per cent of value added). The EEC study mentioned above examines the increase in concentration, and suggests that in several cases (margarine, butter and cheese, yoghurt, baby foods, ice cream, breakfast foods, biscuits) there is perhaps a connection between extremely high levels of concentration and advertising promotion expenditure. In other cases (e.g. sugar), economies of scale contribute to high concentration, but in general it appears that barriers to entry arise more from marketing factors than from technical ones. Let us then turn to a consideration of such factors.

CONDUCT AND PERFORMANCE

The conduct and performance of the industry can best be understood in the context of (i) its technology; (ii) the changing nature of demand; and (iii) its marketing structure.

(i) *Technology.* The technology of food processing is relatively stable, well-known and essentially simple, although most processes can be heavily mechanised and automated. As Horst notes: 'Many of the basic food manufacturing processes—pasteurisation, canning and processing, milling, baking, and others—go back decades, centuries or even millenia.'[15] As studies done for the ILO have demonstrated, there does exist in this industry a considerable range of viable technologies, ranging from the crudest of processes for making the traditional foods for developing countries to very capital-intensive methods of producing the highly refined, preserved and packaged foods for the developed countries. Although the suppliers of capital goods for the food industries have, like other equipment suppliers, produced devices to replace labour, raise productivity and employ more tightly controlled production methods, innovation *within* the food firms themselves has mainly concentrated on products rather than processes. All the available evidence indicates that the industry is, in terms of R and D spending, a very 'low technology' industry, and such innovation as does take place is, with some exceptions which we shall note later, relatively trivial as far as the basic properties of the product are concerned.

Let us review the most recent evidence on R and D activity in food processing given in a publication of the United States National Science Foundation (NSF) (1975). This shows that R and D as a percentage of sales in 1973 came to 0.4 per cent for a sample of large food processing firms as compared to 3.1 per cent for manufacturing as a whole; the employment of R and D personnel as compared to total employment came to 0.7 per cent and 2.5 per cent respectively. By either measure, food firms devoted on average one-seventh to one-third of their resources to this activity as compared with manufacturing generally, and far less than other transnational industries based on high technology like electronics equipment or chemicals. While the largest 4 companies spent more on R and D (1.3 per cent of sales) than the next 4 (0.5 per cent), which spent marginally more than the next 12 (0.4 per cent), the group of larger firms (employment of 10,000 and over) did not seem to spend more on R and D than the smallest firms. Table 4.11 presents figures on the size distribution of R and D spending for the 101 firms covered by the NSF survey. It may be noted that this survey covers the major R and D spenders only: the large number of small firms which do no research are excluded, and the over-all percentage of R and D spending is consequently overstated.

The NSF also classifies R and D spending into basic, applied and development research. The food industry divided R and D into 7.7 per cent, 40.3 per cent and 51.8 per cent respectively, as compared to 2.8 per

TABLE 4.11   R and D and sales of main food firms in the US 1973

| No. employed | Nos. | R and D ($m.) | Net sales ($m.) | R and D per firm ($m.) | R and D/ Sales (%) |
|---|---|---|---|---|---|
| Less than 5,000 | 51 | 49 | 9,432 | 0.96 | 0.5 |
| 5,000 to 9,999 | 20 | 29 | 10,792 | 1.45 | 0.2 |
| 10,000 to 24,999 | 20 | 111 | 21,956 | 5.55 | 0.5 |
| 25,000 and over | 10 | 81 | 21,302 | 8.10 | 0.3 |
| Total | 101 | 270 | 63,482 | 2.70 | 0.4 |

SOURCE
United States National Science Foundation (1975).

cent, 17.9 per cent and 79.1 per cent for all manufacturing. This division shows, somewhat surprisingly, that food firms spend more on basic research than others and that, of the 14 firms in the sample of 101 conducting basic research, 6 (43 per cent) are small firms with under 5,000 employees. Clearly the definition of 'basic' research is flexible, and to think that what is 'basic' in food manufacturing is the same as that which is basic in pharmaceuticals or electronics would be misleading. The NSF also gives the distribution of R and D by 'product field': food firms spend 68 per cent on food products, 8 per cent on non-pharmaceutical chemicals, 6 per cent on pharmaceuticals and the rest on rubber, fabricated metal, etc. (and only 3 per cent on machinery). This, more than other data, illustrates the product-based function of R and D in the sector.

More recent figures on R and D by United States firms have been

TABLE 4.12   R and D and sales of 36 large food firms in the US, 1976

| Turnover | Nos. | R and D ($m.) | Net Sales ($m.) | R and D per firm ($m.) | R and D/ Sales (%) |
|---|---|---|---|---|---|
| Over $3 billion | 6 | 103 | 24,031 | 17 | 0.4 |
| $1 to 3 billion | 18 | 169 | 31,252 | 9 | 0.5 |
| Under $1 billion | 12 | 30 | 4,605 | 3 | 0.7 |
| Total | 36 | 302 | 59,888 | 8 | 0.5 |

SOURCE
*Business Week* (1977).

provided by *Business Week* for a sample of 36 large food and beverage firms for 1976 (Table 4.12). The average R and D on sales for these firms comes to 0.5 per cent of sales, and the expenditure on R and D per employee comes to $337, as compared to $1,149 for all industry (including non-manfacturing). The most interesting fact shown by the *Business Week* sample (covering most of the large United States TNCs in this sector) is the tendency for the technological intensity of firms (R and D over sales) to decline with increasing size. While R and D expenditure per firm continues to rise with size, its falling importance in proportion to the value of output may indicate one or both of two things: first, that there are diseconomies of scale in innovation in the food processing industry; and/or second, that a certain minimum effort (in relation to the size of sales) is necessary for the very large food firms to stay abreast of competition in new product introductions, but that beyond this level research requirements rise less rapidly than output (i.e., the commercial 'need' for further product innovation declines, even if there are no diseconomies of R and D, because the market can only absorb so many 'new' food products). The very small firms which do not compete in the highly differentiated fields need not, of course, be involved in any process innovation.

The United Kingdom data confirm the low-technology status of the food processing industry. In 1968, R and D as a percentage of value added came to 1.6 for food firms and 5.4 for all manufacturing; in that year the food industry ranked fifteenth out of 19 sectors in the country according to this criterion.[16] As with the United States, however, we find surprisingly that the industry spends much more on 'basic' R and D than manufacturing as a whole: 9.4 per cent in 1972/73 as compared to 3.3 per cent for all manufacturing[17] (the comparable figures for the United States are 7.7 per cent and 2.8 per cent). As before, however, we cannot account for this satisfactorily.

(ii) *The changing nature of demand.* There are several factors related to the growth and evolution of the developed economies which lead to changes in the nature of demand for processed foods.

Casual observation suggests that the consumption of more highly processed foods rises steadily with the standard of living: the income elasticity of demand for such foods is for several reasons higher than that for food as a whole. A Unilever report explains the growth in demand for highly processed foods thus:

First, people have more money to buy foods they find more palatable and which offer more variety in each season of the year, as well as foods in which the manufacture saves them time and labour in preparation. Second, changes are taking place in the way people live. More people can afford to eat out. With television, with greater independence among young people, with the weakening of traditions, families eat more snacks and tend to eat separately at different times. Increasing ownership of refrigerators with storage compartments for frozen foods, and of deep freezers, have a major influence on frozen food and ice cream consumption. The growth of car ownership, of caravanning, camping and other leisure activities have all influenced opportunities in the food market.[18]

We may add to this such factors as the increasing tendency of housewives to seek outside work, changes in the pattern of retailing— primarily the growth of supermarkets—and exposure to advertising, mainly through television, factors discussed in detail by Horst (1974). Not all these changes have been conducive to the growth of large food manufacturers: the increasing consciousness about health foods has affected the demand for certain highly processed foods and has in some instances driven the firms to provide health foods themselves; the growth of 'countervailing power' by retailers has, as noted above, led to some reduction in the market power of the large processors, to which they have retaliated by putting more effort into the production of their national brands. By and large, however, the evolution of tastes, urbanisation, living conditions and family habits have caused a greater demand for modern processed foods.

It may be useful to try and distinguish, conceptually if not in statistical terms, between the set of forces related to rising incomes and urbanisation and those linked to the strategies of the firms themselves. Although economic growth generally leads to the increasing need for a wider range of foods and for 'convenience' foods (since people have less time to cook), and these forces are largely outside the control of the food processors, the precise direction and content of this change is determined to some extent by the product innovation and promotion activities of the firms themselves. Thus, some new food products genuinely add to convenience, storability and nourishment; others are simply product differentiation, based on slight changes in presentation, colours and sizes, packaging and composition. It is clearly difficult to separate one from the other in the constant stream of 'new' foods provided by the processors, but the distinction is an important one, especially when we come to consider the effects in LDCs.

(iii) *The marketing structure.* Given the secondary importance of process innovation in the industry and the need to compete for the growing demand for processed foods by means of 'new' product introductions, it is natural that advertising and product differentiation should become the main element in competition among food companies. This tendency has been strengthened by competition from the private brands of retailers, forcing national brand owners to promote their products even more heavily, in order to ensure shelf space in super-markets. The most effective means of advertising is television; the growth of television ownership impels the bulk of advertising to be spent on this medium. Thus, we have a situation in which:

(*a*) there is a constant pressure to bring out 'new' and 'different' processed foods, which allegedly have better flavours, shapes or other attributes, and which are more convenient;

(*b*) these foods must be attractively packaged and heavily promoted, generally by means of television advertising; and

(*c*) the variety of processed foods must be changed frequently in order to sustain the momentum of growth and demand.

The effect of such marketing practices has been to raise significant barriers to the entry of further competitors and to make successful marketing the key to success in general. While some food firms capitalised on a real 'innovation' in their food (e.g., Coca Cola, Wrigley's chewing gum, Unilever's 'vanaspati' or Carnation's con-densed milk), 'their corporate success was usually linked to a particular product, be it sugarless canned milk or a bowl of cold corn flakes. A few of these products were protected by a registered patent or a secret ingredient, but most were fair game of emulators and imitators. The real secret of these firms' success was their willingness to lavish large sums on advertising campaigns, promotional schemes and other methods of brand promotion.'[19] And, as far as conglomerates are concerned, the picture is similar. 'About the only economies of firm size in most food processing industries have been the potential savings enhancing a common distributional network and in using national advertising media . . . Having lost direct control of shelf space (particularly after supermarkets started to introduce their own competing but non-advertised brands), the food manufacturers have had to pay increasing attention to packaging, to spend more money on advertising, especially for television, and to put more time and money into new product innovation and testing' (Horst (1974), p. 124).

The effects of such marketing practices have been the following:

(*a*) There has been a *general increase* in advertising expenditures by the United States food processing industry; these expenditures rose by over 300 per cent during 1950–64, about 33 per cent greater than the rate at which manufacturing companies generally increased their advertising. The food industry spent some $1.4 billion on advertising in 1964, accounting for about 20 per cent of all manufacturing advertising in the United States (see United States FTC (1966a), p. 103).

(*b*) *Large firms* have raised their advertising expenditure far more than small firms. As a percentage of sales, advertising remained roughly constant for small firms since 1947, while the large firms were spending in 1961 at about *four times* the rate of small firms, and at *twice* the rate of medium-sized firms.

(*c*) Advertising is *highly concentrated* among the largest firms. The largest 20 account for 40 per cent and the largest 50 for over 80 per cent of total advertising. The concentration is even higher for television advertising, the largest 50 accounting for about 90 per cent of the total; this is encouraged by the discounts which large advertisers obtain (or used to obtain) from the television companies.

(*d*) The extent of advertising is *highest on differentiable products* (like soft drinks, frozen foods or chocolate) and lowest on non-differentiable products (like packaged fresh meat).

(*e*) Advertising economies (and discriminatory rate structures) have been a stimulus for *mergers*, and large firms have substantially increased the level of advertising of acquired smaller companies. On the average, the advertising expenditures of 39 sample acquired companies in a sample examined by the Federal Trade Commission nearly *doubled* within a year of acquisition by large firms (see United States FTC (1969), p. 147).

The evidence available for food manufacturing in the United Kingdom and the EEC strongly suggests that a similar pattern has emerged outside the United States.[20] As we saw earlier, the level of concentration in Britain is fairly high, with 15 firms accounting for nearly half of the market. This is supposed to give these firms a strong competitive edge over food firms in the EEC, where the level of concentration is much lower. 'The three leading brands [in the United Kingdom] have from 70 per cent to 90 per cent of the total market of modern food products and over 50 per cent of the total for most traditional markets.'[21] The British firms are similar to their American counterparts, widely diversified, and there is a strong trend towards vertical integration in both primary production (by contracts as well as direct entry into farming) and distribution. Furthermore, British food companies spend heavily on advertising as compared to France (twice as much), and concentrate their efforts on television advertising. Half the industry's advertising expenditure is incurred by 30 firms.[22] These factors account for the emerging dominance of British firms (and of Nestlé) on the EEC market in a number of processed foods like ice cream, margarine, coffee, soups and vegetable oils.[23]

The heavy emphasis on promotion which is now characteristic of the food processing industry in the developed world naturally requiries a great and expanding variety of 'new' food products as well as frequent 'model' changes. Thus, one study found that in the United States the number of items carried in 21 well-defined product categories (by a warehouse of a major food retailer) increased almost 300 per cent in 1954–62 and that 'the overwhelming majority of this increase represented *slight modifications of existing products*, rather than really new types of food' (Horst (1974), p. 53, emphasis added). The rapidity with which products are changed is illustrated by a recent report: 'At Campbell Soup Co., today's new product push is being redirected around products that will have a market life of more than two or three years, rather than *the 12 or 14 months that has become an industry standard for some categories.*'[24]

Industrial organisation theory would lead us to expect that in an industry in which concentration is rising rapidly and is accompanied by marked increases in marketing efforts by the largest firms, the profit performance of the industry would vary significantly according to the level of concentration and the expenditures on marketing. Statistical work on United States data confirms this strongly.[25] Once distributional requirements in particular processed foods are suitable for the emergence of nationally-based food companies, the level of seller concentration is related to the level of advertising and the profitability of particular food processing sectors is related to the level of concentration and advertising. The following table (4.13) taken from the FTC's 1969 study, illustrates this clearly for a period around 1950. It is based on statistical relations between these factors, holding other influences constant.

Horst analyses later figures and tests for other influences on structure and profitability. He concludes that:

> Product differentiation was obviously the primary source of high concentration, multiplant operations and excess profitability among

TABLE 4.13   Profit rates of US food manufacturing firms associated with levels of concentration and advertising/sales ratio

| 4-Firm concentration ratio | Associated net profit rates on equity advertising/sales ratio (%) | | | | |
|---|---|---|---|---|---|
| | 2% | 4% | 5% | 6% | 7% |
| 40 | 6.3 | 7.4 | 8.5 | 9.6 | 10.7 |
| 45 | 8.0 | 9.1 | 10.2 | 11.3 | 12.4 |
| 50 | 9.3 | 10.4 | 11.5 | 12.6 | 13.7 |
| 55 | 10.3 | 11.4 | 12.5 | 13.6 | 14.7 |
| 60 | 11.0 | 12.1 | 13.2 | 14.3 | 15.4 |
| 65 | 11.4 | 12.5 | 13.6 | 14.7 | 15.8 |
| 70 | 11.5 | 12.6 | 13.7 | 14.8 | 15.9 |

SOURCE
United States FTC (1969), p. 7.

food processors, product differentiation being measured by a combination of advertising expenditure and competition from private labelling . . . Neither technological change, plant size or industry growth appeared to be an important element in the post-war structure of the food processing industry.

These factors would lead us to expect that large firms would be significantly more profitable than small ones, and that they would tend to predominate in the heavily concentrated and marketing-orientated sub-sectors of the industry. The available evidence for the United States confirms these expectations. It has also been noted in the European case that United Kingdom firms are far more profitable than French ones (two to four times), apparently due to their greater size and higher advertising (see *European Review* (1972)).

This discussion of the conduct and performance of food processing firms within developed countries has important implications for their transnational activities. Recent theories of foreign investment and transnational growth,[26] drawing upon the literature on industrial organisation, have posited a close relationship between the growth of large oligopolistic firms within developed countries and the growth of transnational companies. The same factors – the barriers to entry to new competition – that give rise to the emergence of high concentration and of market power in the hands of the dominant firms also provide the element of "monopolistic advantage" that enables firms to operate profitably across large distances and over national boundaries. In the case of the food processing industry, we would expect, therefore, to find that the leading transnationals would be (*a*) the largest firms in the industry in the capital-exporting countries, and (*b*) the ones relying most heavily on the main source of market power in this industry (advertising and product differentiation). Horst finds that this is indeed so for the United States. A multiple regression shows that the extent of the foreign operations of United States Firms is positively and significantly related to size and advertising intensity (and negatively to high levels of regional market segmentation).[27]

The technological and economic effects of food TNCs on developing host countries are to a large extent determined by their industrial characteristics as described in this section. They are, in other words, heavily influenced by the facts that food TNCs are large, diversified, conglomerate firms; that their innovative activity centres around the introduction of a variety of highly promoted, slighly differentiated products; that their main sources of technology lie in labour-scarce, capital- and skill-abundant developed economies; and that their *raison d'être* is the large-scale, continuous production of standardised, packaged food products primarily for affluent urban consumers. These issues will be taken up again in section V; let us now look at the operations of the world's largest food transnational.

## IV   UNILEVER AS A FOOD TRANSNATIONAL

### THE BACKGROUND

The importance of Unilever's experience in a study of food processing TNCs need hardly be emphasised. Not only is it the world's largest food firm,[28] it is one of the oldest and most international.[29] It has some 220 'principal subsidiaries' throughout the world, 49 of them in developing countries, engaged in manufacturing, servicing and selling. It dominates European and several developing country markets in margarine and vegetable oils, and European ones in frozen foods. About half of its activities are non-food, covering detergents, soaps, chemicals, paper, plastics, animal feeds, plantations and so on.

Table 4.14 summarises some of the salient features of its operations since 1970. The last column shows a very healthy growth of the company over a rather depressed period for the world economy, with profits high and rising and exports increasing considerably faster than sales. The fall in employment is due to a fall in the 1974–6 period; it may be due to rationalisation of operations or to the recession (the latter seems

TABLE 4.14    Unilever: salient features 1970–6 (£m.)

|  | 1970 | 1972 | 1974 | 1976 | % change 1970–6 |
|---|---|---|---|---|---|
| 1. Total sales | 3,539 | 3,982 | 6,554 | 9,547 | 169.0 |
| 2. Internal sales* | 681 | 437 | 711 | 816 | 19.8 |
| 3. Row 2 as a % of 1 | 19.1 | 10.9 | 10.8 | 8.5 | — |
| 4. Profits before tax | 150 | 243 | 333 | 602 | 301.3 |
| 5. Row 4 as a % of capital employed | 13.1 | 17.7 | 17.2 | 20.3 | — |
| 6. Profits after tax | 72 | 129 | 155 | 283 | 293.0 |
| 7. Row 6 as a % of equity | 9.1 | 13.7 | 12.7 | 15.8 | — |
| 8. Employment (000s) | 335 | 337 | 357 | 317 | − 5.3 |
| 9. Total food sales | 1,440 | 1,869 | 3,596 | 4,792 | 232.7 |
| 10. Row 9 as a % of 1 | 40.5 | 46.9 | 53.9 | 50.1 | — |
| 11. Margarine and oil sales | 627 | 779 | 1,968 | 2,346 | 274.1 |
| 12. Row 11 as a % of 9 | 43.5 | 41.6 | 55.6 | 48.9 | — |
| 13. Exports | 293.6 | 387.9 | 767.8 | 1,143.7 | 289.5 |

NOTE
* i.e. intrafirm sales
SOURCE
Unilever, *Annual Report and Accounts* (various).

unlikely in view of sales growth). A special point of interest is the firm's export performance. Exports have risen from 8.3 per cent of sales in 1970 to 12.0 per cent in 1976. Most exports originate, however, in three developed countries: the United Kingdom, Netherlands and West Germany. These have accounted for 81 per cent of exports in 1970 and 84 per cent in 1976. While exports from developing countries have also risen, reaching £0.9 million for Sri Lanka (1975), about £8 million for India (1975) and US $1 million for Indonesia (1975), to take some scattered examples at hand,[30] clearly most trade is still concentrated in the developed countries.

Let us look at Unilever's geographical spread. Table 4.15 sets out the distribution of sales and profitability in different regions of the world. Over 80 per cent of Unilever's sales (if we attribute about half of the sales to Asia and Oceania to the latter) are to the developed world, and the proportion has not changed very much since 1970.

The developing world has, however, proved considerably more profitable than the developed, with the average pre-tax return on capital employed rising steadily from 21.1 per cent to 42.6 per cent in developing countries, and only from 13.0 per cent to 16.6 per cent in the developed countries.[31] While returns in Latin America have been somewhat

TABLE 4.15  Unilever: distribution of sales and profitability on capital employed by region

| | 1970 | | 1972 | | 1974 | | 1976 | |
|---|---|---|---|---|---|---|---|---|
| | Sales (%) | Profit/ Capital | Sales (%) | Profit/ Capital | Sales (%) | Profit/ Capital | Sales (%) | Profit/ Capital |
| Europe | 64.9 | 11.9 | 65.4 | 17.0 | 70.2 | 14.7 | 66.4 | 16.4 |
| US and Canada | 12.3 | 19.3 | 11.7 | 14.7 | 9.5 | 20.9 | 9.9 | 18.3 |
| Latin America | 2.1 | 12.0 | 2.1 | 37.5 | 2.1 | 20.0 | 2.5 | 18.6 |
| Africa | 13.1 | 22.2 | 12.6 | 26.0 | 10.7 | 36.9 | 12.9 | 50.8 |
| Asia and Oceania | 7.4 | 18.0 | 8.1 | 32.0 | 7.2 | 36.6 | 8.0 | 38.7 |
| Total | 100.0 | 14.4 | 100.0 | 18.8 | 100.0 | 18.5 | 100.0 | 21.3 |
| LDCs (including Oceania) | 22.6 | 21.1 | 22.8 | 29.4 | 20.0 | 34.6 | 23.4 | 42.6 |

NOTE
(1) Refers to total sales, including non-food products.
(2) Capital is at historic cost.
(3) Includes trading activities of UAC International.
SOURCE
Unilever, *Annual Report and Accounts* (various).

erratic, those in Africa and Asia have increased steadily—in Africa to a spectacular 50.8 per cent in 1976.[32] While it is generally accepted that TNCs aim for higher profits in LDCs as compared to other regions, mainly to compensate for risk, such differentials must be exceptional by any standards.

So much for the background: let us now pull together the few facts that we have to see how Unilever does in developing countries by some of the criteria of TNC performance relevant to this paper. We have selected three: the transfer and adaptation of technology; product characteristics and marketing; and linkages with local suppliers.

### TRANSFER AND ADAPTATION OF TECHNOLOGY

The transfer of technology—here we are confining ourselves to production technology—by transnational companies is a vast and complex subject, to which we cannot do full justice in this paper. Some of the issues which have been raised in the literature on TNC operations in developing countries,[33] which we discuss here, concern: (i) the extent of R and D performed in the host countries; (ii) the means of transfer; and (iii) the adaptation of technology to suit the labour-abundant conditions in poor countries. Other important issues, like the explicit and hidden costs of technology transfer or local alternatives to imported technology, cannot be discussed meaningfully for Unilever with the information at hand.

*(i) Research and development in developing countries.* Most R and D by Unilever is performed in developed areas. In 1960, however, the Indian subsidiary of the firm set up a research centre in Bombay to develop products and processes suitable to Indian conditions and to maximise the use of local raw materials (for details see Unilever (1976b)). This centre has a research staff of 210, of whom 30 are scientists directing research. The firm has six major factories in different parts of India, the largest one (also in Bombay) running a development unit with 12 scientists, which works with the research centre on technology transfer, product development, process improvement, cost control and quality improvement. The total capital expenditure on R and D up to end-1971 came to Rs. 16.6 million (about £1 million), and current expenditures in 1971 came to Rs. 7.2 million (under £0.5 million). In current terms this was roughly 1 per cent of the firm's estimated total R and D for that year.[34]

The bulk of R and D effort in India seems to have been directed to non-food products. In food, two major lines of research have been undertaken. First, in *edible oil products*, to pioneer the use of cotton-seed oil in 'vanaspati', the use of sal fat in cocoa butter (leading to exports of this fat), the incorporation of polyunsaturates in vegetable oil products and the development of margarine for Indian conditions; second, in *food technology and nutrition*, the development of technology for dehydrated foods, leading to the introduction of 20 new products, many of them special Indian preparations; the formulation of processes for high quality ghee and milk powder from buffalo milk; baby food; and high quality protein foods which are being used in government nutrition programmes. R and D has also been used to design and fabricate sophisticated analytical laboratory equipment, the import of which has been restricted by the government.

The Unilever centre has co-operated actively with official research bodies and sponsored programmes in other centres in India. The parent company has provided 'substantial encouragement and assistance' by the training of Indian personnel abroad and exchange of scientists.

Without detailed information on the social costs, benefits and alternatives to R and D conducted by Hindustan Lever, it is impossible to judge the implications of this activity for the host economy. On the one hand, it is likely that it has yielded benefits in terms of new products and processes suitable for local conditions,[35] conserved or earned foreign exchange, and drawn upon the immense technological resources of the parent firm. On the other, it is possible that the benefits may have been internal to the firm and have not 'spilled over' sufficiently to the indigenous sector, and that some of the 'new' products may have exhibited market-orientated differentiation rather than genuine innovation. (We shall return to this point below.) On balance, it is likely that the effort has been beneficial to India, and possibly to other developing countries, mainly because of the efforts made—and this has been done by the firm in several areas—to develop the use of local raw materials which were previously discarded or not exploited. Part of the credit may also be due to the Indian Government for having forced the pace and extent of import substitution.

*(ii) Means of transfer.* As a director of Unilever has noted: 'In the main, the major Unilever processes are not complex. Edible fat manufacture is basically a matter of purifying crude edible oils, hardening them, blending them with water in the appropriate proportions and crystallising them under carefully controlled conditions' (see Veldhuis (1976), p. 12). This does not mean that these processes have remained stagnant; rather that advances in technology have not been very large,

discontinuous or complex, so that technology transfer remains a relatively informal and autonomous process. In other words, subsidiaries are accorded considerable freedom in their choice of technology—the Indian subsidiary has even developed the capability to 'fabricate all the equipment necessary for the manufacture of detergents' (Veldhuis (1976), p. 15) and are simply provided with free access to all technical knowledge available in the company and with extensive personnel interchange. This is a very different structure from that implicit in the formal, complex and hierarchical procedures used in high-technology industries,[36] where the need to keep abreast of difficult technological progress renders the Unilever organisation model unworkable at least as far as LDCs are concerned. The stability of production technology does not, of course, imply that several product, packaging, promotional and other changes cannot occur continuously: the large number of 'technical' bulletins that are sent around by the firm leads one to believe that in these fields the firm is very dynamic.[37]

Much of the technology transfer within Unilever is thus of the 'disembodied' type: technical news-sheets, personal contact, services of various types, and training, as far as processes are concerned, and trade marks as far as products are concerned. 'Embodied' transfer by the parent company in the form of capital equipment also takes place, but seems to be less important than in other industries, both because of the low technological intensity of the processes and because food processing machinery manufacturers are distinct from the processing firms themselves. In general, the parent seems to act as a channel for the purchase of capital equipment, while the choice of equipment and design of plant is made on the basis of 'a proposal which examines in detail market opportunities, the degree of adaptation necessary, research and development/engineering/maintenance/operating/management requirements, capital and running costs, labour requirements and availability. The degree of sophistication of equipment and control mechanisms has to be tailored to suit local conditions . . . ' (Veldhuis (1976), p. 23). The actual contribution of the parent firm to the transfer is thus in the form of guidance and approval of choices made by subsidiaries, and the provision of specialist services where necessary, rather than the direct provision of 'embodied' technology. Even such guidance may, of course, impart a bias towards the choice of technologies with which the head office is familiar, but it is less restrictive than the practices of technology transfer in more high-technology industries.

*(iii) Adaptation.* The product case studies presented in Chapter III

demonstrate that there is scope, at least for certain products, for using labour-intensive technology in food processing. As far as TNCs are concerned, there are three separate questions to be investigated: whether they adapt the technology they transfer from developed to less-developed countries; whether they adapt better or worse than compara-ble local firms; and whether more adaptation is both possible and desirable.[38]

As regards the first question, there seems little doubt that Unilever undertakes and permits considerable technology adaptation in develop-ing countries.[39] There are three ways of doing this: firstly, the passive one of letting old technology continue unchanged much longer in labour-abundant areas; secondly, to actively adapt processes and products, or to transfer processes and products which are less auto-mated and more labour-intensive; and thirdly, to let subsidiaries use local equipment in countries where such capability exists. It seems that all three tendencies are operative in Unilever, and that the capital intensity of operations in developing countries is much lower than in developed countries. We do not have very detailed figures to test this, but the firm's last annual report enables a comparison of capital employed per employee in different regions of the world (see Table 4.16).

TABLE 4.16   Unilever: capital employed per employee in different areas, 1975–6

|  | 1975 | | 1976 | |
|---|---|---|---|---|
| *Area* | Total *employment* (000s) | *Capital/ Employee* | Total *employment* (000s) | *Capital/ Employee* |
| Europe | 196 | 8.33 | 194 | 10.9 |
| US and Canada | 20 | 11.30 | 20 | 15.3 |
| Total developed | 216 | 8.60 | 214 | 11.33 |
| Latin America | 10 | 5.40 | 11 | 6.82 |
| Africa | 54 | 3.70 | 51 | 5.86 |
| Asia and Oceania | 42 | 3.07 | 41 | 3.90 |
| Total LDCs | 106 | 3.61 | 103 | 5.18 |
| Total | 322 | 6.96 | 317 | 9.33 |
| LDCs as % of DCs | — | 41.9 | — | 45.7 |

NOTE
See previous table.
SOURCE
Calculated from Unilever, *Annual Report and Accounts*, 1976.

The distinction between developed and developing countries is not a very precise one and there are several analytical problems in using such ratios to measure the nature of the technology used (as discussed by Bhalla (1975)). Furthermore, there are practical problems, as mentioned above, in using balance-sheet data for capital, especially in Africa. However, since better data are not at hand, the table must serve to illustrate the main trends: the United States and Canada have the highest capital per employee, followed at some distance by Europe, while within the developing regions Latin America has the highest, followed by Africa and Asia. This ranking might be expected given the levels of labour costs in these regions, and tends to support the impression that considerable adaptation does take place within the company.

As for its performance vis-à-vis local firms, we do not have any information which would allow us to make a comparison. The evidence on TNCs in general does not support any proposition that they are better or worse than local firms in adapting technology once the nature of the market and products is given, but this evidence is patchy, unsatisfactory and often wrongly interpreted.[40] As for further adaptation, there is again a lack of appropriate studies (on the products made by Unilever). The company was a pioneer in the manufacture of vanaspati, so that it is unlikely that traditional (more labour-intensive) techniques existed which could replace it. As for its other products, however, it is very likely that more labour-intensive alternatives do exist for some, especially if the product is made to different specifications. Generalisations are practically impossible: clearly, for new products (like dehydrated peas) there may be no substitute processes, but for products which are more highly processed versions of traditional products (soups, condiments) there probably are viable alternatives which generate more employment.

To end this section then, the available evidence on Unilever does not allow us to come to any clear conclusions about the transfer of technology to developing countries by transnationals. Some of the criticisms directed at the latter—lack of R and D in developing countries, insufficient transfer of technology or technological 'rigidity'—become more questionable in the light of the information we have on this firm. Others, for example, that technology transfers could be better diffused within host countries, that further adaptation of techniques is necessary, and that local firms are better at adaptation, cannot be evaluated on the basis of the information available.

PRODUCTS AND MARKETING

As with technology, there is a list of issues which are of significance in the area of products and marketing, and few of them can be resolved without further research. We may consider the following: are the products modified by the firm in accordance with the environment of the host country? Are they appropriate to the basic needs of the host country? Are advanced marketing techniques transferred from the developed to less-developed countries? Are they beneficial to host countries?

*Products.*
Unilever produces four main types of food products: margarine, oil and dairy products; frozen foods; meat products; and sundry processed foods. The *Annual Report* for 1976 gives a breakdown of majority-owned production and distribution subsidiaries in different countries according to product; this information is summarised in Table 4.17. Although figures for the value of output of the various products in different regions are not given, it is clear that there is a relative concentration of 'traditional' products like oils and margarine in developing countries and 'modern' products like frozen foods in developed countries. (This may partly explain the different capital – labour ratios shown in Table 4.16.) Sundry foods are evenly spread and processed meats are concentrated in rich countries.

The developing countries producing frozen foods are those with a substantial consuming élite and advanced retailing systems—i.e. Brazil, Nigeria, Malaysia, Hong Kong, Philippines and Singapore. There is, therefore, some evidence that products are adapted to suit the income levels of different regions. Discussions between Unilever officials and the author also suggest that at the detailed product level considerable effort is made to develop products suited to local tastes, cultures, climates and distribution systems, which is perhaps hardly surprising in a marketing-based firm like Unilever. Products developed for one market are not automatically transferred to another without considerable market research and adaptation. Several product introductions have failed when they were unsuited to local market conditions.

This does not, however, answer the question about their *appropriateness* to the food and nutrition needs of the host countries. The question of appropriateness is a very tricky one, since it involves judgements at two levels: firstly, whether patterns of income distribution, urbanisation, industrialisation and so on are acceptable as such in a developing

TABLE 4.17   Unilever: number of production, service and distribution outlets by product, 1976

| Region | Total | (%) | Marg-arine, oils, dairy | (%) | Frozen food | (%) | Sundry | (%) | Meat | (%) |
|--------|-------|-----|-------------------------|-----|-------------|-----|--------|-----|------|-----|
| Developed | 58 | (53) | 17 | (40) | 16 | (73) | 19 | (51) | 6 | (75) |
| LDCs | 52 | (47) | 26 | (60) | 6 | (17) | 18 | (49) | 2 | (25) |
| Total | 110 | (100) | 43 | (100) | 22 | (100) | 37 | (100) | 8 | (100) |

SOURCE
Unilever, *Annual Report and Accounts*, 1976.

country, and, secondly, given all these, whether the resulting market demand for processed foods reflects 'real' needs or is conditioned by foreign consumption patterns and the advertising of food companies. As we noted previously, the growth of demand for processed foods results from a complex of all these factors, and several products meet the 'real' needs of urban populations for economy, nutrition or convenience, while several others are trivial, sometimes less nutritious, variations of traditional products.

In Unilever's range, for instance, vanaspati, margarine, enriched protein foods, and some convenience foods may be regarded as appropriate for the needs of the population at large or for urban populations in particular. Other foods, like 'instant' noodles, 'instant' porridge, new varieties of spreads and sweets, etc.,[41] may be considered over-processed, not particularly nourishing, and in many ways unsuited to the needs of host countries. This is not an issue which can be decided simply by reference to 'the facts'; much depends on one's value judgements about what is appropriate in a country which allows income disparities to exist or urbanisation to continue; whether advertising and promotion can make people buy what they do not need, or what is not good for them; and, ultimately, what is the 'welfare' of the host country as a whole. We can only argue for our own point of view: that many of the products developed and sold by the firm are not appropriate to the basic food needs of developing countries (while others are).

### Marketing

This brings us to the role of marketing. It is apparent from a reading of the various monographs prepared by the company that primary emphasis is placed on the transfer of marketing know-how (market research, packaging, promotion) to subsidiaries, and on its subsequent development. This is perhaps the most important skill or asset transferred abroad by the transnational and, while its application to each case is bound to be unique, the nature of the know-how transferred is fairly uniform. Is this a good thing for developing countries? That part of marketing know-how which consists in discovering market needs, presenting products in a form acceptable to consumers and reaching consumers in adequate supply is obviously desirable. That part which consists in creating new needs, causing changes in consumption habits that either cost more for the same nutrition and convenience content or actually decrease nutritional content, is obviously not beneficial. We do not have data on the promotional expenses (and its effects) of Unilever in LDCs as far as food is concerned, but the arguments advanced earlier tend to suggest that the undesirable aspects of promotion and packaging are liberally mixed with the beneficial aspects of presentation, market research and distribution.

The nature of the food processing industry encourages significant linkages with local farmers, and sometimes with local equipment suppliers, consultants, advertising firms, packaging manufacturers and so on. Unilever seems, in varying degrees depending on the nature of the host country, to have developed such linkages. In India and Sri Lanka, for instance, local farmers have been given incentives and know-how to grow various kinds of plants and foods for use by the company. In India, local engineering firms, packaging manufacturers, consultants and scientists have provided various goods and services to the firm— although the strict import substitution policies of Government may have had more to do with this than the wishes of the company. In Indonesia, consulting and advertising services are provided by the company itself,[42] and the level of local purchasing seems quite low although some packaging materials are purchased locally. In Ghana, the firm has (through UAC International) entered into a joint venture with the Government to set up a palm oil plantation.

There is no way of judging whether the linkages of Unilever's subsidiaries with the agricultural sector have had the disruptive socio-economic effects attributed to agri-business firms in Latin America (see below). Certainly no evidence on this has emerged in countries like India where the firm has been active for decades and where there is a suspicious press and a watchful Government.

A proper cost-benefit evaluation of linkages should take into account the 'alternative situation' of what would have happened in the absence of the particular firm we are considering. Would the same linkages have been created? Would they have been created at lower cost? Would they have had more widespread effects? Such an evaluation is clearly not possible at this stage and we must await further evidence before it can be attempted.

This concludes the section on Unilever's food processing activities in developing countries. Although the discussion has been based on rather limited factual evidence, it has permitted us to consider some of the implications of TNC activities in poor host countries. The fact that the conclusions are hesitant is inevitable, and not due simply to the lack of data. There *are* grave difficulties of generalisation and interpretation which must be taken into account in any such analysis: limitations in the evidence also temper our discussion in the next section on TNCs generally.

## V FOOD TRANSNATIONALS AND DEVELOPING COUNTRIES

We may consider the general effects of transfer of technology by food TNCs under the same headings as those in the previous section.

TRANSFER AND ADAPTATION OF TECHNOLOGY

Unilever seems to be something of an exception in the industry as far as the location of major R and D activities in LDCs is concerned. Scattered data on United States TNCs indicate that they do conduct some R and D abroad in food processing,[43] but the research effort is mainly confined to developed countries (with the exception of Brazil and Mexico), and to 'applied' and 'development' work, which in this context entails adapting packaging, flavours, etc., to local tastes and habits. There is no evidence that any major United States TNC conducts basic R and D in developing countries on a scale comparable to that of Unilever's operations in India.

This need not imply, however, that US-based and other food TNCs have not undertaken measures similar to Unilever's to adapt their technology to low-wage conditions in developing countries or to make use of local resources. It is possible, indeed quite likely, that in developing countries with strong pressures for increasing the local content of production and investment, with lower levels of income and less sophisticated tastes, and with abundant supplies of cheap labour, food TNCs in general have made efforts to develop local supplies of food, packaging and machinery, produced 'older' or simpler products, and used older, more labour-intensive technology as compared to their home countries. However, in those developing countries with higher income levels (or a substantial middle class), a greater degree of urbanisation and stronger American influence—the best examples may be Brazil, Mexico, Argentina and Venezuela, the main recipients of United States food processing investment in the developing world—it is possible that the most 'advanced' products of the TNCs have been transferred with little adaptation. The impressionistic evidence which exists in respect of Latin America confirms that the transnational food industry operates with a large array of brand names,[44] and provides a variety of products as large as in developed countries, backed by powerful sales promotion (see Ledogar (1975), George (1976) and Lappé and Collins (1977)).

There are two separate sets of issues at stake here: whether the products themselves are appropriate to the social needs of the host countries, and whether they are produced by techniques appropriate to their factor endowments. Earlier discussion in this paper, and the evidence advanced elsewhere in this book, should have demonstrated that no definite answer can be given to either question. The appropriateness of processed foods must be evaluated in the context of given socio-economic conditions like income equality, urbanisation, the need to expand exports and the need for greater variety and convenience. Some highly processed foods are desirable because they last longer, need less time to prepare, taste better, cost less or are more capable of being exported than traditional foods. Others are less desirable because they are less nutritious, more costly, provide no gain in convenience and cannot be exported. Similarly, some of the technologies used by TNCs in developing countries which are at the large-scale, capital-intensive end of the available range,[45] have alternatives which are socially desirable, economically efficient and technically feasible. Others have no feasible alternatives, or they have alternatives which are very costly and inefficient (especially when export markets are taken into account).

To the extent that the transfer of technology by TNCs involves a transfer of inappropriate products and technologies—and we believe that there may well be an element of inappropriateness even after all qualifications have been taken into account—their operations entail a social cost. Much more detailed evidence is needed, however, to gauge the true extent of this cost and to formulate policy recommendations: at the moment we are still confined to scattered evidence, anecdotes and impressions.

MARKETING AND PRODUCTS

The previous section argued that it is difficult to make a straightforward distinction between appropriate and inappropriate products in the food industry. Clearly, some products meet clearly specific needs of certain classes in certain areas, and some meet more general needs. Others are not so easily viewed as desirable or appropriate, and their introduction into developing countries may be regarded as socially undesirable.

The most important costs derive from the effects of product

differentiation and advertising which are the essence of the growth of large firms and TNCs in this industry. The entry into developing country markets of food TNCs from the rich countries is accompanied by many of the promotional tactics which characterise their operations there, and lead to various social and economic costs:

(a) the economic waste involved in the advertising and promotion of 'new' food products;

(b) the cost of frequent and expensive changes in packaging and composition of the product which add little or nothing (sometimes even detract) from the nutritional content of previous 'models';

(c) the cost of various flavourings, colourings and other additives which help to differentiate and sell particular products but which offer little or nothing in the nutritional sense;

(d) the diversion of demand away from traditional foods which may have been nutritionally superior and which were produced from local components, and towards foods which have a much higher import content (in terms of additives, ingredients, machinery and technology), but which offer no particular nutritional benefit. The normal defence that advertising has no effect on consumption patterns and that people switch 'rationally' to foods which are in some objective sense 'better' for them sometimes rings hollow in the case of this industry. There is persuasive, albeit impressionistic, evidence in developing countries that advertising has a strong influence on taste,[46] even when the nutritional benefit offered by a successful product is virtually zero (take chewing gum or Coke).

A particularly grotesque example of the modern promotional techniques employed by the food TNCs is the famous allegation that 'Nestle kills babies'. Not only did the extensive and powerful local advertising of Nestle's baby foods cause poor mothers in Africa and the Caribbean to switch away from 'traditional' foods (including mother's milk) to costly processed foods, an obvious 'misallocation' of resources, but the fact that these mothers were unable to provide adequate quantities of baby food in sufficiently sterile conditions also led to babies becoming undernourished and sometimes more seriously ill.[47]

We cannot, of course, infer anything from this example about the whole range of highly processed foods but the lesson is obvious—the net nutritional contribution of the sorts of products in which the large food firms specialise may not be great, and may even occasionally be negative, while their cost is much higher. Much more research is needed in particular developing countries to ascertain exactly what sort of processed foods are sold, what other foods they replace, what their contribution is to health and nutrition on the one hand and the economic cost of providing them on the other. Some modern products may be cheaper to produce and better for health; many are certainly not.

It may be argued that the social cost of selling heavily promoted and highly packaged processed foods in developing countries is not as large as appears at first sight, since their consumption is confined to urban élites who are healthy, conscious of advertising techniques and more 'in need' of convenience. There is some truth in this, but the evidence from the baby foods case suggests that advertising has strong spillover effects to the urban poor and to rural populations. It causes preferences to change among people who are highly susceptible to advertising, who are on the borderline of malnutrition and who cannot and do not benefit from the gain in convenience offered by expensive, packaged products.

We may set against this the beneficial aspects of efficient marketing, need fulfilment and presentation afforded by some of the products of food TNCs. Unilever's vanaspati or buffalo-milk based products may be examples of these; protein-rich diets, if they find general acceptance,[48] may be others in the future. It is not the transfer of rich country technology and marketing as such which causes undesirable distortions in developing countries; it is their *indiscriminate and widespread* transfer. Clearly, as incomes rise and living habits change, there is bound to be greater consumption of more processed foods—the problem is to guide this process of change, drawing upon the expertise and resources of TNCs where necessary, in a way which minimises the costs that are to some extent inherent in the TNC mode of operation.

LINKAGES

The linkages that food processing TNCs (or agri-business generally) can create with the agricultural sector has recently become an issue of great economic and political significance. Critics argue, on the one hand, that the entry of large, capitalist, foreign-controlled agri-business has had disastrous effects on community life and on the employment opportunities and incomes of the rural masses, especially in Latin America.[49] Although the agri-business enterprises have run the farms efficiently on developed country lines, and large food processing firms have encouraged the capitalisation of farming, it is asserted that the displaced rural poor have lost their livelihood, suffered declines in nutrition and have seen none of the benefits in export earnings and revenues yielded by such activities. Several governments and international agencies have on the other hand, sponsored the transfer of modern technology to agriculture by agri-business firms,[50] and have promoted the use of capital-intensive techniques in general. There is little doubt that many of the efforts of TNCs (among others) to sponsor the local production of commercial crops have yielded considerable benefits to the host country: they have financed farmers, provided them with technology and inputs, assured them stable prices and improved productivity by demonstrating the viability of new techniques.[51] There is also little doubt that agricultural development in several countries has been inequitable and uneven.

As with marketing, there is a pressing need to separate the desirable from the undesirable effects: and only the host government can do this by defining the structure of land ownership, improving agricultural productivity and infrastructure, and creating opportunities for rural employment. In support of such measures, the government must also ensure that the TNCs involved pay adequate prices to their suppliers, charge fair prices for their exports (especially where intra-firm trade is involved) and part with a sufficient portion of their profits in the form of taxes. Many of the problems concerning linkages with agriculture are of much broader significance than those raised by the operations of food processing firms, and concern the whole nature of agricultural development: we cannot go into them here.

As with TNCs in other sectors, there is a need in this sector to implement measures to deal with potential profit manipulation by means of transfer pricing. We have suggested earlier that the scope for transfer pricing in food processing is small relative to other, more technology-intensive industries, but clearly the danger exists as long as intra-firm trade exists and official controls are imperfect. This subject merits separate discussion, but we cannot enter into it here.[52]

Apart from linkages with the agricultural sector, it is also desirable to maximise the benefits that the presence of TNCs can offer and minimise their costs, in relation to their linkages with locally owned industry. There are two separate sets of problems:

(*a*) to increase beneficial *direct* linkages with suppliers of equipment, packaging, consulting and other services;
(*b*) to reduce undesirable *indirect* linkages such as takeovers of successful local competitors so raising industrial concentration, the increasing use of promotion and product differentiation as key

elements in competitive strategy, and the use of more capital-intensive technology where alternative techniques exist.

Again, these are issues which merit detailed and separate discussion and we cannot do them justice in this chapter.[53] There is little reason to believe that the long-term trends towards increasing concentration, heavier advertising, more rapid product differentiation and greater diversification and conglomeration found in the food industry in developed countries will not be repeated in developing countries if TNCs are given a free hand. It must be recognised that some of these forces are inherent in the industry if private enterprise (local or foreign) is the predominant form of organisation: it must equally be recognised that the entry of TNCs may speed up the process of transforming industrial structure and conduct, and tends to reproduce the conditions of developed countries in a shorter period than otherwise. The foregoing discussion should have clarified why this may entail social costs in developing economies.

A final category of linkage which deserves mention is a subsidiary's *linkage with its parent organisation.* The fact that such linkages exist offers the benefit to the host economy that it gains easier access than an unrelated domestic firm to (*a*) the brand names and know-how of the parent; (*b*) the technology of food processing; and (*c*) to export markets. The social benefits of importing foreign brand names, with the associated paraphernalia of advertising and differentiation, are open to question. The benefits of advanced food processing technology are also, especially where more labour-intensive alternatives exist, not unmixed. The most important potential benefit is therefore that of increasing exports.

As we have seen from United States data, the present contribution of food transnationals to exports from developing countries is very small, although the efforts to increase agri-business investment may raise them in the future. The main problem of integrating into the vertical structure of a TNC is that the firm may resist moves to increase local value added in the producing areas. In part this may be justified by the lack of industrial development of the host countries, but in the main it is likely to be because of the existing pattern of production within the firms concerned (which they would be loath to change) and because of political fears of committing world-wide sourcing to developing countries. It would clearly be much easier to get TNCs involved in producing primary foodstuffs for export than in producing finished products for supplying world markets; this is a constraint that developing countries should bear in mind when contemplating whether to invite TNCs mainly to increase exports. On the other hand, the difficulty of breaking into export markets independently, when the barriers to entry are on the marketing side, should also be borne clearly in mind.

## VI CONCLUDING REMARKS

This paper represents a preliminary attempt to describe the role of foreign investment in food processing in developing countries. It is, of necessity, based on scanty data and scattered evidence, and no firm conclusions about the costs and benefits of the operations of transnational corporations emerge from the analysis. What does seem clear, however, is that a free and unrestricted inflow of foreign capital and technology, accompanied by the strategies that characterise food processing in developed countries, can potentially lead to several undesirable effects in developing countries. A properly controlled inflow should on the other hand prove beneficial. Much more research is needed to define these issues clearly and give them a sound empirical base; into nutritional needs and the role of new processed foods in meeting them; into changes in eating habits caused by changing economic circumstances and by the marketing practices of TNCs; into industrial structure and conduct and the effect of TNC entry on these; and into the balance of payments effects of the operations of large, vertically integrated food firms. Policies can be properly framed only after these complex and controversial issues have been fully investigated: in view of the importance of this industry, the benefits of further research are likely to be substantial.

NOTES

1. This chapter draws upon an unpublished survey by Arthur Domike, 'Issues Relating to Food Industry Transnational Corporations in Less-developed Countries', prepared in 1976 for the UN Centre on Transnational Corporations, and upon published and unpublished papers and reports provided by Doreen Wedderburn of Unilever. I wish to record my gratitude to Mr Domike and Mrs Wedderburn for their kindness, but relieve them of any responsibility for the opinions advanced here. I am grateful to Chris Baron for comments.

2. The main foreign enterprises operating in the Mexican food industry are mentioned by Lopez and Navarro (1976). These authors note the heavy dominance of TNCs in particular product groups like baby foods and soft

drinks, but do not have the data to analyse the industry comprehensively.

3.  Table 4.6 of Newfarmer and Mueller (1975) clearly shows the inverse relationship between the percentage of growth accounted for by acquisition and the technological intensity of the industry. 'High' technology industries like machinery and instruments show a percentage of less than 10, while 'low' technology ones like textiles, paper, rubber, stone, glass and clay show percentages of over 25.

4.  See United Kingdom, Department of Industry (1976), Table 43.

5.  In 1970, United States TNCs accounted for 41 per cent of total United States exports of food products. If we assume that this rose to 45 per cent by 1974 and add the 6 per cent accounted for by affiliates of non-United States TNCs, we get a figure of 51 per cent of exports by all TNCs.

6.  Domike (1976) has drawn up a valuable list of 200 leading food firms, including those known to be non-TNCs, and those in alcoholic beverages and food-related activities other than processing. His study contains a compendium of all sorts of useful data on TNCs in this industry. Also see Horst (1974) for a description of the leading US TNCs in food processing, and Lopez and Navarro (1976) for a list of US firms active in Latin America.

7.  See three studies of the United States FTC (1966a, 1969, 1969, 1966b) and Horst (1974).

8.  Commission of the European Communities (1975).

9.  United States FTC (1966a), p. 58. Domike (1976, p. 21) reports a finding by W. F. Mueller that the average four-firm concentration ratio (i.e. the share of total industry sales accounted for by the largest four firms) rose from 37.7 to 39.3 over 1947–71.

10.  United States FTC (1966a), p. 146.

11.  Ibid., p. 147.

12.  United States FTC (1966b), pp. 67–72.

13.  Domike (1976), p. 23. The process of integration of food processors into agricultural production is also described by Walsh (1975).

14.  For a comparison of the industrial structures of the UK and leading EEC countries, see George and Ward (1975).

15.  Horst (1974), p. 56.

16.  See United Kingdom, *Trade and Industry* (1974a).

17.  See United Kingdom, *Trade and Industry* (1974b).

18.  Unilever (1972).

19.  Horst (1974), p. 123. On the effects of advertising, see Cowling *et al.* (1975) and Comanor and Wilson (1974).

20.  The following evidence is taken from the *European Review* (1972).

21.  Ibid., p. 23.

22.  The latest available estimates on the 25 leading advertisers in the United Kingdom in 1975 show that 15 of them were food processing or food-related firms, led by Unilever. Out of the total advertising expenditure of the 25 on press and television, £162 million, the 15 food firms accounted for £106 million (65 per cent). These estimates were published in *The Times* (1977).

23.  George and Ward (1975) show that of the leading 24 food, drink and tobacco companies in the EEC in 1971, 20½ (half of Unilever) were British, 1 was German, 2 French and ½ Dutch. They explain (pp. 56–7) United Kingdom dominance in terms of exposure to United States competition, Commonwealth

links, different consumption patterns and the greater power of the retailers in the United Kingdom (causing greater concentration among processors).

24. *Business Week* (1976), emphasis added.

25. See Horst (1974), United States FTC (1969, 1966b). The FTC study (1969) also describes a number of instances of undesirable market conduct to which this sort of structure leads: price fixing or market allocation, predatory pricing and discriminatory preferences in favour of large buyers.

26. For a summary, see Lall and Streeten (1977).

27. Horst (1974), p. 106.

28. Its food sales in 1976 came to $7,896 million (50 per cent of total sales), nearly $300 million more than Nestle, its nearest rival.

29. For a history of the firm, see Wilson (1954).

30. Figures from Unilever (1976a, 1976b, 1972).

31. Capital employed is measured at historic cost and profitability figures may be relatively overstated for areas with older investments.

32. African figures are inflated by the inclusion of UAC International's operations which, being mainly trading, involve a low fixed assets-to-sales ratio.

33. See Lall and Streeten (1977); for a survey of the literature concerning the adaptation of technology, see Lall (1978).

34. The total R and D expenditure of Unilever in 1974 came to £63 million, and had risen to £109 million by 1976 (approximately 1·1 per cent of sales). We may estimate 1972 expenditures at £50 million. We should note that this estimate of the firm's R and D is worldwide and not comparable with figures given earlier for the United Kingdom alone.

35. There is, it appears from remarks made by company officials in London, very little transfer of product and process innovations from developing to developed areas in the firm. Indian R and D is however applied to other developing countries.

36. On the evolution of organisation in TNCs, see Stopford and Wells (1972).

37. 'Some 12,000 items of technical information from Unilever companies are collected centrally each year and transmitted if relevant to other companies' (Veldhuis (1976), p. 21).

38. A related question which arises here, which we could not investigate, concerns the cost of imported technology, especially hidden transfers by means of transfer pricing. The quantitative significance of transfer pricing is bound to be limited for this firm, because intra-firm trade represents under 6 per cent of turnover, and under 2 per cent of turnover involves intra-firm trade with developing countries. The 1976 *Annual Report* mentions this problem specifically and notes that market prices are generally used to determine transfer prices; where this is not possible, the two units 'engage in arm's length negotiations' (p. 33), using a cost-plus formula. Host government approval is also obtained.

39. ' . . . there is significantly higher labour content in products in developing countries: in both the edible fats and the soap and detergent industries the average man-hours employed to manufacture a ton of product is two or three times as high as in Europe' (Veldhuis (1976), p. 16).

40. See Lall (1978).

41. These products are being considered for introduction into South East Asia—see Unilever (1976), pp. 9–10.

42. Unilever owns an international advertising agency, SCC, and also

B/Lintas, which has a branch in Jakarta—see Unilever (1976).
43. See the United States Conference Board (1976).
44. See UNCTAD (1977), especially Table 4.12.
45. Although they may be older or more labour-intensive than technologies in the home countries of TNCs.
46. See Ledogar (1975), Barnet and Müller (1974), Lappé and Collins (1977) and George (1976).
47. The latest on the baby food controversy, now involving several firms in the United States and elsewhere, is given in Margulies (1977) and Lappé and Collins (1977).
48. High-protein foods have not as yet proved successful in finding consumer acceptance in developing countries; see Ledogar (1975) and Domike (1976).
49. See Feder (1977), Arroyo (n.d.), George (1976) and Lappé and Collins (1977).
50. According to a recent report, countries all over the world are seeking technology from agri-business firms, and the FAO has set up an 'industry co-operation programme', supported by firms like Kraft, Ralston Purina, General Mills, to encourage direct involvement by private corporations in agricultural production. See *Business Week* (1977).
51. For an example of this in the Mexican dairy industry, see Nestlé (1973).
52. On transfer pricing see Lall (1973).
53. These issues are discussed for TNCs in general terms in Lall (1978); for a review of the issues in the United States, see Parker (1976).

REFERENCES

Arroyo, G. (forthcoming), *Les transnationales et l'Agriculture en Amerique Latine* (Paris).
Barnet, R. J., and Müller, R. E. (1974), *Global Reach* (New York: Simon and Schuster).
Bhalla, A. S. (ed.) (1975), *Technology and Employment in Industry* (Geneva: ILO).
Buckley, P. J. and Casson, M. (1976), *The Future of the Multinational Enterprise* (London: Macmillan).
*Business Week* (1976), 'The Hard Road of the Food Processors' (8 March).
*Business Week* (1977), 'What 600 Companies Spend for Research' (27 June).
*Business Week* (1977), 'Selling US Knowhow to Feed the Hungry' (31 October).
Chung, W. K. (1977), 'Sales by Majority-Owned Affiliates of US Companies', *Survey of Current Business* (February).
Comanor, W. and Wilson, T. (1974), *Advertising and Market Power* (Cambridge (Mass.): Harvard University Press).
Commission of the European Communities (1975), *A Study of the Evolution of Concentration in the Food Industry for the United Kingdom* (Luxembourg).
Connor, J. M. and Mueller, W. F. (1977), *Market Power and Profitability of Multinational Corporations in Brazil and Mexico: Report to the US Senate Subcommittee on Foreign Economic Policy* (Washington, DC).
Cowling, T., Cable, T., Kelly, M. and McGuiness, T. (1975), *Advertising and Economic Behaviour* (London: Macmillan Press).

Domike, A. (1976), *Issues Relating to Food Industry Transnational Corporations in Less-developed Countries*, prepared for the UN Centre on Transnational Corporations.

*European Review* (1972), 'Europe and the British Food Industry' (Spring) pp. 18–31.

Feder, E. (1977), 'Agri-business and the Elimination of Latin America's Rural Proletariat', *World Development* (May–July) pp. 559–72.

*Fortune* (1977a), 'The Fortune Directory of the 500 Largest US Industrial Corporations'.

*Fortune* (1977b), 'The Fortune Directory of the 500 Largest Industrial Corporations Outside the US' (August).

Foster, G. (1977), 'The Changing UK Business Profile', *Management Today* (November) pp. 86–7.

Freidlin, J. N. and Whichard, D. G. (1976), 'US Direct Investment Abroad in 1975', *Survey of Current Business*, no. 49 (August).

George, S. (1976), *How the Other Half Dies* (Harmondsworth: Penguin Books).

George, K. D. and Ward, T. S. (1975), *The Structure of Industry in the EEC*, DAE Occasional Paper No. 43 (Cambridge: Cambridge University Press).

Horst, T. (1974), *At Home Abroad* (Cambridge, Mass.: Ballinger).

Lall, S. (1973), 'Transfer Pricing by Multinational Manufacturing Firms', *Oxford Bulletin of Economics and Statistics* (August) pp. 173–95.

Lall, S. (1978), 'Transnationals, Domestic Enterprises and Industrial Structure in LDCs: A Survey', *Oxford Economic Papers*.

Lall, S. and Streeten, P. (1977), *Foreign Investment, Transnationals and Developing Countries* (London: Macmillan).

Lappé, F. M. and Collins, J. (1977), *Food First* (Boston: Houghton Miffling).

Ledogar, R. J. (1975), *Hungry for Profits* (New York: Simon and Schuster).

Lopez, I. P. and Navarro, Y. G. (1976), 'La industrial alimentariaen Mexico y la penetración de las empresas transnacionales', *Comercio Exterior* (December).

Margulies, L. (1977), 'Cracks in the Bottle', *The New Internationalist*, 20–2 (April).

*Nestlé* (1973), *An Illustration of Nestlé's Role in Developing Countries: Example of the State of Chiapas, Mexico* (Geneva).

Newfarmer, R. S. and Mueller, W. F. (1975), *Multinational Corporations in Brazil and Mexico: Structural Sources of Economic and Non-Economic Power*, Report to US Senate, Washington, DC.

Parker, R. C. (1976), 'Anti-trust Issues in the Food Industries', *American Journal of Agricultural Economics* (December) pp. 854–60.

Stopford, J. M. and Wells, L. T. (1972), *Managing the Multinational Enterprise* (New York: Basic Books).

*The Times* (1977), 'The Times 1000 1976–77'.

Unilever (1976), *Unilever in Indonesia* (London).

Unilever (1976a), *Levers in Sri Lanka*.

Unilever (1976b), *A Note on Hindustan Lever as Part of the Multinational Unilever Limited*.

Unilever (1972), *Annual Report and Accounts*, and supplement on 'Food and Drink'.

Unilever (1972), *Research and Development in Hindustan Lever* (Bombay: Hindustan Lever).

United Kingdom, Department of Industry (1976a), *Census of Overseas Assets 1974* (London: HMSO).

United Kingdom, Department of Industry (1976b), *Overseas Transactions 1974* (London: HMSO).

United Kingdom (1974a), *Trade and Industry*, 'Research and Development by Manufacturing Industry', (2 May).

United Kingdom (1974b), *Trade and Industry*, 'Industrial Expenditure on Scientific Research and Development: Provisional Results on the 1972 Survey', (5 September).

United States Conference Board (1976), *Overseas Research and Development by United States Multinationals, 1966–75* (New York).

United States, Department of Commerce (1975), *US Business Investments in Foreign Countries* (Washington, DC).

United States, Department of Commerce (1976), *Foreign Direct Investment in the US* (Washington, DC).

United States, National Science Foundation (1975), *Research and Development in Industry* (Washington, DC).

United States, Federal Trade Commission (1966a), *The Structure of Food Manufacturing* (Washington, DC).

United States, Federal Trade Commission (1966b), *Economic Report on the Structure and Competitive Behaviour of Food Retailing.*

United States, Federal Trade Commission (1969), *Economic Report on the Influence of Market Structure on the Profit Performance of Food Manufacturing Companies* (Washington, DC).

United Nations (1973), *Multinational Corporations in World Development* (New York), Table 3.

United Nations Conference on Trade and Development (UNCTAD) (1977), *The Impact of Trademarks on the Development Process of Developing Countries*, document TD/B/C.6/AC.3/3.

Veldhuis, K. H. (1976), *Appropriate Industrial Technologies for Developing Countries: Transfer and Adaptation of Technology* (Unilever).

Walsh, J. (1975), 'US Agri-business and Agricultural Trends', in P. H. Abelson, *Food, Politics, Economics, Nutrition and Research* (Washington, DC: American Association for the Advancement of Science).

Wilson, C. (1954), *A History of Unilever* (London: Frank Cass).

# Part Three
# Technology Transfer

# 5 Technology and Developing Countries: a Review and an Agenda for Research[1]

## I INTRODUCTION

Recent years have witnessed a sustained growth of interest, by academics as well as policy-makers, in the subject of technological development in the Third World. While the early development literature had tended to ignore the role of technology in the process of industrial development and in determining changing patterns of comparative advantage, and concentrated on 'gaps' in savings and foreign exchange, later thinking has come to view technological 'gaps' as being almost as significant as gaps in investible resources. Economic historians have always been aware of the crucial role of innovation and diffusion in industrial growth,[2] but the mainstream of economic analysis has never been able to assimilate these into its theory in a meaningful or realistic way.

Development economics has, in its eclectic and *ad hoc* manner, drawn upon new theories of direct investment (*à la* Hymer, Kindleberger and Caves), trade (Vernon, Posner, Hirsch), and information (Arrow, Johnson) to evolve a complex (and often controversial) view of technology in LDCs. This view still lacks coherence, and it still has to forge links with the main body of the industrial literature on technology and innovation in developed countries.[3] But it has thrown up several important issues and has exercised important effects on policy.

The focus of the analysis of technology in LDCs has shifted over time. Early writings focussed on the problems faced by LDC enterprises in absorbing imported modern technology. Then came a concern, which still persists, about the transfer process and its costs: the role of MNCs, the nature of technology markets, monopolistic practices in technology sales, and the like. Slightly later, and from a different perspective, there arose serious doubts about the appropriateness of modern technology for the conditions of labour-surplus, skill- and capital-scarce LDCs. This debate had two components, one concerned with the generation of intermediate technology for rural and small-scale industries, the other with the adaptation of large scale modern technologies.

Most recently, attention has turned back to the question of technological assimilation, but with an important new issue in mind: that of technological 'learning' in LDC enterprises, their growing capability to produce technology and their 'revealed comparative advantage' in exporting technology in competitive international markets. This development corresponds to the growing propensity in official circles in LDCs to formulate 'technology plans' and encourage 'technological cooperation'. There is little doubt that LDC innovation and generation of technology will comprise the main areas of investigation and action in the next decade or so. This will serve to build the missing, but vital, link between the conventional study of technology in industrialised countries and in the Third World.

This paper is intended to provide a brief survey of these various themes in the development literature. It concentrates on manufacturing technology, especially in the 'modern' industrial sector. It selects certain topics which need to be further studied and provides a research agenda which may be appropriate to the international economic setting of the future. Section II discusses the main issues that have arisen in the general area of LDC technology; section III surveys the existing literature on each of the issues; and section IV outlines future directions of research.

## II MAIN ISSUES

We may group the issues that have arisen in the field of 'technology' generally into three main sets, each with several sub-groups: transfer to LDCs; impact on LDCs; and technological progress in LDCs.

### A TRANSFER

The greatest part of the discussion of technology has focussed on how it is transferred to LDCs from the developed countries, and, within this, on the role of the multinational corporation (MNC) as the main agent for generating, controlling and commercialising technology. The issues in this field may be subdivided into the following three sets.

(i) *Nature of technology markets and institutions.* The process by which private enterprise economies produce and commercialize technology has always posed difficult problems for conventional economic theoretical and welfare analysis.[4] The essence of the problem is as follows: once technology has been produced, it is a 'public good' in that its dissemination is socially costless (ignoring any marginal costs involved in transferring it across enterprises or countries—though these could be incorporated without amending the basic argument). In other words, the original holder or innovator of the technology can use his knowledge fully despite the broadcasting of that knowledge to other users. The maximisation of social welfare therefore requires that technological advance be disseminated for free (or at the marginal cost of transfer). Since technology is not costless to produce, however, society has to arrive at a non-optimal solution whereby the innovator is provided a 'just' reward for his investments in technology creation.

Given the inherently non-optimal nature of this situation, the debate revolves around how best society can reconcile the need for a reward (and incentive) for innovation with the need to prevent undue monopolistic exploitation and to ensure its full dissemination. In private enterprise economies, such a reconciliation takes place by granting temporary legal monopolies to innovators. This quasi-monopoly is usually reinforced by commercial secrecy (i.e. the patent may not provide sufficient information to make the innovation usable), by 'embodied knowhow' (i.e. the engineering and technical skills required to implement even a fully-documented patent may be specific to the innovating firm), by commercial practice (goodwill and brand preference created by investments in promotion) and by what are generally known as 'restrictive business practices'. Whether such a strengthening of the quasi-monopoly afforded by patents is socially desirable or not is a highly debatable point: the answer depends crucially on how the risks, costs, and value of innovation in each case are evaluated.

The nature of technology markets reflects these various inherent imperfections. The innovator is granted, or is permitted to set up, various instruments whereby he can appropriate a part of the commercial benefits from the innovation, the exact distribution of the benefits depending (between him and society) upon the strength of the combination of the various mechanisms at his disposal. In the context of technology transfers to LDCs, the technology supplier (not necessarily identical with the innovator, as noted below) has various means of appropriating the benefits of his knowledge: he can sell it outright (for royalties if it is a patent, or fees if it is in the form of technical assistance, or for a price if it is embodied in equipment); he can exploit it directly by investing in productive facilities owned fully by himself; or he can enter into a variety of intermediate arrangements (joint ventures, management contracts, etc.) If none of these yields returns which are sufficient in his view, he can withold the technology altogether.

The nature of the technology market is complex and may take several different forms. The following factors serve to illustrate this complexity:

(a) The age and diffusion of the technology. The older and better diffused the technology, the larger the number of potential suppliers.

(b) The variety of sources. There may be different types of suppliers able to provide the whole or parts of given technologies—e.g. machinery producers which can supply embodied technology in the form of individual pieces of equipment or entire plants; engineering consultants which can design, commission and provide training for particular processes or entire production systems; firms which use the technology themselves, and which can provide it by licensing or direct investment; and firms which possess the technology (but may not be actual users) and which can license it.

(c) Technology may be supplied in a more or less packaged form. The more comprehensive the package, the larger the number of instruments which the seller possesses to appropriate the benefits of new technology, and the higher the 'rent' which the buyer may pay for it. The provision of technology by direct investment (where technology is accompanied by managerial, marketing and other expertise, as well as by resources like capital and access to markets) is perhaps the most broadly based technological 'package'; equipment purchase or the purchase of specialised consulting services perhaps the most 'unpackaged'.

(d) The speed of change of the technology exercises a crucial effect on the structure of the market. The faster the rate of change, the narrower the range of potential suppliers and the greater the appropriating power of the supplier. Thus, in relatively stagnant technologies, the main sellers may be turnkey plant suppliers or engineering consultants; in highly sophisticated and fast-moving technologies, they will be multinational investors.

Thus, technology markets may, depending on the nature of 'supply', range from fairly competitive to highly monopolistic ones. The nature of 'supply' is not, however, the only factor of importance: the 'demand' side also affects the appropriating powers of the seller. The more capable and advanced a purchaser, the greater his ability to 'unpackage' for any given required technology. The less capable the purchaser, the greater his need for a comprehensive package, and the more his liability to pay high rents for the technology acquired.

The lack of capabilities on the purchaser's side may be of two types: first, technological weakness (lack of expertise, skills, experience, R and D, etc.) and second, information gaps (about potential sources of technology supply). The two usually go together, since a technologically capable enterprise is also likely to have a fairly good idea of where to look for more advanced techniques, but analytically they are separate, and call for slightly different policy measures.

Technological weaknesses and information gaps together conspire to compound the imperfections which are inherent on the supply side of technology markets. Thus, what may be fairly competitive markets in the industrialised world may turn out to be highly monopolistic in LDCs; or, what may be a relatively easy 'package' to open for one purchaser may turn out to be an impossible one to open for another. The determinants of the 'packaging' and 'unpackaging' of technology have been much discussed in technology literature, though, as we shall note below, there is an unfortunate lack of specific studies of the costs and benefits of these alternatives.

One feature of the technology market which has received a great deal of attention, and attracted much controversy, is the *patent system*. Since the entire institution of patents is an uneasy compromise between the need to provide incentives for innovation with the need to promote competition and disseminate productive knowledge, there has been a long-standing debate within the industrialised countries about whether the monopolistic costs outweigh the innovational benefits to society. Critics have argued that patents are not really necessary to protect innovation once the major sources of technological growth have become large corporations rather than the individual inspired scientist; that patents do not really serve to disseminate innovations, in that most of them do not provide sufficient information; that their effective scope and life is greatly extended by commercial practices (promotion, restrictive policies of various sorts), and so made to yield far more than a 'just' reward; and that the costs of patent litigation discriminate in favour of larger enterprises.[5] This argument has been extended to LDCs with even greater force[6]: the great majority of patents there are held by foreign companies, and most of them are never used for production; LDCs offer little inducement to innovation in the products and processes in which patent protection if offered; their own enterprises, not being innovators, do not benefit from the system, since they are prevented from imitating the patented technology; and the system is accompanied by a host of undesirable practices such as import-tying, export restrictions and the like, all of which raise the cost of technology transfer to LDCs.

Some of these criticisms need modification and qualification, which will be noted later, but certainly the institution of the patent system has raised issues of great relevance and significance in the areas of technology transfer. These issues still remain to be resolved.

(ii) *Modes of technology transfer.* The issues that arise here are closely related to those arising from the nature of technology markets, but the emphasis here is on the exact nature of the transaction than on the nature of the market forces underlying it. There are several possible ways of classifying the modes of technology transfer, of which two seem to be especially useful.

The first is according to the nature of the technology transaction. Technology is transmitted across enterprises and across countries in a wide variety of forms. Some of these are not commercial in the strict sense: scientific exchange, publications, migration of skilled people, and government assistance. Others are not transfers of 'knowledge' strictly defined; the import of a piece of equipment, while it clearly 'embodies' a certain technology, does not transfer any knowhow in the sense we usually understand the term. Others are commercial transfers of technology in the normal usage: turnkey projects, consulting services of various kinds (engineering, construction, financial, managerial, etc.), sales of patents and trademarks, and direct investment. Cooper and Hoffman (1978) have advanced a three-fold categorisation of technology transactions:

(a) 'simple direct' sales of technology, which consist of outright sales of embodied (machinery) or disembodied (specific consulting services) technology by unrelated firms for prices which are more or less competitive;

(b) 'process packaged' sales of technology, where a complete industrial process or plant is supplied (together with various types of studies and design, commissioning, supervision and training services) by machinery manufactures, independent engineering firms or final manufacturers of products; and

(c) 'project packaged' sales of technology, where the technology is accompanied by other requirements for the commercial operation of a project—i.e. management, capital, brand names, etc.—

and by some element of continuous link or control by the seller (this encompasses licensing contracts, joint ventures and wholly owned foreign subsidiaries).

This categorisation is useful in that it diverts attention from the traditional preoccupation with packaging and unpackaging technology in the last group of transactions. While project-packaged technology may well be the most important form of technology imports by LDCs (ignoring straightforward capital goods imports), other sorts of transactions (turnkey projects for the 'newcomers', various international consultancy services for the others) are becoming increasingly important. Furthermore, depending upon the speed of change of technology, suppliers which have traditionally remained in one category (say, MNCs) are increasingly diversifying the sorts of arrangements they are prepared to undertake (turnkey projects or specialised services). Furthermore, the LDCs themselves are showing a growing capability to enter technology markets as sellers of all sorts of technology, though they face certain strict limits to their capabilities.

The second way of classifying technology transactions is by the nature of the instrument used: i.e., whether technology is sold in the form of equipment, studies, designing of plant, commissioning, supervision, management, training, licenses or direct investment. This particular categorisation is particularly useful for an 'unpackaging' policy, since it enables the buyer to assess just what it is he is buying, and to compare it to what his specific needs are.

General discussions of this sort about the modes of technology transfer have not really given rise to separate issues of any significance. They have been undertaken to support arguments about the *costs* of technology purchase by LDCs (which we come to in a moment); this is unfortunate, because there are problems of great interest and significance in this area of modes of transfer which need further explanation. What, for instance, determines the pace at which alternative technology suppliers become available; how does the strategy of one sort of seller differ from that of another; what is the extent of linkage between different kinds of technology suppliers; how large are the different segments of the market; and, more simply, how does the international consultancy/turnkey market operate?

(iii) *Costs of transfer.* Given the fragmented and uncompetitive nature of many technology markets on the one hand and the weak technological capabilities and poor knowledge on the part of LDC buyers on the other, it is to be expected that LDCs often get a rough deal in international technology transactions. They may have to pay high *direct* costs for what they buy (profits, royalties, fees and the like); and they may be subjected to various types of *indirect* costs (in the form of restrictive clauses, transfer pricing and monopolistic pricing practices, use of predatory market tactics to suppress local competition, etc.). Furthermore, the buyers themselves may worsen their situation by indulging in repetitive purchases of the same technology, by offering very high effective rates of protection that attract inefficient investments, and by not doing enough to encourage bargaining and technological development by local enterprises.

These issues have been so well aired that it seems unnecessary to repeat the debate here. Several UNCTAD studies on transfer of technology[7] have assembled information on the incidence of restrictive practices in technology contracts, and various studies in Latin America (especially Vaitsos (1974)) have described the problems in depth. More recent literature has focussed on another sort of problem arising from technology imports: the impact of 'technological dependence' upon the development of (or lack thereof) local technological capabilities in the LDCs. This is an issue of major importance which is likely to exercise academics and policy makers for some time to come: what is the right balance between importing and developing technology? Can LDCs 'do a Japan' in terms of protecting and fostering their technology and emerge as major suppliers of technology in their own right?

The main fear which 'technological dependence' raises is that a passive policy of importing advanced technology from abroad will not enable LDC enterprises to invest even in local 'learning' of technology in which they have a comparative advantage. In every sort of industry there are technologies which are stable, somewhat 'out of date' and usually somewhat smaller and less capital-intensive as compared to technologies on the frontier: for these technologies, local enterprises may well be able to develop the capability to design, adapt and even export them efficiently. Yet a general policy of technological dependence may prevent the basic infrastructure of 'learning' from being set up, and the necessary costs and risks from being undertaken.

These long-term dynamic costs of technology imports (and they apply to a certain sort of import, not to all) may well be much more important than the financial (direct or indirect) costs of buying technology. But much work needs to be done to define LDCs' comparative advantage in technology.

B IMPACT

The impact of technology on LDCs may be subdivided into the following sets of issues: its appropriateness and adaptation to the needs of LDCs; its diffusion within LDCs; and its linkages with trade.

(i) *Appropriateness and adaptation.* The discussion till now has assumed that the technology transferred to LDCs was socially beneficial to them—that, in other words, it was appropriate to their factor endowments and needs. Several writers (see Stewart (1977)) have questioned this assumption, and argued strongly that much of modern technology is 'inappropriate' in one or both of two senses: it uses too much capital and too little labour, and it produces commodities which are unnecessary, over-sophisticated or overspecified in relation to the needs of poor countries. In this context, MNCs have been singled out for particular criticism, not only for directly transferring inappropriate technologies but also for creating pressures on local enterprises to follow them in using and commercialising such technologies.

The 'appropriateness' of technology raises several complex and difficult issues of theory, fact and judgement. To mention the more important ones:

(*a*) How much scope is there for efficient factor substitution, given the product, at feasible sets of factor prices? How does factor substitutability vary across industries? What are its limits and how are they affected by scale, skills, changes in technology, commercial viability and so on? What are the distributional, technological, trade and growth implications of choosing particular sets of techniques?

(*b*) How can appropriateness of product be defined? What political, social and economic assumptions lie behind the application of such concepts as 'basic needs' which provide one, currently fashionable, possible criterion? To what extent do 'modern' products meet given needs efficiently?

(*c*) What is the relationship between 'appropriate' products and 'appropriate' techniques?

(*d*) Given the scope for efficient and desirable factor substitution, how do different sets of enterprises fare in achieving adaption of technology? In particular, how do foreign-owned firms compare with domestic firms? What determines the response of enterprises (factor prices, government policy, internal rigidities, extent of competition, etc.)?

(*e*) How does appropriate technology fit in with international markets? Is it compatible with the dynamic comparative advantage of LDCs? Should the definition of appropriateness vary with the extent of technological sophistication of the LDC in question, and with its degree of integration into world markets? Does a thoroughgoing programme of implementing appropriate technology lead to autarky?

These are issues which are exercising many economists, governments and international bodies, and by their nature they do not admit to easy solutions. Not only do fundamental political and social value judgements differ between them, but hard facts are also rather scarce.

(ii) *Diffusion within LDCs.* In contrast to the attention given to the process of international transfers of technology, that of diffusion within LDCs has received very little—yet it is clearly of equal significance to the long-term growth of the industrial sector. The issue has arisen rather peripherally in the context of discussions of sub-contracting and 'linkages', but the questions which have been extensively studied in the industrialised countries (see Rosenberg (1976), Mansfield (1968) Nasbeth and Ray (1974)) have not really been explored in LDCs. These concern the industrial and firm-level determinants of the process of technological diffusion: factors such as the amount of capital required, the riskiness of the new technology, its profitability, the role of information flows, managerial attitudes, industrial market structures and the like. It is reasonable to expect that some of the relationships found in the industrialised countries will also obtain in LDCs: the familiar s-shaped diffusion curve (slow at first, speeding up and then slowing down again) probably also characterises the diffusion process in the poor countries. However, there are, for obvious reasons, bound to be important differences: the perception of new technologies may be much slower and the attendant risks greater; the lack of accompanying facilities (equipment, spares, skills) may retard diffusion; the dualistic production structure will impose its own imprint on technical change; the nature of protection offered will be significant; and so on.

(iii) *Linkages with trade.* Technological change is closely linked with comparative advantage—an obvious proposition, but one which has gained acceptance in conventional trade theory only recently, and which has not received its full due in the study of evolving trade patterns of the Third World.[8] The emergence of a few LDCs as very dynamic exporters of labour-intensive products has aroused widespread interest (and concern among the developed nations), but the role of technology in promoting exports as a whole, and in enabling LDCs to enter non-traditional markets (chemicals, machinery, transport equipment) has mainly been considered from one viewpoint: that of the MNC as the agent of dynamic comparative advantage. This is no doubt an important issue, but it is not the only one in this context.

A number of agents have been active in the process of 'restructuring' world industry: technology sellers from developed countries who do not invest in LDCs; retailing organisations in developed countries who provide only marketing (and sometimes design) technology; small firms in developed countries who enter into joint ventures in LDCs, or completely shift their production there; LDC enterprises who adapt, imitate and innovate of their own accord; and the MNCs proper, who enter into buy-back agreements, set up export-orientated affiliates, transfer entire technologies or only the labour-intensive parts of technologies, and gradually integrate LDC affiliates in a system of global 'sourcing'. There is a complex interplay of different forces at work, some increasing the significance of MNCs in LDC trade, others reducing it, depending very much on the speed, costs and nature of technological progress. Where technology is relatively stable, a number of different alternatives appear which can help LDCs to establish themselves as exporters; where it is growing rapidly, on the other hand, only the transfer of the whole 'package' of techniques, management, marketing, etc., can enable them to do this successfully.

This brings us back to questions related to the nature of technology markets and the relationships between the various sellers of technology. When concentrating specifically on LDC exports of manufactures, however, they have to be seen in a different light. Clearly, several kinds of industrial technology which have been imported into LDCs, especially the larger ones still intent on import-substitution and diversification of their industrial bases, are not relevant to their export potential. Given this, however, there are still a number of advanced technologies, with high skill and capital requirements, in which these large LDCs have proved themselves internationally viable, even without the entry of MNCs. A number of indigenous Indian firms are, for instance, now able to sell sophisticated engineering and electronic goods on world markets, using technology which they have adapted and improved from initial licences.

The precise relationships which obtain between different forms of technology transfer and the export performance of LDCs in different industries are thus an important area for investigation.

C  TECHNOLOGICAL PROGRESS IN LDCS

Technical progress can take a variety of forms when viewed from the perspective of the manufacturing enterprise: it covers everything from a major innovations in products or processes, the adoption of new techniques innovated elsewhere and the improvement of existing techniques or products, to the raising of the productivity of given techniques by better management, organisation and 'learning by doing'. Economic literature on innovation has generally concerned itself with major innovations—the Schumpeterian 'break-through' syndrome—and has generally neglected the very important part played by minor changes and improvements in the progress of technology.[9] And it has virtually totally neglected the process of technological development (of all sorts) in the LDCs, reflecting partly an implicit belief that poor countries had little ability to generate technological progress and partly a feeling that modern technology (and innovation) was really irrelevant to the needs of LDCs and should be replaced by older, more appropriate technologies (where the role of innovation was bound to be fairly minor).

This neglect is totally unwarranted. Evidence, scattered and fragmentary though it may be, is now being collected that a substantial and diverse range of technological activity is now going on in the modern industrial sectors of LDCs. This activity is leading to the (a) assimilation of technology (i.e. the capability of the recipient to reproduce the entire technology), (b) adaptation of technology (to domestic raw materials, conditions, scales and skills), (c) improvement of technology, (d) generation of new technology, and (e) commercial export of locally generated technology. While much of the progress made on this front by LDCs may be in terms of 'catching up' with relatively stable technologies rather than competing on the frontiers of technological progress, it does indicate that there may be emerging an international division of technological work, in which (over a long term) the more advanced and larger of the LDCs increasingly assuming the more 'labour intensive' functions (consulting, detailed engineering, training, etc.) of technological work and also taking over the sales of certain types of technologies (slightly out-of-date, standardised, adapted, smaller scale) to other LDCs.

If this is so, the phenomenon is clearly one of major significance to policy and to the conventional wisdom on the comparative advantage of LDCs. Policy makers must take their technological potential (and limitations) into account in formulating decisions on education, science, industrial strategy, foreign investment, and trade. Economists must adapt their usual theories about LDCs specialising in low skill, labour-intensive activities. The dividing line may not always be high-skill and low-skill between the advanced and the poor countries, but *specific types of high skills*, based on scientific advance, massive R and D and high-income markets, on the one hand, and those based on 'mature' technologies, smaller scales, and lower-income markets on the other. Some of the issues of interest here are:

(*a*) What determines the pace and form of technological progress in the industrialising LDCs? What sorts of technologies are particularly suited to 'learning' and export by LDCs? What are the limits to technological progress in LDCs?

(*b*) What is the role of enterprise level R and D in generating technology? How does this compare with the contributions of research institutions separately established by governments?

(*c*) What sorts of educational and scientific structures promote local technological development?

(*d*) What is the role of the capital goods sector in innovation in LDCs? What are the different stages of 'learning' in the design and construction of capital goods? How is this 'learning' influenced by different forms of technology imports from the advanced countries?

(*e*) What role do engineering consultants play in technological progress and diffusion? What is their comparative advantage in international markets and can they enter the markets of advanced countries with their cheap-skills competitive edge?

(*f*) What has been the experience of indigenous technologies within the given LDCs and, when they have been exported, in other countries?

(*g*) How capable are small-scale enterprises of sharing in the innovative process? How can small and large scale enterprises coordinate in technological progress? What special policies are needed to help small-scale enterprises?

(*h*) How do indigenous enterprises compare with foreign affiliates in the generation, application and export of technology? How can MNCs assist LDCs in becoming technologically capable—e.g. by subcontracting design work, by commissioning specific research projects, by transferring their own R and D work?

(*i*) Finally, what role can international organisations (UNCTAD, World Bank, UNESCO) play in promoting the development of

LDCs' technological capabilities, and how can aid donors assist in this process?

It is clear, at least to the present author, that these (unduly neglected) issues are of crucial significance to the whole progress of industrialisation in the larger Third World countries, and that they will come to occupy an increasing part of our attention in the future.

## III   THE LITERATURE

In this section we shall quickly survey the existing literature on each of the main issues noted above. A comprehensive survey would involve thousands of references and hundreds of pages of analysis: this is neither possible nor necessary for present purposes, so we shall pick the more important works and simply state some of the significant conclusions.

### A   TRANSFER

(i) *Nature of technology markets and institutions.* Besides the theoretical works on the welfare aspects of knowledge creation (Kenneth Arrow and Harry Johnson) and the relationship of knowledge creation to the expansion of multinational corporation (Magee), several works have focused on the nature of the market which confronts LDCs, and the costs which it imposes on them. Cooper and Hoffman (1978), Streeten (1972), Pavitt (1972), Chudson and Wells (1974), UNCTAD (1975), Balasubramanyam (1973), Cooper and Sercovitch (1971), Parker (1974) and Vaitsos (1974) have analysed the imperfections in technology markets and the possible reasons for LDCs to be in exceptionally weak bargaining positions.

The patent system in LDCs has been analysed by Vaitsos (1972), Penrose (1973), Greer (1973), Lall (1976), O'Brien (1974) and UNCTAD (1973). The strongest critics (Vaitsos, O'Brien and UNCTAD) have argued that patent systems serve to *retard* the transfer of technology to LDCs, since they only help to set up import monopolies for the large foreign corporations, prevent local technological absorption and enable all sorts of restrictive practices to be implemented. Penrose, Greer and Lall have adopted more moderate positions, arguing that some of the costs attributed to the patent system are simply reflections of the monopoly power of the innovators (which in turn may reflect the high costs of conducting and commercialising R and D); that in many industries (engineering and equipment) the development and transfer of technology is not strongly linked to the patent system because of the importance of 'software' in the technological system; that many patents cannot be economically 'used' in LDCs in any case; and that the patent system may be useful in creating a favourable ambiance for foreign investment and for local innovation. This still admits of high potential costs of the patent system: for some sectors where patents *are* very significant for innovation (e.g. pharmaceuticals) innovators may be particularly prone to abuse them by charging exceptionally high prices for new products and by holding back local production (see Lall (1975)). A tightening of patent regulation and stricter implementation of safeguards and penalties (compulsory licensing) may then be called for to remedy these faults. The revision of the patent system is being strongly urged by UNCTAD, though earlier calls for more extreme action (LDCs to opt out of the Paris Convention altogether) have been dropped. Vaitsos (1976) presents a concise and clear statement of the revisions needed, though it is impossible to say what the final outcome will be.

(ii) *Modes of transfer.* Several of the references given above have also dealt with the modes of technology transfer to the LDCs. Baranson's (1967) rather dated bibliography provides a guide to earlier writings on this subject; Roberts (1973) has provided an excellent analysis of the role of engineering consultants in developing countries; Teece (1976), Helleiner (1975), Parker (1974), Germidis (1977) and Lall and Streeten (1977) have analysed different aspects of technology transfer through the MNC. No detailed studies exist, to my knowledge, of the economic costs and benefits of 'unpackaging' technology—i.e. of switching from one mode of transfer to another—though Balasubramanyam (1973) attempts a comparison of the performance of foreign subsidiaries with licensees and other domestic firms.

(iii) *Costs of transfer.* The costs of technology transfer for LDCs have been amply described in the literature by the authors named above. Vaitsos (1974) and UNCTAD (various publications under the general heading of 'Studies in Transfer of Technology to Developing Countries' and 'Restrictive Business Practices') in particular have made major contributions to this subject. The bulk of the work has emanated from Latin America, though some UNCTAD studies have also produced data on India, Spain, Ethiopia and Sri Lanka. The findings generally confirm that there is a wide variation in prices charged for the same technology in different countries, that markets are highly fragmented and oligopolistic and leave a great deal to the precise outcome of bargaining between buyer and seller, that hidden costs are as important as—and sometimes more important than—the explicit costs. In the absence of detailed studies of 'unpackaging', however, it remains difficult to say what the alternative situation might have been—would a tighter control of technology transfer merely lower its costs or would it also choke off the inflow of advanced techniques? How much are the high costs simply 'monopolistic rents' and how far are they necessary to sustain innovation? Granted the undoubted market power wielded by the large MNCs, are there other channels of technology transmission which (at least in techniques where they excel) are as effective and rapid? Some of these complicated issues (touched on in Lall and Streeten (1977)) need to be analysed further in the discussion of costs.

The issue of technological dependence was raised by UNCTAD in the context of its promotion of 'technological self-reliance' at the last general session of the Conference. While its analysis was confused, and overly influenced by the *dependencia* school of Latin America, it made the valid point that a certain lessening of the passive reliance on imported technology (which is characteristic of most LDCs) might be necessary for the growth of local efforts to generate technology. The statement was more one of faith than an assessment of how technological development actually occurs within enterprises and industries, or of where the comparative advantage of LDCs (and their limits) in technological development lay. It also reflected the growing feeling in countries like Mexico (at least in the Echevarria days) that a certain assertion of technological independence was needed, and that a 'Technology Plan' was a precondition to this. India has, for a long time, pursued a policy of local technological development under the auspices of its CSIR laboratories and the NRDC's promotion of local technologies. Countries like South Korea have combined, with their aggressive policies of export promotion, a Japanese-style protection of local technological development in certain sectors.

A few attempts have been made to evaluate these various experiences: Mytelka (1978) has studied the effect of licensing and foreign investment on local adaptive efforts in the Andean Pact countries; Erber (1978) has made a similar (and more detailed) study of the capital goods sector in Brazil; Newfarmer (1978) has drawn some indirect inferences in his study of market power in the international electrical equipment industry; and Lall (1980) has analysed the evidence on different sorts of 'revealed comparative advantage' in technology exports by LDCs to conclude that there may be a valid 'infant industry' argument for protecting technological efforts. The main conclusion of these various studies seems to be that there are substantial 'learning costs' inherent in the process of developing a viable technological base. The costs are greatest when it comes to the basic design of sophisticated machinery, a function which is not normally transferred to LDCs by the foreign transferrors of technology. To develop this level of technological capability, therefore, LDCs need to encourage local firms (especially locally owned or controlled firms) to invest in their own design and R and D, but the risks and costs of such investments are high enough to warrant a period of protection. This anticipates the section below on local generation of technology, so we shall not pursue it further now.

B  IMPACT

(i) *Appropriateness.* The literature on 'appropriate' technology has now reached massive proportions, and it is difficult in this sort of paper to even highlight the salient findings, but readers are referred to Stewart (1970), Jenkins (1975), Bhalla (1975), Morawetz (1974), Pickett (1977), Rhee and Westphal (1977), Wells (1973), White (1976), Cooper and Kaplinsky (1974) and Pack (1974) for a sample of different approaches, findings and surveys.

Despite this flood of writing—or, perhaps, because of it—the precise definition of 'appropriate' technology is not clear, and the exact scope for its efficient (and commercially viable) application in different branches of manufacturing industry has not been delineated. Different people use 'appropriate' technology to stand for different things: in a weak form appropriateness may mean a greater use of labour and local materials, given the nature of the product; in an intermediate form, it may mean the use of the most labour-intensive technique available with which a given product may be manufactured; and in a strong form, it may mean a more appropriate product made with a technique which is not known but needs to be developed. What is considered 'appropriate' on one definition may be inappropriate on another. Some authors even incorporate appropriate technology into a broader programme of socio-political reform (an 'appropriate' society which will use 'appropriate' products made with 'appropriate' techniques): this is an ultra-strong use of the term with which many proponents of 'more appropriate' (i.e. somewhat more labour-intensive technology given the structure of demand and the more-or-less free play of market forces) technology may well disagree. The choice of definitions clearly depends on the user's value judgement about the 'right' aims of industrialisation and the proper trade-offs between equity, employment-creation, efficiency, growth and international integration.

As far as the scope for efficient factor substitution is concerned, there is again a confusing array of different approaches, ranging from the use of production–function estimates, through detailed examination of particular technologies in use and engineering data, to anecdotal analysis of particular techniques.[10] It seems widely accepted now that *some* substitution is possible in most manufacturing industries, and that a great deal is possible in the more traditional sectors (where both products and processes can be 'simplified' enormously). Even in very 'modern' sectors some substitution is possible by using less automated methods, more labour-intensive peripheral processes, more shifts and more subcontracting to small units (see Helleiner (1975)). However, it is apparent that in many industries with precision engineering, continuous processes, rapid technical progress and large scale-economies, the overall scope for increasing the use of labour is not very great—at least if the product is taken as appropriate and efficiency is an important criterion. This is not to deny that efforts directed at developing new labour-intensive technologies may not be worthwhile: the evidence on this is too scanty to permit generalisations.

The role of MNCs in adapting technology has come in for much discussion in this context.[11] In a recent review of this literature, the present author (Lall (1978)) has concluded that there is some evidence of minor adaptation of techniques and products by MNCs, but that in general these are transferred unchanged from developed to less-developed areas; furthermore, there is no basis to conclude that foreign firms are better or worse at adapting technologies to local conditions than local firms. These issues seem to have been so fully thrashed out that there is little to be gained by further investigation or analysis: 'foreignness' as such does not seem to be a major factor in determining choice of technique.

At the broader level of factor substitution, however, there do remain important issues which have been skated over in the general enthusiasm for applying intermediate technologies. As noted above, these concern the exact scope for their efficient application and their limitations. The conventional wisdom on the Chinese success in applying such technology needs, in this context, a much more sceptical investigation: the sudden reversal in Chinese policy in favour of buying the most advanced technologies from the West surely indicates some severe limitations in 'doing without' modern techniques.

(ii) *Diffusion*. There is little literature on diffusion within LDCs, with the exception of some studies of subcontracting (see references in Lall (1978)) and small-scale industries (OECD (1974) and Germidis (1977)).

The existing studies have not gone into a broad-based analysis of the process of technology diffusion (its pace, determinants, etc.) in LDCs; clearly much remains to be done here.

(iii) *Trade.* Much of the literature on trade and technology tends to relegate LDCs to exporters of labour-intensive, low-skill products at the end of their 'life-cycles'. Some recent authors do, however, recognise the increasing potential for LDCs to export high-skill products based on relatively standardised techniques (e.g. television sets) or on designs which meet smaller scales or use simpler controls (machinery) than the 'most modern' ones (see Pack (1978) Lall (1980)). The different agents for transmitting the requisite technologies and know-how to LDCs are: retailing agencies and trading houses in developed countries (Helleiner (1973), Watanabe (1972), Hone (1974)); small manufacturing firms in developed countries; the large TNCs (de la Torre (1974), Sharpston (1975), Helleiner (1973), Finger (1975)); and local enterprises in the LDCs themselves (Katz and Ablin (1977), Lall (1980)). These relationships are evolving rapidly and there is still a time lag between reality and academic analysis. There is a massive restructuring of world industry under way, and the variety of mechanisms involved needs much greater study. While to some extent this goes beyond the scope of 'technology' as such, clearly the transfer of technology is one crucial element in such restructuring. The MNC has received considerable attention as the agent of 'dynamic comparative advantage'; but there are others, and they may well be more significant over the long run (Nayyar (1978)). The export performance of particular LDCs has also received attention, but the relationships between technological development and exports remain to be properly studied.

C  TECHNOLOGICAL PROGRESS IN LDCS

Only a few studies have attempted to describe technological progress in LDCs: Katz (various), Lall (1979), Cortez (1978), Mytelka (1978), Fairchild (1977), Jha (forthcoming). Nevertheless, all of them point in the same direction: a significant amount of technical progress is going on in LDCs in both foreign and local firms. This progress takes a variety of forms, ranging from minor adaptations to major changes and innovations, and it has important consequences: improved productivity, better export performance, a considerable amount of local learning, better use of local resources and (in some more advanced countries) increasing exports of technology (Lall (1980)), Katz and Ablin (1977), Cortez (1978), Wells (1977, 1978), Diaz Alejandro (1977) and Lecraw

(1977). In my (1980) paper, reproduced in this book (Chapter 8), I take an optimistic view of the capabilities of LDCs: with the restructuring of manufacturing industry there will also be a restructuring of technological work. The LDCs will increasingly take over the export of relatively standardised (but high-skill) technologies; they may also increasingly undertake the more labour-intensive parts of design, engineering and consulting work even in the advanced countries. The growing subcontracting of engineering activity by MNCs to firms from LDCs is the first sign of this emerging trend: the comparative cost advantage of the LDCs is so great that there is no reason why it should not progress further.

Very little is, however, known about the potential for and limitations to technological development in the LDCs. The potential is enormous, but there are also stringent limits: LDCs cannot keep up with changes in areas of rapidly evolving technologies with massive R and D expenditures; they cannot compete with technologies whose commercialisation requires large marketing networks, high-income markets and well-known brandnames; they do not have the ability to mount enormous investments or undertake very long production runs; and so on. All these matters need considerable study and analysis, since this remains, for some inexplicable reason, an area of neglect.

This completes our brief survey of the literature, and enables us to go on to make concrete suggestions for future research.


IV   FUTURE DIRECTIONS

Any selection of promising areas of research is bound to be highly subjective. This paper has touched on dozens of potential research topics: not all of them are equally useful or practicable. Some are intellectual *cul de sacs*; some are worth study, but are already adequately analysed or are being analysed; some are worth study but cannot be properly analysed for lack of theoretical tools or adequate data. I shall be arbitrary and select some which are under-studied, yet which are useful and practicable.

(i) *Role of turnkey contractors and engineering consultants in technology transfer to LDCs.* Among the various avenues for technology transfer to LDCs, those of turnkey contractors and engineering consultants remains the least understood. OECD has already conducted preliminary study of engineering consultants (Brown and Perrin (1977)), and there is a valuable earlier paper by Roberts (1973) on this subject, but as a relative outsider to this subject I find that these have just scratched the surface of the problem. It would be valuable to know (a) the general dimensions of turnkey and consultancy activity by foreign enterprises in LDCs, (b) the dimensions in specific sectors, (c) the experience of particular developing countries.

The existing studies make general references to the growth of consultancy intensive technologies in modern industry and the vital role of consultants in transferring technology. This needs much more clarification. What precisely *are* the functions? How do the functions of feasibility study, project report, project design, detailed engineering, equipment procurement, construction, start up training, etc., link up together—or are they separable in terms of the expertise required? How does their relative importance differ from industry to industry? How do the organisations concerned link (in terms of equity, expertise, language, etc.) with equipment suppliers, technology owners, technology users, etc., in the developed countries? What is the value of the turnkey and consultancy work done each year in different parts of the Third World? In contrast to the steady accretion of data on trade and direct investment, this area, which falls between the two, is relatively blank (although the UN Centre on Transnational Corporations is launching a study of international consultants).

The general questions noted above need to be supplemented by a detailed examination of the operations of foreign consultants and turnkey sellers in one or two LDCs. The previous OECD study makes a few statements about the low level of development of local engineering capabilities in LDCs, but clearly this needs more study. Some LDCs do, as described earlier, sell their own engineering services abroad while they import certain highly advanced services from the industrialised countries. There is some division of comparative advantage between them which needs to be analysed in terms of R and D intensity, skills, type of activity, scale of operations, training structures and so on. A simple citation of the number of firms which indicated one thing or the other in questionnaires or interviews, with the occasional use of ranking by 'important', 'very important', etc., is a very good way to start a study— but it does not take us far enough. Much greater analysis is required of particular cases *in the field* before we can understand what consultants have to offer and where local capabilities are deficient. It is only such a study which could enable a rough quantification of the alternatives, and of the costs and benefits of foreign versus local consultancy.

Clearly such a detailed study would need to be undertaken in relatively advanced developing countries—India, Brazil, Argentina, Mexico. Ideally it should cover different sectors, some in which local capabilities are quite advanced, others where they are backward. A critical eye should be cast at the efforts made by foreign firms to encourage local linkages and to adapt processes to local conditions (though I suspect that, as Brown and Perrin indicate, the latter is sometimes a 'non-issue'). The perspective should essentially be that of the developing country: how best can local capabilities be fully utilised and advanced?

(ii) *Transfer of technology and relocation of production by small firms in developed countries.* The conventional concern with the giant multinational companies has tended to obscure the role of the small manufacturing enterprise in the 'restructuring' of industry between developed and less-developed countries. Yet some work at UNIDO indicates that small firms in Europe are actively engaged in (or are scouting for opportunities) selling technology, subcontracting, offshore assembly (under duty drawback provisions), selling complete plants, etc., in LDCs. What is the extent of this phenomenon? What industries does it effect? What forms does it take? What are its determinants?

Such research will have to be directed mainly at the developed countries themselves, and will involve, first, locating a fair-sized sample and, second, collecting data on the following items: the value and nature of involvement in LDCs; the role of cost competition, fiscal factors, technology, trade unions, etc., in the move abroad; the various inflows and outflows from and to LDCs (capital equipment, intermediate products, finished goods, profits, royalties, interest); experience in LDCs; and future prospects. The hypotheses of interest which may be tested are:

(*a*) Are the industries which are more prone to small firm relocation of 'low' technology and using simpler skills than the average?

(*b*) Are they industries which are less dominated by large MNCs, less concentrated in market structure, less prone to heavy product differentiation?

(*c*) Are there differences between these industries and others in terms of the nature of the process (e.g. batch work as opposed to assembly lines continuous processes), of the diversity of product range, of the final consumer?

(*d*) Are 'low' technology relocators more prone to strike up joint ventures with LDC firms than 'high' technology ones? What role do labour-cost factors play in the decisions of these two groups?

(*e*) What are the employment implications of such relocation? Is it the case (as Finger has argued) that it actually serves to increase employment in the developed countries, because in the absence of relocation the firms would become uncompetitive in the long run?

(*f*) What are the costs and benefits for the host LDCs? Does it promote the development of local enterprises, skills, exports, technologies? What should they do to increase (or decrease) the inflow of such technology, capital and skills?

(iii) *Diffusion of technology within LDCs.* This research is intended primarily to do within LDCs what Mansfield and others have done within the industrialised countries. It would take specific innovations (perhaps introduced from abroad by a foreign firm or by licence) and analyse the process of diffusion, the length of time taken, the firms affected, the factors affecting diffusion within and across industries and the role of government policy. It would pay particular attention to three sorts of relationships:

(*a*) between large firms and small firms;
(*b*) between the 'modern' organised sector and the traditional sectors; and
(*c*) between the foreign and indigenous sectors.

It is obvious that the process of technology diffusion is as central to the process of development as technological innovation, and that the relationships just noted are of particular significance for policy in LDCs. The methodology for conducting such a study is well established (see Nasbeth and Ray (1974) and Mansfield (1968)), though clearly the process of collecting data is bound to be a slow and difficult one. Again, the countries chosen for study should be relatively advanced; for purposes of comparing the effects of different kinds of government policy it would be useful to pick a 'liberal' economic regime and a very tightly controlled one (e.g. Brazil and India). Perhaps some local academic institution would be best suited to handle this sort of research, though there are sometimes grave difficulties of 'quality control' in such a procedure. It may be practicable to study the diffusion of only three or four selected technologies across countries.

(iv) *Trade and technology.* Katz has already demonstrated for Argentina a statistically significant relationship between technological activity (broadly defined to include R and D, engineering, design, production engineering, trouble-shooting) and export performance. This is a finding of great importance, which needs to be extended to other countries and to be broken down into finer categories:

(*a*) export performance and technological activity between different types of industries;

(*b*) between different types of firms (large and small, local and foreign);

(*c*) between different types of technological activity (R and D, design work, process improvements, learning by doing); and

(*d*) between LDCs at different levels of industrial development and pursuing different policies.

This research has to rely on firm level data on exports and technological activity; here the main difficulties lie in obtaining information for a broad sample of different types of firms. In particular, the construction of meaningful comparable data on (accumulated) technological activity is likely to raise problems. At the very least, it will call for extensive interviews with firms and some acquaintance with their production techniques and processes. For reasons advanced by Katz (1976, 1978), however, such data are likely to be far more useful than the standard measures of technology and skills used in the trade literature: R and D as a percentage of sales, scientists per thousand employees, skilled as a proportion of total labour, or wage levels of different classes of employees. However, these standard variables may also be employed in the analysis to discover the sources of comparative advantage of LDC firms.

Another possible way to approach this problem—easier in terms of data collection but less revealing in terms of the role of technological 'learning'—would be to collect data on all manufacturing products (at the 3 or 4 digit level) in which LDCs have registered high growth rates recently (a sort of 'dynamic comparative advantage' measure) relative to the growth of world exports. These can then be correlated to standard indicators of labour/capital intensity, scale variables, skill levels and the like (see Hirsch (1977) ) for different groups of industries—low and high technology; modern and traditional; MNC dominated and other; and so on. Such an exercise would provide more insights into the emerging comparative advantage of LDCs than the usual run of trade-theory testing.

(v) *Local technical progress in LDCs.* The measurement of technical progress raises severe conceptual and methodological problems (David (1975) Nelson and Winter (1977) ), which may be one reason for the paucity of such studies in LDCs. However, it is perfectly feasible to make sensible analyses of the innovative process within particular firms, as long as the complications raised by the interaction of such factors as scale, *x*-efficiency, factor substitution, various types of 'learning' and innovation proper are kept firmly in mind. Jha (forthcoming) has already conducted studies of some Indian public sector firms, primarily to analyse the organisational requirements of successful innovation. Katz and his colleagues have conducted studies of technical improvements (*within* given technologies) in local and foreign firms in Argentina. But there remain huge gaps in our knowledge and understanding of the phenomenon of technical change in LDCs (not to say the developed countries). What leads a firm to invest efforts in improving existing processes? What leads it to search for new products and processes? How successful are its efforts and what does success depend on? What is the particular experience of firms in LDCs, with underdeveloped technological infrastructures, poor supplier networks and a vast technological gap to bridge? Do they benefit by being latecomers or are they permanently handicapped? And does this vary from one industry to another? What sorts of skills, investments and structures are particularly helpful for innovation?

These questions are, in my view, probably the most important ones to ask in the whole field of technology, and they are the least studied at present. It would be extremely valuable to take a sample (say 50 firms of different sorts) in a country like India or Brazil and to make in-depth studies of the process of technical absorption, improvement and innovation. The choice of the sample should be dictated by the need to illustrate innovation for industries of different levels of technical 'intensity' for local and foreign firms, for public and private firms, and large and small firms. It should aim to illustrate the nature of technical progress (imitative or innovative, minor or major, product or process, capital or labour saving, etc.), its determinants (cost or demand factors, government policy, competition, etc.) and its future potential.

(vi) *Technology exports by LDCs.* Everyone has a hobby-horse. This one happens to be mine, so I may as well ride it. The present state of knowledge on technology exports by LDCs is grossly inadequate, though the information that exists testifies that it is growing rapidly (at a much higher rate than manufactured exports). The first step should obviously be to map out what is happening: who is exporting what, how much and to whom. The next step would be (ideally in conjunction with a study of the previous item) to analyse the comparative advantage of LDCs in such activity. The two hypotheses to test are whether LDCs can successfully export technologies which are stable, not of the largest scale and not based on 'high' marketing skills; and whether the ability to export technology depends on achieving a certain 'independence' from foreign technology suppliers. If these hypotheses are verified (or rejected), implications for policy can be drawn for the LDCs, and for trade and collaboration for the developed countries.

As noted above, a certain amount of data on such technology exports as turnkey projects, consultancy services and direct investments by LDCs already exist, and more may be gathered with little difficulty from various ministries in the larger LDCs. Comprehensive information may not, however, be kept even by ministries on all such activities—especially on licensing turnkey scales, training schemes, or various exports of 'know-how' to back up commodity exports. Some hunting around the major export houses may be required, supplemented by interviews with consulting firms and overseas investors and banks. Only a few countries figure as significant technology exporters—India, Argentina, Brazil, Mexico, South Korea, Taiwan, Singapore and Hong Kong (the last two mainly export managerial skills)—and most of these keep good official records; a research project of this sort is perfectly feasible.

This concludes the proposed research agenda. It will be obvious that I have steered away from the traditional concerns of the technology literature on LDCs: MNCs, costs of transfer, appropriateness and the like. This is not because these subjects are not worth studying—on the contrary, I have myself spent several years on them. But these issues are now well known and it is doubtful if the marginal return on further research into them will be very high. On the other hand, there are several important issues which remain unstudied, even unnoticed, in the field of technology. It is these I have tried to concentrate on, not just for academic purposes but because many of them are, or will become, important for policy in developing and developed countries.

NOTES

1. I am grateful to Constantine Vaitsos for having induced me to write this, but absolve him of any responsibility for the views expressed here.

2. See, for instance, David (1975), Rosenberg (1976), and, of course, Schumpeter (1936).

3. See Mansfield (1968), Freeman (1974), Johnson (1975), Nelson and Winter (1977), Kamien and Schwartz (1975), Parker (1974).

4. See Arrow (1969), (1962), Johnson (1970), Magee (1977) and Cooper and Hoffman (1978).

5. On the general debate see Machlup (1957) and Taylor and Silberston (1973).

6. See Vaitsos (1972), Greer (1973), O'Brien (1974) and UNCTAD (1973).

7. Especially 'Major Issues Arising from the Transfer of Technology to Developing Countries', TD/B/AC11/Rev. 2, 1975.

8. The best recent study of trade patterns is by Hirsch (1977).
9. Recently, however, economists have begun to advance new theories of technical change which emphasise the evolutionary nature of innovation and which do not differentiate between minor and major innovation between moves along a production function and shifts of the function itself. For a review see Nelson and Winter (1977).
10. For revues of methodology, see Gaude (1975), Morawetz (1976) and O'Herlihy (1972).
11. See Germidis (1977, vol. 1), Helleiner (1975), Fairchild (1977), Reuber (1973), Vaitsos (1974 b), Morley and Smith (1974).

REFERENCES

Arrow, K. J. (1962), 'Economic Welfare and the Allocation of Resources for Invention', in *The Rate and Direction of Inventive Activities*, NBER (Princeton: Princeton University Press).
Arrow, K. J. (1969), 'Classificatory Notes on the Production and Transmission of Technical Knowledge', *American Economic Review, Papers and Proceedings*.
Balasubramanyam, V. N. (1973), *International Transfer of Technology to India* (New York: Praeger).
Baranson, J. (1967), *Technology for Underdeveloped Areas: An Annotated Bibliography* (Oxford: Pergamon).
Bhalla, A. S. (ed.) (1975), *Technology and Employment in Industry* (Geneva: ILO).
Brown, M., and Perrin, J. (1977), *Engineering and Industrial Projects: A Survey of Engineering Service Organisations* (Paris: OECD).
Chudson, W. A., and Wells, L. T. (1974), *The Acquisition of Technology from Multinational Corporations to Developing Countries* (New York: UN) ST/ESA/12.
Cooper, C., and Sercovitch, F. (1971), *The Channels and Mechanisms for the Transfer of Technology from Developed to Developing Countries* (Geneva: UNCTAD) TD/B/AC.11/5.
Cooper, C., and Kaplinsky, R. (1974), *Second-Hand Equipment in a Developing Country* (Geneva: ILO).
Cooper, C. and Hoffman, H. K. (1978), 'Transactions in Technology and Implications for Developing Countries' (Science Policy Research Unit: University of Sussex) (mimeo).
Cortez, M. (1978), 'Technological Development and Technology Exports to Other LDCs', in *Argentina: Structural Changes in the Industrial Sector* (Washington, DC: World Bank) (mimeo).
David, P. A. (1975), *Technical Change, Innovation and Economic Growth* (London: Cambridge University Press).
de la Torre, J. (1974), 'Foreign Investment and Export Dependency', *Economic Development and Cultural Change*.
Diaz-Alejandro, C. F. (1977) 'Foreign Direct Investment by Latin Americans', in T. Agmon and C. P. Kindleberger (ed.), *Multinationals from Small Countries* (Cambridge, Mass.: MIT Press).

Erber, F. (1978), 'Technological Development and State Intervention: a Study of the Brazilian Capital Goods Industry' (Sussex University: Ph.D. Thesis) (unpublished).

Fairchild, L. G. (1977), 'Performance and Technology of US and National Firms in Mexico', *Journal of Development Economics* (October).

Findlay, R. (1978), 'Some Aspects of Technology Transfer and Direct Foreign Investment', *American Economic Review, Papers and Proceedings*.

Finger, J. M. (1975), 'Tariff Provisions for Offshore Assembly and the Exports of Developing Countries', *Economic Journal*.

Freeman, C. (1974), *The Economics of Industrial Innovation* (Harmondsworth: Penguin).

Gaude, J. (1975), 'Capital–Labour Substitution Possibilities: a Review of Empirical Evidence', in Bhalla (1975).

Germidis, D. (1977) (ed.), *Transfer of Technology by Multinational Corporations*, 2 vols (Paris: OECD).

Greer, D. F. (1973), 'The Case Against Patent Systems in Less Developed Countries', *Journal of International Law and Economics*.

Helleiner, G. K. (1973), 'Manufactured Exports from Less-Developed Countries and Multinational Firms', *Economic Journal*.

Helleiner, G. K. (1975), 'The Role of Multinational Corporations in the Less Developed Countries' Trade in Technology', *World Development*.

Hirsch, S. (1977), *Rich Man's Goods, Poor Man's Goods and Everyman's Goods: Aspects of Industrialisation* (Tübingen: J. C. B. Mohr).

Hone, A. (1974), 'Multinational Corporations and Multinational Buying Groups', *World Development* (February).

Jenkins, G. (1975), *Non-Agricultural Choice of Technique: An Annotated Bibliography* (Oxford: Institute of Commonwealth Studies).

Jha, P. (forthcoming), *Technological Development and Organisation in the Indian Public Sector: an Appraisal* (Bombay and Delhi: Oxford University Press (India)).

Johnson, H. G. (1970), 'The Efficiency and Welfare Implications of the International Corporation', in C. P. Kindleberger (ed.), *The International Corporation* (Cambridge, Mass.: MIT Press).

Johnson, P. S. (1975), *The Economics of Invention and Innovation* (London: Martin Robertson).

Kamien, M. J., and Schwartz, N. L. (1975), 'Market Structure and Innovation: a Survey', *Journal of Economic Literature* (March).

Katz, J. (1976), *Importacion de Technologia, Aprendizaje e Industrializacion Dependiente* (Mexico: Fondo de Cultura Economica).

Katz, J. (1978), 'Creacion de Technologia en el Sector Manufacturero Argentino', *El Trimestre Economico* (January–March).

Katz, J., and Ablin, E. (1977), 'Technologia y Exportaciones Industriales: Un Analysis Microeconomico de la Experiencia Argentina Reciente', *Desarrollo Economico* (April–June).

Lall, S. (1973), 'Transfer Pricing by Multinational Manufacturing Firms', *Oxford Bulletin of Economics and Statistics*.

Lall, S. (1975), *Major Issues in Transfer of Technology to Developing Countries: a Case Study of the Pharmaceutical Industry* (Geneva: UNCTAD).

Lall, S. (1976), 'The Patent System and the Transfer of Technology to Less-Developed Countries', Chapter 6 below.

Lall, S. (1978), 'Transnationals, Domestic Enterprises and Industrial Structure in Host LDCs: a Survey', *Oxford Economic Papers* (July).

Lall, S. (1980), 'Developing Countries as Exporters of Industrial Technology', Chapter 9 below.

Lall, S., and Streeten, P. P. (1977), *Foreign Investment, Transnationals and Developing Countries* (London: Macmillan).

Lecraw, D. (1977), 'Direct Investment by Firms from Less Developed Countries', *Oxford Economic Papers.*

Machlup, F. (1957), 'An Economic Review of the Patent System' (Washington, DC: US Senate).

Magee, S. P. (1977), 'Information and the Multinational Corporation: an Appropriability Theory of Direct Foreign Investment', in J. N. Bhagwati (ed.), *The New International Economic Order* (Cambridge, Mass.: MIT Press).

Mansfield, E. (1968), *The Economics of Technological Change* (London: Longmans).

Morawetz, D. (1974), 'Employment Implications of Industrialization in Developing Countries: a Survey', *Economic Journal.*

Morawetz, D. (1976), 'Elasticities of Substitution in Industry: What Do We Learn from Econometric Estimates', *World Development.*

Morley, S. A. D. and Smith, G. W. (1974), 'The Choice of Technology; Multinational Firms in Brazil'. Rice University, Program in Development Studies, No. 58.

Mytelka, L. K. (1978), 'Licensing and Technology Dependency in the Andean Group', *World Development.*

Nasbeth, L. and Ray, G. F. (ed.) (1974), *The Diffusion of New Industrial Processes* (London: Cambridge University Press).

Nayyar, D. (1978), 'Transnational Corporations and Manufactured Exports from Poor Countries', *Economic Journal.*

Nelson, R. R. and Winter, S. G. (1977), 'In Search of Useful Theory of Innovation', *Research Policy.*

Newfarmer, R. S. (1978), *The International Market Power of Transnational Corporations: a Case Study of the Electrical Industry* (Geneva: UNCTAD).

O'Brien, P. (1974), 'Developing Countries and the Patent System: an Economic Appraisal', *World Development* (October).

O'Herlihy, C. S. J. (1972), 'Capital/Labour Substitution and Developing Countries: a Problem of Measurement', *Bulletin of the Oxford University Institute of Economics and Statistics.*

OECD (1974), *Transfer of Technology for Small Industries* (Paris).

Pack, H. (1974), 'Capital–Labour Substitution—a Microeconomic Appraisal', *Oxford Economic Papers.*

Pack, H. (1978), 'The Capital Goods Sector in LDCs: a Survey' (Washington, DC: World Bank) (mimeo).

Parker, J. E. S. (1978), *The Economics of Innovation* (London: Longman).

Pavitt, K. (1972), 'The Multinational Enterprise and the Transfer of Technology', in J. H. Dunning (ed.), *The Multinational Enterprise* (London: Allen & Unwin).

Penrose, E. T. (1973), 'International Patenting and Developing Countries', *Economic Journal.*

Pickett, J. (ed.) (1977), 'The Choice of Technology in Developing Countries', in special issue of *World Development* (September/October).

Reuber, G. L. *et. al.* (1973), *Private Foreign Investment in Development* (Oxford: Clarendon Press).

Rhee, Y. W. and Westphal, L. E. (1977), 'A Micro, Econometric Investigation of Choice of Technology', *Journal of Development Economics.*

Roberts, J. (1973), 'Engineering Consultancy, Industrialization and Development', in C. Cooper (ed.), *Science, Technology and Development* (London: Cass).

Rosenberg, N. (1976), *Perspectives on Technology* (London: Cambridge University Press).

Schumpeter, J. (1936), *The Theory of Economic Development* (Cambridge, Mass.: MIT Press).

Stewart, F. (1977), *Technology and Underdevelopment* (London: Macmillan).

Streeten, P. P. (1972), 'Technology Gaps between Rich and Poor Nations', *Scottish Journal of Political Economy.*

Taylor, C. T. and Silberston, Z. A. (1973), *The Economic Impact of the Patent System* (London: Cambridge University Press).

Teece, D. J. (1976), *The Multinational Corporation and the Resource Cost of International Technology Transfer* (Cambridge, Mass.: Ballinger).

UNCTAD (1973), *The Role of the Patent System in the Transfer of Technology to Developing Countries* (Geneva) TD/B/AC.11/90.

UNCTAD (1975), *Major Issues Arising from the Transfer of Technology to Developing Countries* (Geneva) TD/B/AC.11/Rev. 2.

Vaitsos, C. V. (1972), 'Patents Revisited: Their Function in Developing Countries', *Journal of Development Studies.*

Vaitsos, C. V. (1974a), *Intercountry Income Distribution and Transnational Enterprises* (Oxford: Clarendon Press).

Vaitsos, C. V. (1974b), 'Employment Effects of Foreign Direct Investment in Developing Countries', in E. O. Edwards (ed.), *Employment in Developing Nations* (New York: Columbia University Press).

Vaitsos, C. V. (1976), 'The Revision of the International Patent System: Legal Considerations for a Third World Position', *World Development.*

Watanabe, S. (1972), 'International Subcontracting, Employment and Skill Promotion', *International Labour Review.*

Wells, L. T. (1973), 'Economic Man and Engineering Man: Choice in a Low-Wage Country', *Public Policy.*

Wells, L. T. (1977), 'The Internationalization of Firms from Developing Countries', in T. Agmon and C. P. Kindleberger (ed.), *Multinationals from Small Countries* (Cambridge, Mass.: MIT Press).

Wells, L. T. (1978), 'Foreign Investment from the Third World: the Experience of Chinese Firms from Hong Kong', *Columbia Journal of World Business* (Spring).

White, L. T. (1976), 'Appropriate Factor Proportions for Manufacturing in Less Developed Countries: a Survey of the Evidence' (Princeton: Woodrow Wilson School). Research Program in Development studies No. 64 (mimeo).

# 6 The Patent System and the Transfer of Technology to Less-Developed Countries

## I INTRODUCTION

As concern has grown in recent years with the transfer of technology[1] as a prime mover in promoting the economic development of the less-developed countries (LDCs), attention has focused increasingly on the institutions and channels which govern this transfer. The international patent system has, therefore, come under careful scrutiny, and its role at the centre of the legal structure within which a large proportion of technological transfers are effected has been severely criticised. Thus, several authors, such as Greer (1973), O'Brien (1974), Penrose (1973) and Vaitsos (1972), have analysed the implications of the patent system in the particular context of LDCs, and have arrived at conclusions ranging from the agnostic to the highly unfavourable. The United Nations Conference on Trade and Development has entered the fray, after an earlier UN Study (1964), with a strong bid to reassess and reform the international structure of the patent system as embodied in the Paris Convention (UNCTAD (1974) and Patel 1974)). And all this activity has accompanied several sober evaluations of the workings of the patent system in the developed world (Sherer (1971), Firestone (1972), and Taylor and Silberston (1973)).[2]

It now appears to be generally accepted that some sort of reform in the patent system, at the international as well as national levels, is required, and even those who firmly believe in the virtues of an international system of granting special protection to innovators agree that the system is liable to abuse[3] in LDCs in its present form. The debate then ranges around how drastic the reforms should be, whether more stringent laws (such as those recently passed by countries like India, Brazil or

Argentina) will be able to deal effectively with the abuses, and whether it would not be to the advantage of some LDCs to opt out of the system altogether.

It is the aim of this paper to clarify some fundamental issues about the 'transfer of technology' and 'development' which have got rather obscured in this debate, and so created a misleading impression of what the real problems are and how they should be tackled in LDCs. It will be argued that the relationship between technology and development has been over-simplified and the role of the instruments of transferring technology over-stressed (Section II); that the role of the patent system in the present LDC framework has not been clearly understood (Section III); and that its function in a different socio-political framework is quite different (Section IV). The main conclusions will be presented in Section V.

## II    SOME NEGLECTED PROBLEMS OF TECHNOLOGY AND DEVELOPMENT

Much of the discussion of technological progress in LDCs, the transfer of technology, bargaining and the role of MNCs (multinational corporations), in promoting technological development has proceeded along lines which can be summed up as follows:

(a) 'Technological progress' is a necessary condition for economic 'development', because it enables a more 'productive' use of factors of production, provides the fruits of such progress in 'modern' consumption goods and is conducive to more 'progressive' or 'dynamic' attitudes or socio-economic patterns in society.

(b) Such technological progress can occur in LDCs in two ways: its 'transfer' from abroad and its 'production' locally. The latter is bound to be a relatively insignificant source for a long time to come, though of course it must be encouraged; the former is the main source for all LDCs until a certain (unspecified) level of industrial and scientific development is achieved locally.

(c) There are in general two ways of getting foreign technology transferred to LDCs: its sale to local enterprises by licensing (patented and unpatented knowhow) and its transfer by means of direct investment. The technology 'market' is fragmented and oligopolistic, so that a great deal is to be gained by LDCs by bargaining, getting more information and removing restrictive practices associated with licensing contracts. It is, however, recognised that a part, perhaps a major part, of the latest technology is not for sale and can only be obtained by direct investment. Since the bulk of direct investment and modern technology is accounted for by MNCs, policies have to be formulated to encourage more investment on terms 'regulated' by the government in the host countries' favour.

(d) Some of the technology transferred by MNCs, and some of their products, may be 'inappropriate' for the factor endowments and income levels of the host countries, and must also be 'regulated' so that proper adaptation is ensured, or at least, the undesirable effects of such transfers are minimised. There may be considerable scope for international action, as well as the use of small technological establishments and firms in developed countries, in the production of more 'appropriate' technology for LDCs.

This seems to be a fair summary of recent thinking in this field; it represents the general position of the UN Group of Eminent Persons, of the Andean Pact, of various LDC governments which do not follow an open door policy to MNCs, and of UNCTAD, in their statements and policies regarding technology and foreign investment.[4] While these views of technology do contain a large element of truth, they may be highly misleading when presented in this general form, since they are not clear about their objectives and contain some unresolved contradictions. The terms put in inverted commas are particularly susceptible of misinterpretation, because they are in common use as vehicles for concepts which seem to be generally acceptable and generally well understood, yet which need far greater clarification and qualification if they are to serve their actual purpose.

This is neither the place for a full discussion of terminological and conceptual issues, nor is it possible for me to fully explain my criticisms of the conventional approach to development. Let me, therefore, blandly state my own views, in the hope that any ensuing discussion will provide a fuller understanding of the problems. Taking the above propositions in turn:

(a) Recent 'dependence' literature, supported by studies from such respectable institutions as the World Bank, has cast serious doubt on the whole conventional measure of 'development' as the growth of *per capita* GNP.[5] Such broad, aggregate measures are now seen to cover enormous and unacceptable disparities in its distribution, and much of recent economic 'growth' is seen to have lead to no improvement, if not actual impoverishment, of the majority of LDC populations. The 'technological progress' which has accompanied such growth has supported, and often reinforced, the inequitable pattern, leading to the production of goods and a pattern of employment promoting the welfare of a small élite, whose consumption patterns (and general life styles) closely emulate those of the élite in developed countries. Thus, while 'technology' in some abstract sense does increase productivity, and provide better standards of living, it is imperative to go behind conventional measures to see *who* benefits, *what* the products actually are, and whether the resultant *structure* of society is in fact conducive to the well-being of the people in LDCs.

   (*b*) Once the socio-economic structure of society is specified, the form of technology required to produce its consumption requirements is defined in general terms. Within given structures in most LDCs, therefore, the need for advanced technology to produce a wide range of modern consumer goods is overwhelming, and must indeed, as conventional reasoning goes, be provided from abroad. Two things must be understood in this context. First, there cannot be a 'transfer' of of technology in the sense of a once-for-all phenomenon, and there cannot be an elimination of the transfer process within a foreseeable period of industrial development: as 'technology' in developed countries keeps evolving the needs it creates keep pace, and it is difficult to see how this process can be halted. It must be noted that a lot of so-called 'technological progress' in developed countries (carried out mainly by MNCs) consists merely of product differentiation, model changes, slight improvements in packaging or design, and so on, all of which are costly and necessary for selling in developed markets, but which ensure a constant and increasing demand in LDCs.

   Secondly, technological innovation is not a 'production' process in the sense that a given combination of inputs leads to a predictable quantity or quality of output. It is basically a cumulative process of learning and experience, of making mistakes and taking risks, which is initially quite costly and perhaps unproductive, but which must be undertaken seriously if LDCs are to build up any capacity to do things themselves. Conventional thinking relegates it to too minor a place *vis-à-vis* imported technology, and the actual policies of governments, operating in the sorts of political and social environments mentioned above, ensure that there is little independent research geared to local needs, and that there is practically no industrial demand for whatever is produced. Thus, the given patterns of consumption dictate the pattern of industrialization and technology utilised; they necessarily imply a heavy reliance on MNC technology because in the sophisticated products demanded local R and D cannot hope to compete with foreign R and D; and local R and D never gets off the ground because it never gets over the large initial barrier of learning, making mistakes, gaining confidence and building what Charles Cooper calls the 'organic' links with industry and society.[6]

(c) The technology 'market' is indeed fragmented and oligopolistic, and heavily dominated by MNCs. It is, however, somewhat misleading to think of it in terms of a market where commodities are bought and sold because of the importance of the organisational element in handling complex technologies. The bulk of modern technology cannot be sold on its own, even by one MNC to another in some cases and certainly not to a relatively inexperienced non-technological LDC firm, without transferring a lot of skill and experience with it. This is clearly recognized in a lot of literature (especially on patents).[7] It must also be recognised that most technology is developed by MNCs as part of their oligopolistic strategy which is increasingly encompassing the whole world market, so that the nature of the 'market' is continuously changing. Thus, technology which was for sale a few years ago may not be for sale now because the MNC concerned has expanded enough to wish to exploit it by direct investment rather than licensing. Moreover, as particular oligopolies gain more stability world-wide, MNCs may be willing to license *each other* but not newcomers or LDC firm which could threaten the *status quo*. The 'market' may therefore be continuously getting smaller from the LDCs' point of view, in that more and more advanced technology is only available as part of a direct-investment package; this process may well accompany one in which the 'market' is expanding for older forms of technology as small firms and some industrialised LDCs enter the stage.

Enough has been written about the 'regulation' of MNCs to make it clear that not only is it difficult for an LDC government *wanting* to control them effectively, but also that for various socio-political factors hinted at already many governments *do not want* to control them very strictly. They may tax them and bargain with them, but ultimately the need for their technology, products and capital is so pressing (and growing over time) that they will be willing to provide the necessary inducements for MNCs to operate with relative freedom.

(d) A lot of MNC technology and products may well be 'inappropriate', distortionary and harmful for the welfare of the majority. It is, however, useless to talk of 'regulation' in the present framework, for two reasons: first, MNCs expand precisely *because* they are in the forefront of product differentiation, marketing, technology, etc., and their advantage lies in using a given package as widely as possible at the lowest possible cost of adaptation. It is not, therefore, in their line of business, as the leading capitalist enterprises, to change their technology, limit product innovation or stop creating demands for new products. If LDCs want to have a different sort of technology-output composition, they must look elsewhere. Second, and more important, is the fact that LDCs do not want 'appropriate' products and technologies. Their governments are concerned to promote 'development' in the conventional sense, and perceive their world very much through the eyes of the élite; they may not be ill-intentioned or hypocritical, but certainly their policies have shown that they reveal a preference for 'dependent' development.

In sum, therefore, it is not enough to discuss policies to promote transfers of technology for appropriate products within a bargaining framework. We must also specify:

(*a*) which products are conducive to national welfare defined broadly;

(*b*) what technologies are available to produce these products, and of them which are the most appropriate;

(*c*) how these technologies are to be got at the lowest social cost, bearing in mind the necessity of developing local scientific/technological expertise;

(*d*) and, finally, if they are to be bought abroad, how best to get them, in terms of buying them outright or having them transferred by means of direct-investment.

It is clear that the problem as posed conventionally *only deals with the last item*, and ignores the others, *implicitly assuming that all technologies promote development, 'latest' is best*, and *local capacities are fundamentally inadequate*. As the Chinese experience shows, and as many economists have argued in different contexts, each of these assumptions may be false. The *patent* problem is usually approached in the conventional manner, so its discussion also suffers from the same limitations: it presupposes that the only issue is the improvement of LDCs' position in bargaining for technology, and assumes away the larger socio-economic issues. Yet it can be strongly and, to my mind, convincingly argued that the problems of bargaining are secondary relative to the others, and that it is *positively dis-functional to divert interest from the basic issues to peripheral ones.*

One final point before we leave the general issues. The discussion of the last few paragraphs may be misleading if it gives the impression that the problem is simply one of turning LDC governments' attention to the larger issues of technology and development. If the previous reasoning has any validity, the problem is to change the political economic structure underlying the government, and so is not one of 'policy' in the sense economists have been traditionally trained to use the term.

If this is true, we have before us two different frameworks within which to evaluate the role of the patent system: a predominantly capitalist one, as is the present case with most LDCs, and a socialist one, such as China. If we are not prepared to question the existing capitalist structure of ownership and production, we should, to be consistent:

(*a*) consciously accept the view that LDCs should undertake a predominantly capitalist form of development, in which case such considerations as 'appropriateness' of technology and products become redundant, and 'technology' is taken to be generally desirable;

(*b*) endorse the legal, political and cultural framework in which free enterprise can function, and MNCs operate, with or without official controls and bargaining.

If, on the other hand, we are prepared to analyse the problem in a socialist framework, we may assume:

(*a*) that the problem of *foreign* technology transfer arises only in cases where the technology is 'appropriate'; and

(*b*) that there is a problem of encouraging local research and promoting local technological capability.

Let us proceed with our discussion along these lines. The usual approach to the patent problem is, of course, within the capitalist framework, and we consider this in the following section. The alternative approach, under a socialist system, is discussed in section IV.


## III PATENTS IN A CAPITALIST FRAMEWORK

There are two separate functions which patents are required to perform in this framework in LDCs: to promote the transfer of technology from abroad, and to promote local R and D and technical innovation. Let us take them in turn.

A FOREIGN TECHNOLOGY TRANSFER

The discussion of the patent system has usually centred around the model, applicable to most LDCs today, where a developing country has a predominantly capitalist system of internal production, seeks to integrate itself to a greater or lesser extent with the international capitalist trading system, and permits, with more or less freedom, direct investment by foreign private enterprises. Most LDCs in this setting also envisage future development on predominantly capitalist lines, though some, like India, also have large public sector enterprises, sometimes competing with private firms. To facilitate discussion, let us assume that they will pursue policies to achieve development along capitalist lines and continue to integrate with the world capitalist system.

In order to understand the importance of patents in the transfer of technology to LDCs, we must first understand the role of patents in the developed countries themselves. There are apparent and growing contradictions in the economics of patenting, noted in the literature, especially by Taylor and Silberston (1973), which are worth mentioning. With the increasing concentration of economic resources in the hands of a relatively few firms, which have mostly (but not in every industry) gone multinational, R and D and technological innovation have also become extremely concentrated. Thus, some 30 firms account for about 65 per cent of total R and D expenditure in the United States, some 20 for about 45 per cent in France, and so on.[8] These are also the firms which take out the bulk of patents, both nationally and internationally. The sectoral incidence of patenting is, however, fairly narrow, and is important only in chemicals, electrical (especially electronic) products, mechanical engineering and artificial fibres—all 'high technology' industries as defined by the percentage of R and D in total expenditures. The contradictions arise from the facts that, despite the theoretical significance of granting patent protection to private innovation,

(*a*) a very large proportion of patents actually taken out seem to be unimportant for innovative activity in the industries concerned; and

(*b*) a large amount of research activity goes on in industries which do not go in much for patenting (high technology industries like aircraft and automobiles, and low technology industries like detergents, food products, and other consumer oriented industries).

In fact, the only industries where patenting is found to have a significant effect on R and D are pharmaceuticals and other specialty chemicals. There are, therefore, two questions to be answered regarding the failure of patents to operate according to their theoretical rationale.

First, *why is private R. and D. less and less dependent on patenting?* The answer lies in the following:

(a) With the growth of modern technology in *domestic* industry in developed countries, the importance of patenting in securing *technological market power* has declined steadily—with the exception of pharmaceuticals noted above—and non-patent sources of technological monopoly, mainly economies of scale in R and D (basic chemicals) and the complexity of non-patented knowhow (electronics, engineering, etc.), have become far more significant.

(b) With the increasingly oligopolistic structure of domestic industries in the developed countries, and the spread of these industries *internationally*, the importance of *marketing* (advertising, product differentiation, etc. ) in securing market power has grown enormously *vis-à-vis* the role of technology. The existence of this source of market power is in fact the *essential condition* for multinationalization; we find that even very low technology industries go multinational if they can market their products effectively, while in the absence of product differentiation a high technology industry may well prefer to stay in its home country and sell its technology or export its products. Even in a highly innovative industry like pharamceuticals, the essence of market power and high profits lies not so much in the patenting system as in marketing techniques.[9] The growing importance of product differentiation in capitalistic enterprise means that more and more research is directed to non-patentable innovation, and that the hold of marketing is such that other sources of market-power become practically redundant.

The second question then arises: if this is so, why do firms with non-patent sources of technological market power bother to take out patents at all? The answer to this is not clear, but various reasons may be suggested from the literature:

(a) A reflex action learnt in earlier days when patent *were* important.
(b) A bargaining counter against other equally technological firms, which can be used in technology swaps.

(*c*)   A device to limit areas of operation on cartel-like lines (as in chemicals).

(*d*)   A device to get around possible anti-monopoly action.

(*e*)   A convenient legal device to base licensing contracts on, and to frighten off smaller innovators with (by threats of expensive litigation).

(*f*)   A monopolistic device to strengthen marketing/knowhow market power by an especially strong and predatory leader in an oligopoly. This is illustrated by the case of Xerox in the recent U.S. investigations; and it may also be true of pharmaceuticals in LDCs, where patents do not really add to the MNCs' effective control of the markets but help to prevent potential threats by local or other foreign firms. Pharmaceutical firms can, however, retain their market dominance even without patents (Italy).

All in all, therefore, patents emerge very much as a *subsidiary device for supporting strongly oligopolistic market structures*, with the leading firms co-operating with each other in exchanging patents in some cases, and using patents together with their secret knowhow and marketing in others to keep competition out. In a few cases patents *are* (or *have been*) important in stimulating innovation, so permitting Taylor and Silberston to conclude that there are some positive, though small, beneficial effects to be set against no significant harmful ones. This appears—given the framework of private enterprise production—to be an eminently fair assessment,[10] and can serve as the basis of discussing policy implications for LDCs.

In the context of technology transfer to LDCs, we may agree with the various commentators who argue that patent laws are not particularly significant in promoting direct investment or technology transfers. The reasoning above should have explained why multinational expansion is only tenuously based on patent protection; furthermore, a large number of industries do not seem to bother with patenting at all, and the transfer of their technology is totally unrelated to the patent system.

Are there any *costs* to LDCs of the present system? Various costs have been noted in the literature:

(i)   *Non-use*: It is misleading to simply cite figures for patents taken out by MNCs in developing countries and not used for local production as a straightforward cost for LDCs. The only case where non-use can be seen as a social cost is when local production is *proved beneficial on economic grounds* and is *actually prevented by the patent holder* (either for another MNC or a local firm desiring to start production). If local production is neither economic nor likely to be undertaken by another firm, the unused patent has no extra cost to the economy. It would appear, therefore, that the costs of non-use may in fact be quite small, and we must be careful not to over-rate them.[11]

(ii) *Import monopoly*: Patents impose a cost if the price paid for imports of patented products is higher than it would in their absence (i.e. if there were no other sources of market power), and if the products were available at lower prices from other producers. This may be important for pharmaceuticals but is probably less so for other industries.

(iii) *Restrictive practices* in licensing contracts: These are obviously undesirable, but not necessarily caused by patents unless other sources of market and bargaining power are absent.[12]

(iv) *Overpricing of intermediate imports* and *excessive royalties*: As with restrictive practises, it is difficult to attribute these solely to patents. In the drug industry, where the bulk of transfer-pricing takes place, other sources of market power seem much stronger than patents. In all these cases, patents seem to get an unfair share of the blame which should really be attached to the whole oligopolistic structure of international industry. However, there *may* be some instances where the above costs do depend on patents, and may provide a case for a stricter enforcement of standard checks and regulations like compulsory licensing, vetting of individual contracts, revocation of patents, and the like.[13] The evidence does not as yet seem strong enough to support a case for a complete abolition of the patent system, since there may well be some advantages to LDCs to stay within it.

What are these advantages? In very general terms, there may be significant *political* and *psychological* benefits for LDCs following a capitalist pattern of development of adhering to the international legal system which promotes private enterprise. These advantages would show up not only in attracting more foreign capital (if only indirectly, by showing the 'right' attitude) but also in promoting trade, getting aid, access to markets and so on. The point is clearly put by Penrose: ' . . . given the existence of national patent systems, and given the interests, motives and policies of multinational firms, which are the chief international investors, it may be that co-operation in this system on the part of less-developed countries will help them to obtain the co-operation of such firms in introducing and developing new technology.'[14] These advantages can be realised even if regulations were tightened—after all, the developed countries themselves operate patent laws and check abuses with great vigour. The basic fact remains that if LDCs want to play the capitalist game they should play by the rules—

especially regarding property (real or intellectual)—if they want to derive maximum benefit from the other players.

### B    LOCAL INNOVATION IN A CAPITALIST SYSTEM

Since in a capitalist system most R and D in LDCs would take place, to the extent that it takes place at all, in private firms (government R and D does not need special protection under any system), there is a strong case for maintaining a patent system to encourage local innovation. There is hardly a need to argue this case very strongly,since the merits of patent system in the early days of industrialisation are amply established in history; a few points are, however, worth noting.

First, it may be desirable to have special inducements for local innovators by granting them preferential treatment. This would, however, run into great political problems with MNCs and their home governments, especially if the local enterprises in the LDCs were large and powerful.

Second, there would be no necessity for special devices like inventor's certificates (which are aimed at the individual inventor, a rare bird these days), though the government may offer rewards for especially valuable innovations.

If one were realistic, of course, one would not expect very much real innovation to emerge from the present structure of capitalist enterprise in LDCs. It may also be the case that subsidiaries of MNCs would conduct most of the peripheral R and D which does take place, and pass the benefits on to the parent companies, but the existence or renunciation of the patent system would not have any effect on this.

## IV    PATENTS IN A SOCIALIST FRAMEWORK

While in a capitalistic system an LDC would probably promote economic growth and integration with world markets by retaining the patent system, in a socialistic system the domestic economy would necessarily be far more isolated from the world free enterprise system, and would not face the same need to promote direct foreign investment and transfers of technology. China provides the obvious example of a poor socialist country, but it can serve as an illustration only for the few LDCs which have fairly large markets and a long bureaucratic tradition. We shall return to small countries later; let us first consider a Chinese-type case.

The need for technology from MNCs would certainly exist in a socialist LDC, but the sort of technology sought would be very limited as compared to a capitalist country. Most of product-differentiation technology, marketing knowhow, and technology required for the production of sophisticated consumer goods, would not be necessary—this rules a substantial portion of present technological transfers by MNCs—and even in the industries for which foreign technology was thought beneficial (medicines, telecommunications, transport, data processing, etc.) the scope for its purchase would be restricted by:

(a) the need to promote local science and technology;
(b) the need to use a much less capital-intensive technology; and
(c) the need to have products made to lower specifications, with simpler packaging, fewer models, less model changes and fewer unnecessary characteristics generally.

If technology transfers could be achieved in a way which suited the needs of the LDC in question—and it is an empirical question as to which technologies were actually available in such conditions—a process of bargaining would resolve the problem of the costs of the transfer. The market power of the MNC selling the technology, determined now only by its technological prowess and not its marketing strategy, would show up in the terms of the bargain. Patents may or may not be an important consideration affecting technological market power, but clearly for the LDC there would be no need at all to adhere to any system of industrial property. Similarly, there would be no commercial advantage to the MNC in insisting upon patent rights in the LDC, since a commercial exploitation of the patent is ruled out by assumption.

If an LDC were fairly industrialised, it would be to its great advantage to '*steal*' *foreign technology* by imitation and adaptation. For this reason alone, it may be advantageous not even to have a nominal adherence to the international patent system. Furthermore, as it built up its own technological capacities and depended less on foreign non-patented knowhow, the advantage of 'stealing' would grow much greater. This sort of policy would only be open to socialist countries, since a capitalist one would face all sorts of pressures and threats of economic retaliation which would be intolerable to its continued growth.

It may be thought that a socialist LDC would not be *able* to buy necessary technology from advanced countries. This would be un-realistic. As a matter of fact, many MNCs would prefer to do business with socialist countries which offered reasonable and secure terms for technology sales than with nationalistic capitalist regimes which threatened to expropriate direct investments or arbitrarily limit commercial operations. This is *not* to argue, however, than in political terms MNCs or their home governments would permit an LDC to go socialist rather than have a capitalist, though dictatorial, regime. On the contrary, pressures would be exerted to preserve a capitalistic system at all costs, since the inherent logic of capitalist growth must ultimately compel even the most nationalistic country to re-enter the free enterprise, multinational fold. This is far outside the concern of this paper, but must be borne in mind when discussing 'policy' options.

Small countries which go socialist face very difficult problems. Certainly they face equally difficult problems in a capitalist framework, but if they are endowed with natural resources (minerals, agricultural products or scenery) they can sell them to developed countries, or else turn into a tax haven and benefit from some revenue; if they are not capable of either, they are doomed to stagnation. In a socialist framework it would be more problematic to market natural resources to capitalist countries, though it should not be impossible; they can also trade with developed socialist countries, but this also entails a sort of dependence which may prove undesirable. In any case, since industrialisation may not be feasible, the role of patents is irrelevant. If they wanted to invite export-oriented 'foot-loose' MNCs to set up there, the procedure would be one of case-by-case bargaining, and patents would not enter the picture.

So much for transferring foreign technology in a socialist framework: what about local innovation? Since the fundamental rationale of granting a patent monopoly is to permit a protected commercial exploitation of an innovation, it clearly has no role to play in stimulating innovation where private commercial production is not possible. Some other instrument may, however, be necessary to stimulate private invention. This instrument may be financial (inventor's certificate or some form of reward) or non-financial (promotion, award, recognition), or some combination of the two. There may be problems in deciding about the correctness of the reward in relation to the social value of the invention, a function undertaken somewhat imperfectly by the market in a capitalist system, but there is little that we can say about it in general *a priori* terms. Experience does not tell us that innovation in a socialist framework is any poorer than in a capitalist one—compare India and China—so that there does not seem to be too much cause to worry on this score.

## V SUMMARY AND CONCLUSIONS

In this paper I have argued that:

(i) The issues concerning bargaining and improving the terms on which technology is transferred to LDCs—the normal context for discussing the patent system—are less significant than those concerning who benefits from the transfer, what goods are produced by the technology and how the political-economic structure of the recipient country determines the nature and demand for foreign technology over the long run.

(ii) Once the political-economic structure—defined broadly here to be either capitalistic or socialistic—is defined, the sort of technology to be transferred is also determined in general terms. If a capitalist structure is envisaged, then the issues concerning technology transfer do indeed boil down to bargaining and regulation, and there is little to be served by bringing in considerations concerning the 'appropriateness' of products or technology. If a socialist structure is envisaged, the role of foreign technology is far more limited because of its 'inappropriateness' and because of the need to promote domestic technological capability.

(iii) In a capitalist system, the costs of the patent system to LDCs seem to have been overemphasised in some recent literature. The rise in importance of non-patented knowhow as a source of technological superiority, and of other sources of market power over technology as such, has reduced its significance as an inducement to innovation and direct investment by MNCs, with the major exception of the pharmaceutical industry where it still appears to promote innovation. The costs to LDCs, in terms of non-use, import monopoly and various restrictive practices, are exaggerated and cannot be attributed to patents as distinct from other sources of market power (with the possible exception of pharmaceuticals).

(iv) To LDCs which will remain capitalist, it seems on balance better to remain within the international patent system and to implement stricter checks and bargaining to counter its present abuses and to obtain the best terms. This will facilitate their integration into the developed capitalist world and also promote domestic innovation.

(v) For developing countries which follow a socialist pattern, the international patent system has nothing to offer in terms either of getting foreign technology or of promoting domestic innovation. Technology which is required abroad can be purchased under case-by-case agreements which do not require adherence to the patent system, and domestic innovation can be promoted by 'stealing' foreign technology and by offering specific rewards, not based on commercial monopoly, to deserving innovators.

In sum, therefore, the role of the patent system in the transfer of technology cannot be understood properly unless the political-economic structure of the country which is supposed to receive the technology is clearly specified: the 'intellectual property' system is, after all, an intrinsic part of a certain system of property ownership, and its role in development is inextricably tied up with the part that the whole system plays in the growth of LDCs. The patent system cannot be judged on the rather simple cost-benefit rules which seem to have been applied to it (without the broader context being mentioned): if it is seen to promote an undesirable form of technology transfer and to per-petuate a 'dependent' form of technological development, it is the system in its entirety which must be looked at and not one particular, and relatively minor, component.

NOTES
    1. I am grateful to Edith Penrose and Peter O'Brien for helpful discussions. I retain full responsibility for the views expressed here.
    2. See also important earlier works by Penrose (1951), Machlup (1958) and Vernon (1957).
    3. On the legal aspects of patent 'abuse' see Roffe (1974) and the references mentioned there.
    4. See, for instance, UN (1973), UNCTAD (1971) and various other studies by the UNCTAD Secretariat on the transfer of technology. On the problem of 'inappropriate' technology see Stewart (1974).
    5. On 'dependence' literature see a survey by O'Brien (1975) and Chapter 1 above; for the World Bank Study, conducted jointly with the Institute of Development Studies, Sussex, see Chenery, *et al.* (1974).
    6. Cooper (1974).
    7. For instance, Penrose (1973).
    8. See the UN (1973) and Parker (1974).
    9. See Lall (1974). This is not to deny that patents are of great importance to large pharmaceutical firms in preventing competition from *other large* firms with comparable marketing resources.
    10. Although it is generally agreed that even in pharmaceuticals, the main industry justifying the system today, the costs of innovation are very heavy in terms of imitative patenting, molecule manipulation, and so on.
    11. Vaitsos (1972) places a great deal of emphasis on this cost (and the others mentioned), and is chastised by Penrose (1973).
    12. The latest figures for India show that, while restrictive clauses regarding exports, imports, and so on were still quite prevalent in technology contracts, of the 620 firms having technical agreements in 1970, *only nine bought patents as*

*such,* 316 bought *unpatented* knowhow, 207 bought some combination of patented and unpatented knowhow, and the rest some combination of trademarks, patents and knowhow (RBI, 1974). Clearly patents *as such* were not responsible for the existence or incidence of restrictive clauses.
13. There may, however, be great difficulties for governments in reforming the existing patent laws. See Kochanek (1974), ch. XIV, for an account of how local and foreign business acted in concert to delay and modify a revision of the Indian patent law.
14. Penrose (1973) p. 785.

REFERENCES

Chenery, H. B. *et al.* (1974), *Redistribution With Growth* (London: Oxford University Press).
Cooper, C. (1974), 'Science Policy and Technological Change in Underdeveloped Economics', *World Development* (March).
Firestone, O. J. (1972), *Economic Implications of Patents* (Ottawa: University of Ottawa Press).
Greer, D. F. (1973), 'The Case Against Patent Systems in Less-Developed Countries', *Journal of International Law & Economics.*
Kochanek, S. (1974), *Business & Politics in India* (Berkeley: University of California Press).
Lall, S. (1974), 'The International Pharmaceutical Industry and Less-Developed Countries, with Special Reference to India', *Oxford Bulletin of Economics & Statistics* (August).
Machlup, F. (1958), 'An Economic Review of the Patent System', Study prepared for the US Senate Sub-Committee on Patents, Trademarks & Copyrights (Washington, DC: US Government).
O'Brien, Peter (1974), 'Developing Countries and the Patent System: an Economic Appraisal', *World Development* (September).
O'Brien, Philip (1975), 'A Critique of Latin American Theories of Dependency', in I. Oxaal, T. Barnett, D. Booth (eds), *Beyond the Sociology of Development* (London: Routledge & Kegan Paul).
Parker, J. E. S. (1974), *The Economics of Innovation* (London: Longman).
Patel, S. J. (1974), 'The Patent System and the Third World', *World Development* (September).
Penrose, E. (1951), *The Economics of The International Patent System* (Baltimore: Johns Hopkins Press).
Penrose, E. (1973), 'International Patenting and the Less-Developed Countries', *Economic Journal* (September).
RBI (1974), 'Survey of Foreign Financial and Technical Collaboration in Indian Industry—1964–70—Main Findings', *Reserve Bank of India Bulletin* (June).
Roffe, P. (1974), 'Abuses of Patent Monopoly: a Legal Appraisal', *World Development* (September).
Sherer, F. M. (1971), *Industrial Market Structure & Economic Performance* (Chicago: Rand Mc-Nally).
Stewart F. (1974), 'Technology and Employment in LDCs', *World Development* (March).

Taylor, C. T. and Silberston, Z. A. (1973), *The Economic Impact of The Patent System* (London: Cambridge University Press).

UN (1973), *Multinational Corporations in World Development* (New York: United Nations).

UN (1964), *The Role of Patents in the Transfer of Technology to Developing Countries* (New York: United Nations).

UNCTAD (1971), *Policies Relating to Technology of the Countries of the Andean Pact: their Foundations* (Santiago: UN Conference on Trade & Development) TD/107.

UNCTAD (1973), *The Role of the Patent System in the Transfer of Technology to Developing Countries* (Geneva: UN Conference on Trade & Development) TD/B/AC.11/19.

Vaitsos, C. V. (1972), 'Patents Revisited: their Function in Developing Countries', *Journal of Development Studies* (October).

Vernon, R. (1957), 'The International Patent System and Foreign Policy', Study prepared for the US Senate Sub-Committee on Patents, Trademarks & Copyrights (Washington, DC: US Government).

# Part Four
# Exports

# 7 Recent Trends in Exports of Manufactures by Newly-Industrialising Countries[1]

## I INTRODUCTION

There is now a large literature on the growth of manufactured exports by LDCs, especially on the performance of the NICs (the newly industrialising countries).[2] This paper reviews this literature and presents some data on the recent experience. There is so much written in this area, however, that this survey cannot hope to be exhaustive. It concentrates on certain themes that are likely to be of direct interest to policy-makers and students concerned with this area, and mainly on works, published and unpublished, that have appeared in the past five years or so.

Section II deals with the recent trends in manufactured exports by region, section III with the products exported and studies of the comparative advantage underlying the observed patterns, section IV with market penetration in the developed countries and section V with the main agents responsible for export growth, with special reference to the role of multinational companies. Section VI draws the main conclusions.

It should be noted at the outset that this paper does not cover the large, and increasingly important, issue of protectionism on the part of developed countries towards imports from LDCs. A few crucial works on this are, however, referred to below.

## II TRENDS IN MANUFACTURED EXPORTS BY REGION[3]

In 1965, according to UNCTAD (1978a), the total value of manufactured exports from the Third World came to $4.6 billion or 5.4 per cent of the value of similar exports from developed market economy countries and 4.5 per cent of total world manufactured exports (including centrally planned economies). By 1974, LDC exports had risen to $32.5 billion or 8.4 per cent of DC exports and 7.1 per cent of total world exports. In terms of growth, in the 10 year period 1965–74, LDCs together recorded real growth rates of 16.3 per cent, compared to 10.6 per cent for the world as a whole, 10.8 per cent for developed countries and 9.5 per cent for centrally planned economies. By 1973, manufactures comprised some 22 per cent of the value of all LDC (non-OPEC) exports, and 69 per cent of these were sold to DCs, 28 per cent to other LDCs (including OPEC) and 3 per cent to the Socialist countries.

In 1976, the total value of manufactured exports by LDCs came to $42 billion, as compared to $33 billion for 1975, an increase of 27 per cent in current terms (UNCTAD, 1978d).[4] While the value of exports in dollars rose even faster in the recessionary period of 1973–6 than before, in quantity terms there was in fact a set-back to export growth in this period, especially in 1973–5. As Table 7.1 shows, the oil-importing LDCs (which account for the overwhelming bulk of manufactured exports from the Third World) experienced an average rise of 9.5 per cent in the *volume* of manufactured exports in 1973–6 as compared to 12 per cent in 1963–73. Their rate of growth of manufacturing output also suffered a slight decline. Since 1975, however, the rapid rate of growth of manufactured exports has been resumed and, despite protectionist pressures, seems likely to continue growing in the near future.

TABLE 7.1    Selected indicators of oil-importing developing countries' trade and manufacturing production, 1955 to 1976 (annual average percentage rate of change)

|  | 1955–63 | 1963–73 | 1973–6 |
|---|---|---|---|
| Dollar value of total exports | 2½ | 12 | 20 |
| Volume of total exports | 5 | 6 | 3½ |
| Purchasing power of total exports* | 2 | 7½ | 3 |
| Volume of imports of manufactures | 4 | 7½ | 4 |
| Manufacturing production | 6½ | 7½ | 6 |
| Volume of exports of manufactures | 7 | 12 | 9½ |

NOTE
* Ratio of value of exports to unit value of imports.
SOURCE
Blackhurst *et al.* (1978b).

Different regions of the Third World registered sharply differing rates of growth in manufactured exports. In 1965–74, for instance, Latin America had a real growth rate of 21.1 per cent and East Asia of 20.9 per cent, while South Asia only recorded 12.4 per cent and Sub-Saharan Africa 4.9 per cent. Similarly, in the developed world, Japan and the 'transitional' countries recorded high growth rates of 15.6 per cent and 18.0 per cent respectively, while the more mature economies of Western Europe and North America expanded exports at 10.4 per cent and 8.9 per cent. The centrally planned economies steadily lost their share over the period.

Table 7.2 illustrates the dramatic shifts which have occurred in the share of manufactured exports accounted for by different regions of the Third World in 1965–76. While the value of total exports has risen by 1,800 per cent in this period, those of East Asia had risen by a phenomenal 14,000 per cent and those of Latin America by 10,900 per cent, making these the only groups with rising shares of the total. The initial higher weight of East Asia and its fast growth rate enabled it to account, by 1976, for 60 per cent of total LDC manufactured exports and recent figures show no signs that this growth (apart from the bad recession year of 1974–5) is slowing down.

TABLE 7.2   Shares of exports of manufactures by LDCs, 1965–76

|  | *1965* | *1970* | *1976* |
|---|---|---|---|
| East Asia | 38 | 48 | 60 |
| Latin America | 14 | 16 | 17 |
| Turkey & Yugoslavia | 14 | 10 | 8 |
| South Asia | 22 | 15 | 8 |
| Middle East & N. Africa | 7 | 7 | 5 |
| Sub-Saharan Africa | 5 | 4 | 2 |
|  | 100 | 100 | 100 |
| Total value (current US $bn) | 4.6 | 10.2 | 43.8 |

SOURCE
Keesing (1979).

The main exporters are relatively few in number. If we take manufactured exports to exclude petroleum products and unworked non-ferrous metals,[5] we find that of total LDC exports in 1976 of $27 billion—these figures are taken from UNCTAD (1978d) and exclude Taiwan—eight countries had exports of $1 billion each during that year. These countries (in descending order of importance: Hong Kong, S. Korea, Mexico, Brazil, Yugoslavia, Singapore, India and Malaysia) accounted for 75 per cent of this total. If we take Taiwan's exports to be $5.4 billion (lying between $5.6 billion of Hong Kong and $5.3 billion of South Korea, according to its position in 1975), we get a total of $25.7 billion for the nine leading LDCs, or nearly 80 per cent of total manufactured exports for the Third World.

There is a fairly high degree of concentration within this group of nine. The top three exporters—Hong Kong, Korea and Taiwan—account for nearly two-thirds of their exports in 1976, and the South East Asians together—including Singapore and Malaysia—for nearly three-fourths. The continuing high rates of growth of this region is tending to increase their dominance in Third World manufactured exports. In 1975–6, for instance, Korea's manufactured exports grew by 63 per cent, Taiwan's by 60 per cent, Hong Kong's by 40 per cent, and Singapore's by 39 per cent. Brazil's exports showed a respectable, but lower, growth of 33 per cent and Mexico's a more modest 15 per cent. India showed a sudden spurt in 1975–6 of 48 per cent (and slowed down in 1976–7, revived in 1977–8 and flagged again in 1978–9).

LDCs as a whole recorded increases in manufactured exports of 19 per cent in 1975–6, compared to 11 per cent for developed market economics and 10 per cent for East European economies. Preliminary estimates (see UNCTAD (1978a)) show that non-OPEC LDC exports (total, including non-manufactures) have speeded up from 18 per cent in 1975–6 to over 22 per cent in 1976–8. As Chenery and Keesing (1978) note, on the basis of estimates, 'In the 1976 recovery, LDC manufactured exports leaped forward by over 20 per cent; and in slow growth conditions of 1977, they appear to have expanded once again in real terms by over 10 per cent, despite a decline in clothing and textiles, although world trade increased only 4 per cent' (p. 12).

The phenomenon of rapid growth of Third World manufactured exports thus comprises a number of trends. First, as Keesing (1979) remarks, there are several new entrants to the ranks of 'successful exporters'. Between 1965–74, the number of LDCs with exports of over $2 billion (in constant 1974 dollars) rose from zero to 6, over $1 billion from 3 to 8 and over $100 million from 14 to 30.[6]

Second, there are long-term changes in the structure of Third World exporters, as Table 7.3 shows for 1965–75 for eleven leading LDCs. While Hong Kong remains the leading LDC exporter of manufactures, it has been losing ground to other NICs. South Korea and Taiwan have shown the most remarkable increases in share, while India and Yugoslavia (and on a smaller scale, Pakistan) have suffered substantial declines. The big Latin Americans, especially Brazil, have recorded

TABLE 7.3  Leading developing-economy exporters of manufactures in 1965 and 1975

| Country or Territory | Value (Mil. current US dollars) 1965 | 1975 | Percent share 1965 | 1975 | Cumulative share 1975 |
|---|---|---|---|---|---|
| Hong Kong | | | | | |
| including re-exports | 989 | 5,590 | 21.5 | 16.8 | 16.8 |
| excluding re-exports | n.a. | 4,464 | – | – | |
| Taiwan | 187 | 4,303 | 4.1 | 13.0 | 29.8 |
| Korea | 104 | 4,136 | 2.3 | 12.5 | 42.3 |
| Yugoslavia | 617 | 2,781 | 13.4 | 8.4 | 50.7 |
| Singapore | | | | | |
| including re-exports | 300 | 2,233 | 6.5 | 6.7 | 57.4 |
| excluding re-exports | n.a. | 1,286 | – | – | |
| Brazil | 124 | 2,192 | 2.7 | 6.6 | 64.0 |
| India | 809 | 2,089* | 17.6 | 6.3 | 70.3 |
| Mexico (including border) | 166 | 1,967 | 3.6 | 5.9 | 76.2 |
| Argentina | 84 | 723 | 1.8 | 2.3 | 78.5 |
| Malaysia | 68 | 667 | 1.5 | 2.0 | 80.5 |
| Pakistan | 190† | 589 | 4.1† | 1.8 | 82.3 |
| All developing countries | 4,590 | 33,200 | 100.0 | 100.0 | 100.0 |

NOTES
* Statistical year ending 30 March 1976.
† Including what is now Bangladesh.
SOURCE
Keesing (1979).

increased shares of the total. Malaysia has, from a small base, performed rather well.

Third, on the basis of the evidence at hand, it appears that S. Korea, Taiwan, Brazil and Mexico will continue their rapid penetration of world markets.[7] Hong Kong will also grow, but perhaps slowly lose ground to other NICs. India's performance is difficult to predict because of its erratic recent experience, its heavily regulated trade structure (see Bhagwati and Srinivasan (1978b)) and its variable industrial growth. However, its sustained growth of engineering goods (and complete 'projects') and chemical exports have helped offset a poor performance in traditional manufactures, and this offers some ground for hoping that the future will see a recovery of lost ground by India (see Cable and Weston (1978)). Yugoslavia may also hope to accelerate its export growth, particularly by entering a variety of cooperation agreements with the EEC.

What does the future hold for LDC manufactured exports as a whole? Predictions are obviously hazardous in this as in any other area of economic performance. There are three main aspects of the question of which countries are likely to be the successful exporters of the future, and each of these is beset by uncertainties of different kinds:

(a) How are tariff and non-tariff barriers against LDC exports going to behave?

(b) How far will LDCs go in their policies to promote exports and to remove the heavy legacy of inward-looking industrialisation strategies?

(c) How will their economies fare internally (an especially important question for countries with unstable political situations, large non-industrial sectors or heavy dependence on a narrow range of products)?

As far as the first question is concerned, the precise future of negotiations on reduction of barriers to trade is very uncertain (see Birnberg (1978), Blackhurst *et al* (1977a), Blackhurst *et al* (1977b), Helleiner (1978), International Monetary Fund (1978) and Tracy (1977b)). The major LDC exporters may (as they have done already, (UNCTAD (1978d)) diversify their range of products into more sophisticated, more high-value and less obviously 'cheap labour' categories, and threatened industries may extend the scope of protection demanded, with the outcome depending on the interplay of adjustment, growth, employment and technological progress in the industrialised world. The restoration of growth may facilitate the necessary adjustments that accompany a lowering of protectionist barriers; the continuation of relative stagnation will certainly hinder it. The literature on this aspect of trade is beyond the scope of this paper and will not be explored in any detail.

The second question, about the shift to export-oriented strategies by LDCs, is easier to answer. It seems fairly well established in the literature (Balassa (1978), Bhagwati (1978a), Donges (1976) and Donges and Reidel (1977)) that export promotion strategies, if well-designed, stable and vigorously implemented, can lead to high rates of export growth in a broad range of manufactured products. Hesitant attempts at liberalisation are unsuccessful, and there may be an initial slowdown in growth as the old structure is dismantled, but if the disincentives to export are really removed there will, after a lag, be a healthy response in export growth.

The evidence for this is so strong and drawn from the experience of such different countries that even the most ardent import-substitutionists are starting to advocate liberalisation. The last bastions of the old regime (India, Pakistan and the like) are moving into the initial phases of export-oriented strategies (even China may join in), and the next decades are very likely to see a widespread and concerted effort on the part of many important LDCs to enter world markets (regardless of the outcome of the various North–South 'dialogues').

However, the direction that their export efforts take will be heavily influenced by the evolution of protectionist measures in developed countries (Birnberg (1978), Helleiner (1978)).

Third, not all countries may be as successful in this endeavour as the experience of the South East Asian or Latin American NICs may have led them to believe. Apart from the problem of 'saturating' particular markets,[8] the existing structures, skills, technology, infrastructure (or lack thereof) will influence the ability of each economy to find its 'true' comparative advantage (of which, more below), and such imponderables as political upheaval, labour conditions, or weather, will affect the performance of the economy. To some extent, of course, the very fact of export growth will enable some industries to achieve a degree of independence of their home economy, but for large countries like India or Pakistan the home market will always remain a strong influence.

For obvious reasons, the few predictions that exist on how developing countries will fare in the next decade or two should be treated with great caution. Let us briefly consider a few such predictions.

(a) The OECD's Department of Economics and Statistics' (1978c) study, surveying the recent performance of a large group of 'middle income' NICs (excluding India), provides a particularly useful account of their recent growth, investment and balance of payments experience, and of their impact on OECD trade performance. It has a brief and succinct account of the effects of the recent recession and of structural problems facing the 'mature' industrialised countries (also see Birnberg (1978), Helleiner (1978)). It does not, perhaps wisely, attempt to make any quantitative predictions of trade patterns: the furthest it is prepared to go is to anticipate *continued dynamic export growth on the part of the Far Eastern NICs and Brazil and Mexico*. As for other LDCs, it tentatively forecasts the emergence of four groups as fast export growers:

(i) The large inward-looking economies of Argentina, Chile,

India, Pakistan and Egypt, which, depending on internal situations, may or may not break into world markets successfully;
(ii) Malaysia, Philippines, Thailand and Colombia, which are expected to be very dynamic exporters in the near future;
(iii) small offshore processors (e.g. the Caribbean) which will specialise on low-skill activities but are unlikely to emulate the Singapore or Hong Kong model; and
(iv) the OPEC countries, which may build up substantial export capabilities over the longer run in petro-chemicals, steel and automobiles.

These predictions seem sound[9] but are stated very briefly, so it is impossible to evaluate the underlying argument.

(b) The OECD's Interfutures project has produced, and reviewed, quantitative estimates of future patterns of world trade (OECD (1977), OECD (1978b)). Three such estimates now exist: the UN Input-Output model, the SARU model and the Interfutures model. The UN model predicts the share of LDCs in 'light industry' exports to rise from 12.8 per cent in 1970 to 13.8 per cent in 2000 (which seems on the low side), and in machinery and equipment exports to rise from 1.5 to 2.7 per cent. The SARU model expects the market shares of the LDCs in manufactured trade to rise from 9.1 per cent in 1975 to 10.3 or 15.5 per cent, depending on pessimistic or optimistic assumptions about trade liberalisation and preferences for LDC exports. Both these models expect slower growth of trade than experienced recently and both project country export performance on the basis of historical trends. The Interfutures model is more complex, with different assumptions about exchange rate regimes, aid, energy and GDP growth rates. Its prediction for non-oil exports of LDCs (excluding OPEC) is that the share in world trade will rise from 10.8 per cent in 1976 to 14.0 per cent in 2000 under fixed rates and to 23.0 per cent under flexible rates. It predicts a major change in trade patterns, with a fast growing trade between Japan and LDCs. The LDCs are assumed to increase their share faster under flexible rates because their currencies are assumed to devalue by about 65 per cent in this period—an assumption which, the OECD notes, is rather dubious. Trade between LDCs is excluded from the Interfutures model, while trade between OECD countries is ignored by the SARU model.

(c) The Hayes Committee's (1979) report makes qualitative forecasts about LDC performance as follows:

(i) Many of the NICs will continue to develop their manufacturing industries rapidly, but that

(ii) in accordance with World Bank forecasts (see below) and in view of a number of influences limiting the pace of industrial and GNP growth in the industrialised countries, the rate of growth of exports will be slower than in the past;

(iii) the predominance of the Far Eastern and Latin American NICs is unlikely to be challenged; and

(iv) the successful exporters will continue to move into higher skill activities and to attract MNCs into their export sectors.

(d) Donges and Reidel (1977) take a sample of 15 leading Third World exporters and predict annual rates of export growth till 1985 of 13 per cent on optimistic and 11 % on pessimistic assumptions. This projection, published a year before the World Bank's, is remarkably similar to the latter's calculation for all LDCs' manufactured exports.

(e) The World Bank (1978) provides projections for manufactured exports for 1975–85 and compares these to growth actually achieved in 1970–5 (for all manufactures, average annual growth rates in 1970–5 were 12.3 per cent). On optimistic assumptions (of high growth rates in the developed countries of 4.7 per cent per annum) these exports are expected to grow by 14.2 per cent per annum average over 1975–85; on pessimistic assumptions (developed countries growing by 3.7 per cent) by 10.2 per cent; and on 'base scenario' assumptions (medium growth rates of 4.2 per cent) by 12.2 per cent (pp. 28–32). On the 'base scenario' assumptions, and given existing levels of protection in industrialised countries, LDCs are expected to increase their share of manufactured goods imports of developed countries from 8.9 per cent in 1975 (1.2 per cent of consumption) to 13.6 per cent by 1985 (2.7 per cent of consumption). The Bank expects that the LDCs' share of market *growth* of imports will decline from 18.6 per cent for 1970–5 to 17.5 per cent for 1975–85.

The Bank provides (World Bank (1978), Table 27) a breakdown of its projections by broad sectors, and these are worth mentioning: clothing expanded on average by 20.3 per cent pernum in 1970–5, but is expected to grow by only 8.3 per cent per annum in 1975–85; similarly, textiles (17.8 and 6.2 per cent), chemicals (16.5 and 13.0 per cent); machinery and transport equipment (20.3 and 17.3 per cent) and 'other' (10.2 and 10.0 per cent) are expected to suffer slower growth rates. Only iron and steel (10.7 and 14.5 per cent) is expected to grow faster. Machinery is, however, expected to continue to be the most dynamic sector. We shall return to this in the following section.

## III  THE PRODUCTS EXPORTED

This section is divided into three parts, dealing with

(*a*) the overall commodity composition of LDC manufactured exports,
(*b*) individual commodity studies, and
(*c*) recent empirical studies of the determinants of comparative advantage in LDC manufactured trade.

(A)  COMMODITY COMPOSITION

At the broad statistical level, the most comprehensive collection of data by exporting country, products exported and the relative significance of different products is UNCTAD (1978a). A more digestible summary on the evolution of LDC exports by industry and destination is given in GATT (1978). Several other studies provide information on the changing commodity composition of manufactured exports by LDCs. A few selected tables will suffice to illustrate the present situation for the Third World as a whole and for selected NICs.

Table 7.4, dealing with non-oil exporting LDCs, shows the evolution, over 1963–76, of the broad product structure of manufactured exports. Comparing the first year with the last, the most striking developments seem to be the diversification away from 'semi-manufactures' to engineering and finished products, the sharp decline in textiles counterbalanced by the increase in clothing, the relative stagnation of low-skill manufactures like footwear, toys and leather goods, and the rapid advance in the high technology area of office and electrical/electronic equipment. While iron and steel appears relatively stagnant, the World Bank study (1978) identifies it as a promising growth commodity for the future. Balassa (1978) also includes it in his list of future growth areas, along with machinery, automobiles, components and durable goods accessories.

Table 7.5 is taken from a larger table showing the 50 most important commodities contributing to LDCs export growth in 1970–6 (UNCTAD (1978d)). This shows, at a more detailed (4-digit trade classification) level, the 12 products accounting for the fastest *rates* of growth in this period. While traditional products like textiles and

TABLE 7.4   Product structure of oil-importing developing countries' exports of manufactures (billion dollars, f.o.b. and percentages)

|  | 1963 | 1973 | 1976 |
|---|---|---|---|
|  |  | *Value* |  |
| ALL MANUFACTURES | *3.5* | *23.2* | *42.2* |
|  |  | *Shares* |  |
| *Semi-manufactures* | *60* | *41* | *35* |
| Textiles | 33 | 17 | 14 |
| Iron and steel | 4 | 4 | 4 |
| Plywood and paper | 3 | 4 | 2 |
| Other | 20 | 16 | 15 |
| *Engineering products* | *13* | *26* | *29* |
| Industrial machinery | 4 | 5 | 6 |
| Office, telecommunications and other electrical equipment | 7 | 17 | 18 |
| Transport equipment | 2 | 3 | 5 |
| *Other finished products* | *27* | *33* | *35* |
| Clothing | 9 | 17 | 19 |
| Footwear, toys, leather goods and miscellaneous finished products | 18 | 16 | 16 |

SOURCE
Blackhurst *et al.* (1978b).

TABLE 7.5   Exports of all LDCs

| Product | Growth rate (1976 as multiple of 1970) | Value of increment ($m.) | Share of total DC imports 1970 | 1976 |
|---|---|---|---|---|
| Telecomm. equipment | 9.5 | 444 | 3 | 9 |
| Leather clothes | 9.7 | 411 | 22 | 46 |
| Watches, movements, cases | 34.6 | 290 | 2 | 22 |
| Motor vehicle parts | 10.8 | 207 | 0 | 1 |
| Switchgear | 11.1 | 200 | 1 | 6 |
| Piston engines, non-air | 9.7 | 184 | 1 | 3 |
| Accounting machines | 26.2 | 184 | 1 | 15 |
| Electric power machinery | 9.3 | 182 | 2 | 7 |
| Sound recorders | 40.8 | 166 | 0 | 7 |
| Domestic elec. equipt. | 14.7 | 134 | 1 | 4 |
| Fur clothes | 18.3 | 122 | 7 | 25 |
| Silk yarn and threads | 52.7 | 94 | 10 | 66 |

SOURCE
Extracted from UNCTAD (1978d).

TABLE 7.6   The percentage contribution of individual developing countries to the increment in developing countries'* exports of manufacturers excluding unwrought non-ferrous metals and petroleum products to developed market-economy countries between 1970 and 1976 (percentages based on trade data of 21 DMEC[†] in current dollars)

| Exporting country or territory | Cloth-ing | Engineering, excl. road motor vehicles | Tex-tiles | Misc. light industry products | Wood and furni-ture | Pro-cessed food | Leather and foot-wear | All other product groups | Total |
|---|---|---|---|---|---|---|---|---|---|
| Korea, Republic of | 28.6 | 19.6 | 22.1 | 33.5 | 19.5 | 7.5 | 32.4 | 18.9 | 23.2 |
| Hong Kong | 38.5 | 18.3 | 13.5 | 32.5 | 2.5 | 1.7 | 1.3 | 1.0 | 18.9 |
| Mexico | 2.9 | 17.1 | 4.4 | 6.0 | 2.5 | 4.7 | 2.7 | 12.8 | 8.0 |
| Brazil | 1.3 | 3.9 | 8.6 | 2.8 | 5.5 | 33.3 | 19.2 | 13.6 | 7.8 |
| Singapore | 2.6 | 16.2 | 1.9 | 3.3 | 8.2 | 0.7 | 0.1 | 2.8 | 6.0 |
| Yugoslavia | 6.0 | 5.0 | 1.0 | 1.9 | 10.8 | 4.4 | 6.2 | 8.9 | 5.5 |
| Malaysia | 0.9 | 7.9 | 2.6 | 1.1 | 24.1 | 2.9 | 1.3 | 1.1 | 4.6 |
| India | 5.2 | 1.8 | 10.2 | 2.0 | 0.5 | 0.4 | 13.6 | 1.8 | 4.1 |
| Total of 8 major LDCs | 86.2 | 89.8 | 64.2 | 83.1 | 73.5 | 55.5 | 76.7 | 60.9 | 78.1 |
| All other LDCs* | 13.8 | 10.2 | 35.8 | 11.9 | 26.5 | 44.5 | 23.3 | 39.1 | 21.9 |
| Total LDCs* | 100.0 | 100.0 | 100.0 | 100.0 | 100.0 | 100.0 | 100.0 | 100.0 | 100.0 |

NOTES
* Excluding Taiwan.
† Developed market economy countries.
SOURCE
UNCTAD (1978e)

clothing accounted for the largest absolute value of increases, the most dynamic products (which increased in value nine-fold or more) were either high technology, capital-intensive products (switchgear, telecommunications, vehicle parts, etc.) or high-fashion, 'new' traditional products (leather and fur clothes). Unfortunately, the UNCTAD study makes no attempt to analyse the economic characteristics of 'dynamic' exports, but the impression conveyed by even a cursory examination is one of rapid diversification across a broad spectrum of technologies, skills and scales.

Table 7.6, taken from another UNCTAD study (1978e) shows the commodity composition of the increment in manufactured exports for the leading eight NICs (excluding Taiwan). These countries contributed 78 per cent of the total LDC increase in such exports, and over 75 per cent in clothing, engineering, miscellaneous light industry and leather and footwear. Sectors like textiles, wood and furniture, processed food and 'other' were more widely distributed in the Third World. There were important differences between the contributions of different products to the individual NICs. Korea, for instance, gained particularly in miscellaneous light industry and leather, Hong Kong in clothing and light industry, Mexico in engineering, Brazil in processed food and leather, Singapore in engineering, Yugoslavia and Malaysia in wood and furniture, and India in textiles and leather. However, the dynamism of countries like Korea and Hong Kong (and presumably Taiwan) across a wide range of activities is striking.

Chenery and Keesing (1978) have shown the commodity composition of the exports of 24 LDCs (including South European countries) for 1975, grouping them into four categories (Table 7.7). Group I, with 'early specialisation in manufactures', includes relatively small economies which have shown a comparative advantage in 'light' industry, making labour-intensive and technologically mature products. Group II are the 'large semi-industrial countries' with substantial 'heavy' industry built up behind protective barriers, which have switched to export-oriented policies and are relatively more competitive in capital and intermediate goods. Group III are 'countries emerging from primary specialisation', the more recent entrants into the manufactured export scene, which are more heavily concentrated (with the odd exception of Ivory Coast) on traditional labour intensive products (Iran and Venezuela are naturally specialised in 'other', energy-based products). Group IV, the 'large poor countries', have a diversity of experience: from India, with advanced manufacturing capabilities and 'heavy' exports, to Bangladesh, with its overwhelming dependence on textiles.

TABLE 7.7  Percent composition of manufactures exported from selected LDCs and developed countries in 1975

| Country | Capital goods | Consumer engine-ering | Clothing and footwear | Other clearcut consumer goods | Textiles incl. rugs | Standardised intermediate excl. textiles | Other and miscel-laneous |
|---|---|---|---|---|---|---|---|
| Developed countries | 31.8 | 9.4 | 2.7 | 4.0 | 4.6 | 24.1 | 23.3 |
| Developing countries* | 12.5 | 5.8 | 21.8 | 9.8 | 14.9 | 16.2 | 19.0 |
| Group I | | | | | | | |
| Israel | 8.9 | 1.7 | 6.9 | 4.1 | 3.2 | 6.4 | 68.8 |
| Greece | 5.2 | 1.3 | 17.8 | 3.1 | 17.3 | 40.1 | 15.2 |
| Hong Kong | 2.8 | 11.3 | 45.7 | 19.7 | 9.7 | 0.7 | 10.0 |
| Portugal | 9.0 | 5.9 | 18.4 | 2.5 | 23.0 | 15.2 | 25.9 |
| Taiwan | 9.5 | 9.8 | 27.8 | 14.9 | 15.1 | 8.5 | 14.4 |
| Korea | 7.0 | 5.2 | 32.4 | 12.3 | 15.7 | 14.7 | 12.7 |
| Group II | | | | | | | |
| Spain | 23.5 | 5.6 | 11.4 | 8.4 | 4.6 | 22.3 | 24.2 |
| Yugoslavia | 25.4 | 3.1 | 13.2 | 5.5 | 6.1 | 21.1 | 25.5 |
| Argentina | 18.0 | 7.8 | 2.8 | 4.3 | 0.3 | 24.9 | 41.9 |
| Brazil | 25.4 | 6.1 | 12.2 | 5.0 | 12.4 | 21.1 | 17.8 |
| Turkey | 2.8 | 0.5 | 25.2 | 2.0 | 33.6 | 22.6 | 13.4 |

| | | | | | | | |
|---|---|---|---|---|---|---|---|
| **Group III** | | | | | | | |
| Venezuela | 0.3 | — | — | 0.7 | 2.1 | 40.3 | 56.6 |
| Iran | 0.7 | 0.5 | 10.9 | 1.0 | 60.1 | 6.5 | 20.3 |
| Malaysia | 11.4 | 4.5 | 8.5 | 3.4 | 5.1 | 16.6 | 50.5 |
| Tunisia | 1.1 | 0.4 | 26.7 | 1.4 | 11.5 | 51.8 | 7.1 |
| Colombia | 6.7 | 1.2 | 11.4 | 12.1 | 21.9 | 25.7 | 20.9 |
| Ivory Coast | 20.2 | 0.9 | 2.1 | — | 20.5 | 26.4 | 29.9 |
| Morocco | 2.4 | 0.2 | 26.6 | 6.4 | 29.2 | 20.9 | 14.4 |
| Philippines | — | 0.4 | 14.1 | 25.5 | 8.7 | 22.2 | 29.1 |
| Thailand | 0.9 | 2.9 | 16.2 | 7.4 | 24.5 | 16.5 | 31.6 |
| **Group IV** | | | | | | | |
| Egypt | 1.0 | 0.3 | 22.0 | 6.5 | 47.7 | 13.6 | 8.9 |
| India | 9.3 | 1.2 | 11.2 | 4.4 | 30.6 | 21.0 | 22.3 |
| Pakistan | 2.0 | — | 7.2 | 6.4 | 66.1 | 13.1 | 5.2 |
| Bangladesh | — | 0.4 | — | 0.3 | 88.2 | 9.5 | 1.6 |

NOTE
* Countries listed only. For explanation of groups see text.
SOURCE
Chenery and Keesing (1978).

Chenery and Keesing comment on the changing pattern of exports by the various groups. They note that while in most developed countries the first four product groups, the new manufactures, comprise over 40 per cent total exports, only six LDCs (Hong Kong, Taiwan, Korea, Spain, Yugoslavia and Brazil—note that Mexico is missing in this exercise) exhibit such a specialisation. These are the products requiring advanced technological and marketing capabilities and high capital intensities. Other LDCs are generally in more standardised, less skill intensive and more easily marketed products. However, the share of capital goods and finished consumer goods in manufactured exports has been rising in almost all cases, indicating that for LDCs in general 'export success has been based in part on learning special skills involved in marketing and producing for customer specifications' (p. 32).

These figures do not, of course, show which agent is doing the 'learning': whether it is a highly integrated multinational company which has acquired all its skills in the developed world and has simply transferred the 'easier' processes to LDCs; a local firm which has acquired manufacturing skills but is still dependent upon foreign retailers or buyers for marketing skills; or a local firm which is able to manage the entire manufacturing and marketing function from start to finish. It would be an interesting and valuable refinement to the analysis of the emerging comparative advantage of different LDCs to compare the relative roles of foreign manufacturers, foreign buyers and local manufacturers in each. This would enable us to distinguish 'country specific' performance (i.e. exports as a whole) from 'ownership specific' performance (i.e. by local versus foreign firms), and to add another dimension to our understanding of the 'learning' process which is so crucial to industrial development. We shall return to some of these points below.

(B) COMMODITY STUDIES

A few studies of LDC exports of manufactures by individual industries, dealing with the 'new' industries in which LDCs have shown competitive strength, have appeared in recent years. Institutions such as UNCTAD, GATT (and the joint UNCTAD–GATT trade centre), the World Bank, UNIDO and regional bodies have produced numerous statistical and marketing studies dealing with trade in primary commodities and simple, traditional manufactured products. These are so numerous, and their conclusions so well known, that they will not be reviewed here. We shall concentrate on the papers that deal in the more modern products.

*Electronics.* The most useful studies dealing with the export-based electronics industry in LDCs are UNCTAD (1975b) and Plesch (n.d.). The UNCTAD study, while focusing on subcontracting arrangements (across countries) in this sector, is a valuable if rather dated source of information on production, products, costs and MNCs. The Plesch paper is more recent, and comprehensively covers export performance by LDCs, the role of LDC products in imports by rich countries, offshore assembly provisions, the basis of LDC comparative advantage, the role of MNCs, protectionism and prospects for future exports. Table 7.8 shows the product composition of the leading LDC exporters of electronics and electrical machinery. Two country studies are also worth noting: Pang Eng Fong and Linda Lim (1977) on Singapore and Sang Chul Suh (1975) on Korea. The former is particularly interesting for its analysis, based on questionnaire surveys, of the linkages between foreign and local firms in this industry. Sciberras (1977) discusses the activities of electronic MNCs in detail.

The technology of the electronics industry is changing so rapidly that most publications are out of date by the time they appear. The best source of information on this sector is, therefore, the financial/economic press and specialised trade journals. There seems to be a feeling running through recent discussions that increasing automation of the manufacturing processes will tend to relocate the industry back in the industrialised countries, but the trend still has to show itself in the trade and investment figures. After a visit to Singapore last year (reported in Lall (1979)), I noted that the electronics MNCs there were steadily upgrading the skill and technology content of their work in Singapore and that there was no sign of any impending shift away from the island. UNCTAD (1975b) and Plesch (n.d.) confirm that there is a steady shift of lower-skill, more labour-intensive, activity away from the older centres (Korea, Taiwan, Singapore and Hong Kong) with higher wages to new cheaper locations like Malaysia, Thailand, the Philippines and Central America. The setback in the early recession years (1974–5) seems to have been completely overcome.

*Electrical machinery.* Mrs Kawaguchi (1977) of the World Bank has produced a short note on the LDCs' comparative advantage in this industry (which also includes some electronics), where she concludes that 'LDCs' comparative advantage in the electrical machinery industry lies in relatively low skill (but not necessarily low technology) branches but, in contrast to the picture for manufacturing as a whole, these are characterized as large scale operations in terms of workers and value-added per unit. This can be explained by the fact that the electrical

TABLE 7.8  Product composition of nine major exporting developing countries' exports of electrical and electronic machinery in 1973 (value in US $ million)

| SITC Product description | Taiwan | Hong Kong* | Singa-pore† | Korea | Yugo-slavia | Mexico‡ | Brazil | India | Argen-tina | Nine developing countries Value | % Share |
|---|---|---|---|---|---|---|---|---|---|---|---|
| 722.1 Electric power machinery | 26.2 | 2.5 | 12.9 | 11.2 | 29.1 | 24.6 | 4.2 | 3.9 | 3.7 | 118.3 | 4.3 |
| 722.2 Switchgear, etc. | 10.2 | 0.7 | 19.9 | 12.5 | 23.2 | 35.1 | 7.2 | 4.7 | 2.1 | 115.6 | 4.2 |
| 723.1 Insulated wire and cable | 11.8 | 0.7 | 2.2 | 3.4 | 63.5 | 19.5 | 1.3 | 6.0 | 2.9 | 111.3 | 4.1 |
| 723.2 Electrical insulating equipment | 0.6 | — | 0.1 | — | 4.4 | — | 0.3 | 0.4 | — | 5.8 | 0.2 |
| 724.1 Television receivers | 233.5 | 14.4 | 25.9 | 23.9 | 10.4 | 27.6 | 17.2 | — | 1.1 | 354.0 | 12.9 |
| 724.2 Radio receivers | 142.6 | 241.2 | 65.8 | 32.8 | 0.6 | 6.0 | 18.3 | 3.3 | 0.1 | 510.7 | 18.6 |
| 724.9 Other telecommunications equipment | 162.4 | 14.8 | 9.4 | 23.0 | 20.8 | 135.7 | 10.7 | 1.2 | 5.9 | 383.9 | 14.0 |
| 725 Domestic electrical appliances | 11.1 | 19.6 | 11.0 | 0.9 | 36.3 | 1.9 | 4.9 | 4.3 | 6.1 | 96.1 | 3.5 |
| 726 Electric apparatus for medical purposes | — | — | 0.9 | — | 1.0 | 0.6 | 0.2 | — | 0.1 | 2.8 | 0.1 |
| 729.1 Batteries and accumulators | 7.2 | 6.9 | 13.5 | 0.8 | 14.2 | 2.7 | 1.1 | 3.4 | 0.6 | 50.4 | 1.8 |
| 729.2 Electric lamps | 15.4 | 5.3 | 0.8 | 11.5 | 2.0 | 4.9 | 1.0 | 0.4 | 0.1 | 41.4 | 1.5 |

| | | | | | | | | | | |
|---|---|---|---|---|---|---|---|---|---|---|
| 729.3 Electronic components (transistors, etc.) | 83.2 | 93.0 | 55.1 | 179.7 | 5.5 | 101.8 | 9.6 | 1.6 | 4.3 | 533.8 | 19.5 |
| 729.4 Automotive electrical equipment | 1.2 | 4.5 | 2.0 | 0.8 | 4.6 | 1.3 | 3.8 | 0.2 | 2.7 | 21.1 | 0.8 |
| 729.5 Electronic measuring and contr. instruments | 1.6 | — | 2.4 | 1.0 | 5.8 | 5.9 | 0.6 | 0.2 | 1.5 | 19.0 | 0.7 |
| 729.6 Electro-mechanical hand tools | 0.4 | — | 1.5 | — | 0.6 | 0.1 | — | — | — | 2.6 | 0.1 |
| 729.7 Electron and proton accelerators | — | — | — | — | — | — | — | — | — | — | — |
| 729.9 Other electrical machinery and apparatus | 34.2 | 105.9 | 164.4 | 10.7 | 5.1 | 42.8 | 6.7 | 1.8 | 1.7 | 373.3 | 13.6 |
| 72 Total electrical machinery | 741.8 | 509.5 | 387.8 | 312.5 | 240.5 | 410.5 | 87.1 | 31.4 | 32.9 | 2740.1 | 100.0 |

NOTES
* Excluding re-exports.
† Including re-exports.
‡ Mexico's export data have been modified using US import statistics to reflect border assembly industries.

SOURCE
Plesch (n.d.).

machinery industries in which the LDCs have comparative advantage are strongly associated with foreign investment by the developed countries . . . ' (p. 2). The high level of multinational activity in the electrical equipment sector is explored (critically) by R. S. Newfarmer in an UNCTAD publication, 'The International Market Power of Transnational Corporations: A case study of the Electrical Industry' (1978b) which has a useful collection of data on the leading MNCs. Plesch's (n.d.) study also deals with electrical machinery and presents detailed data on the commodity composition of exports by the leading exporters. (Table 7.8 includes data on electrical machinery.)

A valuable study of electrical machinery exports is by Weiss (1978). The aim of this work is to identify products within this high skill, high technology sector in West Germany which are turning uncompetitive and losing ground to LDCs. A detailed consideration of several branches leads Weiss to conclude that the standardised and unskilled labour-intensive parts of electrical engineering have lost their competitive edge and should be phased out of DCs. It would be useful to identify (which Weiss does not do) which the LDCs are that are gaining in competitive strength, what are the sorts of skills being created, how the technology is being transferred, and what is being done in terms of R and D within the LDCs. Table 7.8 above indicates that Yugoslavia, Mexico, Taiwan, Singapore and Korea are the main exporters (the first two items on the Table), but more detailed information is needed at the firm level.[10]

*Non-electrical engineering.* Kawaguchi (1978) has compiled an exhaustive set of data on trade in non-electrical engineering equipment by LDCs, analysing patterns of growth, comparative advantage, cost structures and the role of MNCs. The destination of LDC exports is also analysed at length, and two case studies (on calculators and sewing machines) are also included. She traces the rapid diversification and growth of market penetration by LDCs and notes that 'the most important factor for the growth of machinery exports would be the behaviour of DC firms. Their decisions on which products, production processes and technology they want for transfer, where they want to transfer, from where they want to purchase and from which LDC to which LDC they want to shift the production site are crucially important in determining the future export patterns of LDCs.' The next wave of exports will come from LDCs which are still in the primary stages of exporting textiles and simple products, like Thailand, the Philippines, Venezuela and El Salvador. Interestingly enough, Kawaguchi places Iran, Egypt and Indonesia as further behind this second wave.

Kawaguchi arrives at the following conclusions: the LDCs' comparative advantage lies in labour-intensive and technologically standardised products with low transport costs (heating and cooling equipment, pumps and centrifuges, mechanical handling equipment and ball and roller bearings);[11] they will increasingly replace Japan in simple types of metal working machinery; and they have a substantial advantage in producing components for and assembling calculators, engine parts, office machine parts and simple sewing machines.

While this was outside the scope of Kawaguchi's paper, it would have been very useful to understand more clearly the exact role of MNCs, retailers and domestic LDC producers in the process of expanding machinery exports. It is not clear which firms, from which DCs, are relocating production processes in LDCs, and it is not clear how much 'learning' and adaptation is going on within the LDCs themselves. India, as before, is 'going it alone' in this sector, with indigenous firms taking the main weight of exporting engineering products. As with electrical machinery India's exports are more embodied in turnkey plant exports. To understand their future prospects, we need a much deeper analysis of their capabilities, costs, techniques and marketing.

A few papers have dealt in general with these problems. M. Frankena (1973) has published a useful paper on engineering products exports by India, and Howard Pack (1978) has produced a more perceptive analysis of the competitive strengths and weaknesses of LDC capital goods manufactures. However, the field is truly vast, and much remains to be done.

*Automobiles.* J. Baranson has written several papers on the world automobile industry (see, for instance, Baranson (1971)) now rather dated. The OECD Interfutures project has prepared a study on 'Long Term Perspectives of the World Car Industries' (1978a), which predicts a shift of production of standard models to countries like Brazil, Argentina, Mexico, Korea and Iran. An article in *The Times* recently (13 November 1978, p. 27) noted 'How Brazil has become Car Supplier to the Third World' under the international sourcing arrangements of three or four MNCs (led by VW). Brazil is not only making cars specially designed for Third World conditions, which it is successfully selling in other LDCs, but it is also acting as an important supplier of components to developed countries. Argentina and Mexico follow in its wake. South Korea is embarking, on the other hand, on an independent export-based car venture. India is a successful exporter of trucks, made by TELCO (from a Daimler-Benz licence, now terminated)[12] and by a Leyland subsidiary; it is also emerging as a major exporter of motorcycles and scooters.

*Other sectors*: UNCTAD and UNIDO have recently produced studies of the iron and steel industry. The UNCTAD study by I. Walter (1978) is mainly concerned with prospects within the industrialized world rather than progress in the LDCs, but is nevertheless very well informed and perceptive (if rather pessimistic about adjustment in the DCs).[13]

R. Stobaugh published a monograph some years ago on the petrochemical industry (1971), but little work seems to have been done on the exports of chemical products from LDCs in more recent years. The chemical industry is not, as yet, a very important one for LDCs, but a number of countries may be expected to make an impact on particular sectors of the market. India's exports of pharmaceuticals, for instance, are expected to reach $90 million in the current fiscal year, and it is entering into coproduction arrangements with the USSR to formulate bulk chemicals for re-export. Singapore is an important centre for petrochemical production and for drug formulation by MNCs. The big Latin American countries are also rapidly increasing drug exports. But, most important of all, the OPEC countries are expected to come on stream in the medium term with massive investments in petrochemicals (see Turner and Bedore (1978/79)).[14] Eastern Europe is also making threatening moves in this industry.

*Technology exports.* A relatively unexplored area of LDC entry into world markets, though one which is likely to assume great significance in the long run, is the provision, by the more industrially advanced LDCs, of manufacturing, construction and other types of technology. Five such areas of technology exports have been identified for the manufacturing sector (Lall (1980)): sale of turnkey projects; engineering consultancy; licensing and provision of managerial services; direct investment; and sale of training services. The export of technology in these forms by indigenous LDC enterprises, on commercial terms and in competition with established sellers of technology from developed countries, has grown impressively in recent years. In part, as noted above, this overlaps with export of various kinds of capital goods, but the implications of the sale of complete plants and related services are rather different from those of simply selling individual items of machinery: the former represents the entry of LDC manufacturers and consultants into a new and much higher level of industrial activity than the latter (which could take place simply under licence from a foreign firm). There are signs that the technology exported by LDC firms is more labour-intensive, smaller-scale and better suited to the conditions of other LDCs than that normally provided by DC firms. It is, however, limited to fairly well-diffused knowhow and to technologies that do not require massive R and D investments or far-flung marketing networks. LDC enterprises have both a complementary and a competitive role with respect to DC firms. They are complementary in two ways: they can take over the sale of techniques which are on the way out in DCs (the sale of technology for making scooters by India to Indonesia is a good example), and they can work as subcontractors to DC firms to provide certain labour-intensive engineering, detailed design and project management functions much more cheaply than the established, high salary firms (a great deal of such subcontracting is now done in Latin America and the Middle East). However, in certain areas where the technology itself is fairly stable and the finances involved are not too large (LDC enterprises cannot compete on credit terms), LDC contractors can be competitive with DC firms, and so pose a threat to them in Third World markets.

There are few papers on this emerging form of international division of labour.[15] Lall (1980) explores the general dimensions and determinants of LDC technology exports, and identifies India as the LDC with the most diverse and highly developed capability (a beneficial fallout from an otherwise inefficient import substitution policy). Katz and Ablin (1978a, 1978b) discuss technology exports (in particular turnkey projects) by Argentina and their findings are further analysed by Cortes (1978). Rhee and Westphal (1978) also at the World Bank, have described exports of turnkey projects by South Korea and Taiwan.

All these papers barely scratch the surface of a new phenomenon which crucially affects the world area of LDC competition: the assimilation, adaptation and creation of industrial technology in developing countries. It is this which ultimately determines the evolution of comparative advantage, and it is this, consequently, which deserves the greatest attention when predictions are made about the future pattern of trade.

(C) RECENT STUDIES OF LDC COMPARATIVE ADVANTAGE

There are two broad groups of studies dealing with the pattern of LDC manufactured exports.

(i) The first tries to analyse the evolution of manufactured exports in total exports, and the composition of the products exported, with reference to *country characteristics*, such as the level of industrialisation, per capita income, population growth and the macro-economic policies pursued. Chenery and Hughes (1973) and Chenery and Keesing (1978) relate the broad composition of LDC exports to a mixture of income and policy characteristics; the findings of the latter have been mentioned in sub-section (*a*) above. Hirsch (1977), in the first part of his book on industrialisation and trade patterns, groups commodities into 'rich man's, poor man's and every man's goods' according to whether these goods are positively, negatively or unrelated with the level of economic development (as measured by per capita GNP). This leads him to identify LDCs' advantage as lying initially in 'poor man's goods' like beverages, tobacco, textiles and similar traditional products,[16] and increasingly in 'everyman's goods' like light manufactures, paper, steel, metal goods and ship building. The rich countries' advantage lies in high technology, skill-intensive goods like machinery, motor vehicles and instruments. While noting exceptions to this categorisation and the statistical weaknesses of his computations, Hirsch concludes there are certain consistent relationships between income levels and export performance. Michaely (1978) conducts a similar exercise and obtains similar results.

Morrison (1976) tests export performance of LDCs against market size, level of development, 'openness', natural resource availability and inflation. He finds that the first three variables have positive and the last two negative effects on overall export performance. Banerji (1972) tests the share of manufactured exports in total exports against income levels, industrial development, population growth and population density. The first two variables exercise, as may be expected, a positive influence while the other two (whose theoretical rationale is dubious) have relatively insignificant effects.

(ii) The second set of studies explores and analyses the revealed comparative advantage (RCA) of LDCs with reference to *industry characteristics* such as factor intensity, skill requirement, scale, and so on. The most commonly used RCA measure is by the so-called 'Balassa' method—exports minus imports of each commodity normalised by the total trade in that commodity. There are several problems with this method (its static nature, the high level of aggregation, the choice of base years, the influence of government policy), but it is difficult to devise one which is 'ideal' given the nature of available data. In particular, the failure to take dynamic export elements into account[17] limits the usefulness of usual RCA exercises in making predictions or even in keeping up with current changes.

One major attempt to counter the static nature of RCA computations is by Donges and Reidel (1977). They calculate RCAs for 119 commodities exported by 15 leading LDCs for 1962–3 and compare it to RCAs for 1972–3 and evaluate the direction of change in LDC exports. They conclude that

the number of branches in which the sample countries revealed comparative advantage increased from 36 items in 1962–3 to 53 items ten years later. The industries exhibiting comparative advantage according to the 1972–3 data are cotton fabrics, footwear, textile clothing, tanneries, canned fruit, household equipment, jewellery and wood products. Not surprisingly, these are all labour-and/or raw material-intensive products. Interestingly, however, the sample countries appear to have developed a comparative advantage in a number of light manufacturing products, of which electrical equipment, metal containers and telecommunication equipment are the most prominent. (p. 69)

A similar computation of RCAs for West Germany *vis-à-vis* other developed as well as less-developed countries by the Institut für Weltwirtschaft (1978) is also worth noting. While the degree of aggregation is very high (2-digit trade classification), the results are interesting. Developed countries tend to specialise more on different products *within* industries in their trade with each other, and on different activities altogether in their trade with LDCs. Germany's advantage lies essentially in innovativeness based on R and D investments, while that of LDCs lies in labour cost advantages in making mature products. This study also remarks on the rapid evolution of LDCs' RCA towards higher skill products.

The UK Department of Industry (1978) undertook an analysis of the Institut für Weltwirtschaft's data to discover the basis for British comparative advantage.[18] The conclusion was that

The U.K. is different from the economies of West Germany and Japan in having a lower level of R & D expenditure, a different balance in the distribution of that expenditure between industrial sectors and between government objectives, and a more important role given to government in the provision and allocation of R & D funds. The result is that in the grouping of industries which tend to be research-intensive (chemicals, electrical engineering and machinery and instruments) the U.K. spends substantially less than either W. Germany or Japan on R & D. (para. 32)

Very similar findings are reported by Pavitt (1978) and Freeman (1978), of the Science Policy Research Unit at Sussex, based on their examination of the link between R and D, innovation and trade performance. The good performances of Germany and Japan, and the poor one of the UK, are found to be strongly correlated to their pace and direction of innovative activity.

As far as the statistical explanation of the RCAs of LDCs are concerned, there is a vast literature on empirical tests of trade theory which cannot be adequately covered here.[19] We shall, therefore, pick the more recent studies, which can be subdivided into two groups.

*First*, there are cross section studies, of either the export performance of groups of countries or of all LDCs together in their performance in exporting to a given importing developed country. The most useful recent countrywise study (for 29 countries) is by Hirsch (1977), who tests different 'new' theories of trade (neo-factor proportions, technology gaps, etc.) and finds that skills and technology are the primary determinants of comparative advantage, that physical capital is not a significant factor but is generally negatively associated with rich countries' export performance, and that LDCs are generally characterised by low-skill exports. It is a 'neo-factor proportions model whose factors, however, are those which are specified by the neo-technology approach' (pp. 63–4), a convenient and long overdue marriage between the two approaches.[20] As for studies of LDC trade as a whole with given developed countries, there are several notable works.

(i) Helleiner (1976), who tests a comprehensive model of the determinants of LDC competitiveness in DC markets and finds that skill (human capital) and scale variables perform best as (negative) influences on LDC exports, and that the degree of product differentiation may also have a negative effect.

(ii) Fels (1972), who examines the imports of West Germany from DCs and LDCs and relates these to physical and human capital intensity, and finds that both kinds of 'capital' influence trade, and that Germany's comparative advantage with respect to LDCs lies in goods which require both more physical capital and higher skills.

(iii) Wolter (1977a, 1977b), who examines West Germany trade with DCs, LDCs and the socialist countries, and finds that different explanations are required for each form of trade. The neo-Heckscher–Ohlin theory works best in trade with LDCs, with 'human capital' intensity (i.e. skills) comprising Germany's comparative advantage. The neo-technology theory works best in Eastern Bloc trade, with R and D intensity comprising Germany's advantage. Both theories seem to have some validity in Germany's trade with other non-socialist developed countries. Physical capital intensity tends to have a negative effect on German competitiveness, yet another indication of Leontieff's classic 'paradox' of US trade patterns.[21]

(iv) Stern (1976), who uses Fels' data to establish that, in non-resource based manufacturing industries, the strongest determinant of German RCA is skills, and that physical capital intensity has an insignificant negative impact;

(v) Weiss (1978), who examines the West German electrical engineering industry and finds that low skill, standardised products are losing ground to LDC competition;[22]

(vi) The UK Government (1978), who, in an unpublished paper, test Britain's advantage with respect to different regions, and find that capital intensity has a uniformly negative impact and that skill intensity and foreign ownership (of UK firms) have positive and generally significant effects as far as trade with LDCs is concerned.

The *second* group of studies of LDC comparative advantage concentrates on individual countries.

(i) Boatler (1975) finds, for Mexico, that, against the predictions of conventional Heckscher–Ohlin theory, 'the greatest marginal comparative advantage of semi-industrialised countries will be found in the most completely modernised and generally capital-intensive industries.' He finds also that very small scale labour-intensive industries have been able to maintain their share in Mexican exports. The small-to-medium scale industries without modern, capital-intensive methods have fared worst of all.

(ii) Cline and Rapoport (1978) on Central America use static and dynamic RCA measures, and find that, besides the usual traditional industries, several 'new' ones (electrical and telecommunications equipment, fertilisers, vehicles, tyres) seem to have high export potential.

(iii) Katz and Ablin (1978a) find a significant positive statistical relationship between the rate of technical progress in the major Argentinian exporting firms and their export performance. They define technical progress broadly to include 'minor' changes and 'troubleshooting' as well as R and D in the conventional sense, and conclude that, once accumulated technical experience reaches a certain level, an LDC enterprise may develop significant competitive advantage in exporting even sophisticated manufactures.

(iv) Lowinger (1971) in an early study of Brazilian exports to developed countries (1966) found that they were intensive in low-skilled labour. In a later study, however, Tyler (1972, 1976) finds that total

Brazilian manufactured exports tend to be highly skill-intensive. He explains partly by the fact that most of its exports are directed to other LDCs, and partly by the existence of 'distortions'. At least in the former category, Brazil would seem to have developed a genuine advantage in high skill activities. This supports the findings for Argentina and for LDC technology exports reported above.

(v) de Vries (1977) on Latin American countries notes, in a similar vein, that the long-term dynamic advantage of the larger economies lies in non-electrical machinery and other capital goods where considerable import substitution has taken place and a stock of experience built up.

These studies bear out the tendencies, reported earlier, about the specialisation of LDC exports in traditional (low skill) activities as well as their propensity to shift increasingly into activities requiring greater skills and technology. Over the longer run, as Hirsch (1977) has noted, the pattern of developed/less-developed country trade will come to resemble that of intra-developed country trade, with LDCs specialising in the more standardised, less innovative portions of the *same* industries rather than in different industries (as compared to industrialised nations). It will, as Lall (1980) concludes, be *special skills*, based on large scale R and D and marketing, which will constitute the comparative advantage of the developed countries within each industry, and not *skills in general*, which had in the past ruled out certain industries from LDCs altogether.[23]

Interestingly, the realisation that technology is a crucial determinant of trading advantages echoes the concerns felt by classical economists a century ago. In a recent paper Bloomfield (1978) shows how the role of 'technology gaps' was debated in nineteenth-century Britain, and the significance of 'learning', technological diffusion and imitation was understood (if not always correctly interpreted). We always seem to be rediscovering things which were known before!

An important point worth making here is that future shifts of LDCs into areas of high-skill and high-technology exports may be artificially accelerated by protectionist measures on the part of developed countries towards 'traditional' labour-intensive products (see Birnberg (1978) and Helleiner (1978)). Such a 'forcing' of the process of dynamic comparative advantage will distort the optimum use of productive factors possessed by LDCs; needless to say, it will also lead to a grave misallocation of industrial resources in the advanced countries.

## IV  THE MARKETS SERVED

GATT's *International Trade 1977/78* (1978, Table L) shows the regional distribution of total exports by LDCs, grouped by geographical area and between oil-exporting and other countries. The same source (Table K) shows the destination of manufactured exports by major industrial categories. UNCTAD (1978a) gives detailed data on import penetration (by source), for 14 industrial groups, into the EEC, the UK, the US and Japan, and for these regions together. Data on penetration for individual commodities are shown in a convenient chart, taken from IMF (1978) in Table 7.9, and, in a summary table taken from the OECD's Department of Economics and Statistics (1978c) in Table 7.10.

It is by now a commonplace that the *total* penetration by the LDCs of DC markets, whether measured as a proportion of total imports or of consumption, is small. Despite the rapid rise of LDCs' share in world trade, by 1977, only 8.1 per cent of total OECD imports of manufacturers came from NICs as defined by the OECD (i.e. including South European countries but excluding India), and only 5.8 per cent came from our list of 6 NICs (again excluding India). The share of all LDCs (excluding European countries) in total OECD imports in 1977 came to 8.2 per cent, having risen from 1.6 per cent in 1963. By contrast, the share of West Germany stood at 17.6 per cent in 1977, of US at 13.1 per cent of Japan at 8.8 per cent. According to the World Bank's (1978) prediction, LDCs will account for about 14 per cent of developed country imports by 1985.

It is the *narrow commodity concentration* of LDC penetration rather than its overall level which is the cause of recent problems.[24] As Tables 7.9 and 7.10 below show, it is the 'traditional' industries (clothing, textiles, wood and leather) which are causing the most trouble, in part because these are relatively low technology sectors in the OECD countries and in part because there is no complementarity in production activities between DC and LDC firms. In the longer term, however, given the propensities of MNCs to seek cheaper locations in order to stay competitive (see below), the developed countries may expect to face severe competition on a much broader front, not just at home but also in their export markets.[25]

In general, the share of LDC manufactured exports going to other LDCs has been declining. After 1973, however, the trend was reversed, and the share of exports going to LDCs rose from 29.4 per cent of the total to 34.4 per cent by 1975, mainly due to the boom in the oil exporting countries. Detailed descriptions of market penetration in

TABLE 7.9   Developing countries: share in world trade, 1974

SOURCE
IMF (45) pp. 102–3 (slightly amended).

**80% and up**
Bananas, fresh plantains, fresh. Raw beet & cane sugar. Coffee in all forms. Cocoa. Tea, Spices. Natural rubber gums, Silk, Jute, Crude fertilizers, Nickel, Jute fabrics, woven

**70 – 80%**
Other vegetable fiber, hard fiber, Fixed vegetable oil, nonsoft, Tin

**60 – 70%**
Edible nuts, fresh or dry, Cotton, Men's underwear, not knit, Petroleum & coal chemicals

**50 – 60%**
Shrimp, shellfish, frozen, Refined sugar, etc., Wood, rough Lumber, shaped, nonconifer, Nonferrous ores & concentrates

**40 – 50%**
Rice, Fruit & nuts, fresh or dry Dried fruit Tobacco unmanufactured Iron ore & concentrates, Copper, refined, etc.

**30 – 40%**
Vegetables, etc. fresh, simply preserved, Vegetable oil residues for feed. Cotton fabrics, woven, Household & other textiles, Travel goods & handbags, Clothing, not of fur, Men's outerwear, not knit, Underwear, knit, not elastic, Outerwear, knit, not elastic

**20 – 30%**
Bovine cattle, Meat, tinned or prepared, Cereals n.e.s., unmilled, Oranges, tangerines, etc. Fruit, preserved, prepared. Animal feeding stuff. Oil seeds, nuts, kernels, Crude animal matter n.e.s., Crude vegetable matter n.e.s., Fixed vegetable oil, soft, Natural abrasives, Other crude minerals, Zinc, Leather, Women's outerwear, not knit, Footwear, rubber or plastic, Radio broadcast receivers, Developed cinema film, Toys, indoor games, sporting goods, Other manufactured goods n.e.s., Plywood, veneers, etc., Dyes n.e.s., tanning products, Essential oils, perfumes, etc.

**10 – 20%**
Meat, fresh, chilled, or frozen, Fish, fresh, chilled, or frozen, Fish, prepared, Maize, preserved, Vegetables, etc., prepared. Margarine, shortening, Food preparations n.e.s. Tobacco manufactures, Hides, skins, undressed, except furs, Wool & animal hair, natural & manufactured, Silver, platinum, etc. Lead, Nonferrous base metals n.e.s., Textile yarn & thread, Woven textiles, noncotton, Lace, ribbons, tulle, Floor coverings, Fur clothing, Footwear of leather, Semiconductors, valves, etc., Precious & semiprecious stones & pearls, Diamonds, etc.

**1 – 10%**
Milk & cream, Barley, unmilled, Wheat, etc.: meal or flour, Cereal, etc., preparations, Chocolate & products, Grape wine, Distilled alcoholic beverages, Animal oils and fats, Processed animal & vegetable oils, etc. Lumber, shaped, conifer, Pulp & waste paper, Stone, sand, gravel, Iron & steel scrap, Nonferrous scrap, Continuous synthetic weaves, Cellulosic fiber fabrics, woven, Knit, etc., fabric, nonelastic, Special textile products, Office machinery, computers, etc., Electric power machinery, Switchgear, etc., Insulated wire & cable, Telecommunications equipment, Television receivers, Microphones, loudspeakers, amplifiers, Domestic electrical equipment, Electric space heaters, Electrical machinery & parts n.e.s., Batteries, accumulators, Works of art, etc. Paper & paperboard Articles of paper & paperboard n.e.s. Furniture, Printed matter, Organic chemicals, Inorganic elements, oxides Other inorganic chemicals, Synthetic dyes, indigo, Paints, pigments, etc., Medicinal products, Fertilizers, Plastic materials, manufactured, Chemicals n.e.s., Pig iron, etc., Iron & steel primary forms, Iron & steel shapes, Iron & steel universals, plate, sheet, Iron & steel tubes, pipe, etc. Metal tanks, boxes, etc. Wire products, nonelectrical, Tools, Metal manufactures n.e.s. Plumbing, heating, lighting equipment, etc.

TABLE 7.10  Penetration of OECD markets by LDCs (1977) (percentages)*

| Commodity group SITC | Year | All† NICs | of which | | | Total OECD | Canada | US | of which | | | | | | Eastern bloc | Other LDCs | Share in total OECD imports of manufactures |
| | | | OECD NICs | Brazil and Mexico | East NICs | | | | Japan | France | Germany | Italy | UK | | | |
|---|---|---|---|---|---|---|---|---|---|---|---|---|---|---|---|---|
| Clothing (84) | 1977 | 39.1 | 5.1 | 1.3 | 29.9 | 51.9 | 0.4 | 1.7 | 1.6 | 6.5 | 7.8 | 12.8 | 3.7 | 5.1 | 8.2 | 4.9 |
| | 1963 | 17.3 | 1.2 | 0.0 | 15.3 | 78.5 | 1.1 | 1.9 | 7.1 | 7.2 | 7.8 | 16.4 | 5.6 | 1.7 | 3.0 | 3.3 |
| Leather, footwear, travel goods (61, 83, 85) | 1977 | 31.3 | 7.9 | 3.9 | 17.7 | 64.5 | 0.6 | 2.2 | 1.3 | 5.8 | 5.9 | 27.7 | 3.2 | 3.9 | 7.8 | 2.4 |
| | 1963 | 7.2 | 2.3 | 0.5 | 3.3 | 83.7 | 1.5 | 6.0 | 7.6 | 10.3 | 9.6 | 20.6 | 10.3 | 3.4 | 7.6 | 2.2 |
| Wood and Cork manufactures (63) | 1977 | 23.8 | 4.7 | 2.4 | 15.9 | 69.8 | 8.6 | 11.7 | 2.6 | 5.0 | 7.8 | 4.0 | 0.9 | 3.2 | 7.4 | 1.2 |
| | 1963 | 12.3 | 6.2 | 1.1 | 3.6 | 80.2 | 14.3 | 4.2 | 13.9 | 5.1 | 6.9 | 3.8 | 1.5 | 4.0 | 8.7 | 1.4 |
| Textiles (65) | 1977 | 12.1 | 4.2 | 1.7 | 5.8 | 79.0 | 0.5 | 6.3 | 4.3 | 8.1 | 14.1 | 9.3 | 6.8 | 4.1 | 8.6 | 5.3 |
| | 1963 | 5.7 | 2.4 | 0.7 | 2.1 | 82.9 | 0.5 | 6.2 | 6.2 | 10.1 | 10.1 | 9.5 | 10.1 | 2.1 | 11.4 | 8.9 |
| Electrical Machinery (72) | 1977 | 12.0 | 1.0 | 2.2 | 8.4 | 85.8 | 1.6 | 14.4 | 14.6 | 5.8 | 18.5 | 4.9 | 5.4 | 1.0 | 2.0 | 10.3 |
| | 1963 | 0.8 | 0.2 | 0.0 | 0.5 | 98.2 | 2.6 | 22.2 | 6.3 | 5.9 | 23.6 | 4.1 | 9.6 | 0.6 | 0.5 | 8.3 |
| Miscellaneous finished manufactures (81, 82, 86, 89) | 1977 | 11.2 | 1.3 | 0.7 | 8.7 | 85.6 | 1.6 | 12.7 | 12.2 | 6.5 | 16.5 | 7.7 | 6.3 | 2.3 | 1.4 | 10.2 |
| | 1963 | 4.2 | 0.7 | 0.2 | 2.7 | 93.5 | 1.0 | 17.9 | 8.1 | 7.3 | 19.8 | 6.1 | 8.5 | 2.0 | 0.8 | 9.0 |
| Rubber manufactures (62) | 1977 | 7.6 | 4.2 | 0.4 | 2.5 | 94.2 | 3.4 | 8.4 | 7.5 | 16.7 | 18.0 | 8.6 | 9.4 | 1.0 | 0.7 | 1.3 |
| | 1963 | 0.5 | 0.2 | 0.0 | 0.2 | 97.8 | 2.0 | 17.0 | 4.5 | 11.2 | 18.1 | 7.2 | 13.6 | 0.5 | 0.7 | 1.1 |
| Manufactures of metal (69) | 1977 | 7.4 | 2.0 | 0.7 | 4.3 | 91.9 | 4.0 | 10.2 | 9.1 | 7.1 | 21.7 | 6.6 | 7.5 | 1.4 | 0.9 | 3.4 |
| | 1963 | 1.5 | 0.5 | 0.1 | 0.6 | 97.8 | 1.7 | 19.4 | 7.3 | 5.4 | 26.2 | 4.1 | 11.1 | 0.6 | 0.4 | 3.7 |
| Non-metallic mineral manufactures (66) | 1977 | 4.9 | 1.5 | 0.9 | 2.3 | 74.9 | 1.5 | 5.9 | 3.6 | 5.8 | 11.7 | 8.1 | 15.6 | 5.7 | 7.0 | 3.3 |
| | 1963 | 2.7 | 0.8 | 0.8 | 0.8 | 84.8 | 0.8 | 8.9 | 6.7 | 6.6 | 13.7 | 4.3 | 17.7 | 3.2 | 3.3 | 3.9 |
| Iron and Steel (67) | 1977 | 4.8 | 2.4 | 1.0 | 1.0 | 90.3 | 2.9 | 2.5 | 15.0 | 10.8 | 17.8 | 5.2 | 4.5 | 3.6 | 1.7 | 6.4 |
| | 1963 | 1.3 | 0.5 | 0.4 | 0.0 | 92.2 | 3.0 | 5.3 | 6.9 | 12.7 | 22.5 | 1.2 | 7.1 | 5.1 | 0.8 | 9.3 |

TABLE 7.10 (*continued*)

| Commodity group SITC | Year | All† NICs | OECD NICs | of which Brazil and Mexico | East NICs | Total OECD | Can-ada | US | Japan | France | Ger-many | Italy | UK | East-ern bloc | Other LDCs | Share in total OECD imports of manu-factures |
|---|---|---|---|---|---|---|---|---|---|---|---|---|---|---|---|---|
| Transport equipment (73) | 1977 | 2.8 | 1.7 | 0.4 | 0.5 | 97.5 | 11.6 | 16.9 | 15.4 | 10.0 | 19.4 | 4.3 | 5.2 | 1.0 | 0.4 | 18.2 |
|  | 1963 | 1.0 | 0.5 | 0.0 | 0.1 | 98.0 | 2.1 | 19.6 | 1.1 | 10.0 | 30.9 | 5.4 | 14.7 | 0.6 | 0.8 | 12.2 |
| Machinery other than electric (71) | 1977 | 2.8 | 1.0 | 0.8 | 0.8 | 96.3 | 4.3 | 21.9 | 5.8 | 7.2 | 22.7 | 6.2 | 8.9 | 1.2 | 0.4 | 16.6 |
|  | 1963 | 0.3 | 0.2 | 0.0 | 0.0 | 98.7 | 2.6 | 28.2 | 0.9 | 5.4 | 26.2 | 4.9 | 13.2 | 0.8 | 0.3 | 20.1 |
| Chemicals (5) | 1977 | 2.5 | 1.1 | 0.6 | 0.6 | 92.3 | 3.2 | 14.2 | 2.1 | 9.6 | 19.5 | 4.2 | 7.9 | 3.1 | 4.1 | 12.9 |
|  | 1963 | 2.1 | 0.9 | 0.8 | 0.2 | 91.7 | 4.0 | 22.1 | 1.2 | 8.8 | 20.3 | 3.9 | 8.9 | 2.6 | 3.5 | 12.1 |
| Paper (64) | 1977 | 2.2 | 1.0 | 0.5 | 0.5 | 97.5 | 21.7 | 8.1 | 1.4 | 5.2 | 10.9 | 2.6 | 3.5 | 1.1 | 0.1 | 2.9 |
|  | 1963 | 0.3 | 0.1 | 0.0 | 0.0 | 98.5 | 38.9 | 7.8 | 0.8 | 2.1 | 4.8 | 0.5 | 2.8 | 0.7 | 0.3 | 4.5 |

NOTE
* In descending order of NIC shares in 1977 world total.
† NICs defined as middle income countries, excluding India, but including South European countries.
SOURCE
OECD (1978c).

developed countries are contained in Hayes Committee (1979), OECD (1978c) and Watkins and Karlik (1978), and occasional predictions are made about areas of greater danger in the future. The several commodity and global (UNIDO, SARU and OECD Interfutures) studies mentioned above also contain predictions about likely future patterns of trade. None of the papers at hand offer any suggestion that the destination of LDCs' exports will change dramatically in the foreseeable future. We may, therefore, expect that, subject to relative GNP growth rates and the rate of trade liberalisation, the pattern of LDC trade will continue to be the same as before: about two thirds going to the OECD and the rest to the other countries.

## V THE AGENTS OF EXPORT GROWTH

It may be analytically helpful to consider the agents behind the export growth of LDCs by grouping the types of activities involved in exporting as in Table 7.11.

This schematisation is simple, and does not contain various intermediate cases of joint ventures and the like, but it is useful in focusing on the two main determinants of the form of export activity: technology and marketing. The table is self-explanatory, but the following papers provide more detailed expositions: G. K. Helleiner (173, 975), A. Hone (1974) and de la Torre (1974).

The quantification of the role of local and foreign producers in the exports of LDCs is difficult because many countries do not collect (or publish) data on this basis.[26] The role of foreign buyers is even more obscure, and, apart from rather impressionistic accounts by Hone (1974) and Chenery and Keesing (1978) little is known of their activity except that they may be 'very important' in simple industries like clothing and radios. The overall role of MNCs in exports depends on the *balance* between products which are at the bottom of the above chart and those at the top.

Nayyar (1978) has pieced together bits of information from a diverse collection of sources on a number of countries, and UNCTAD (1978c), while rather short on hard data, provides a useful collection of references.[27] According to Nayyar, the share of MNCs in the exports of the seven NICs was: Hong Kong 10 per cent (1972); Taiwan, at least 20 per cent (1971); S. Korea, at least 15 per cent (1971); India, approximately 5 per cent (1970); Singapore, nearly 70 per cent (1970); Brazil, 43 per cent (1969); Mexico, 25–30 per cent (1970). No new estimates have become

TABLE 7.11   Export growth agents

| Characteristics of activity | | Agent of production | Main agent and form of export |
|---|---|---|---|
| Technology | Marketing | | |
| (a) Well diffused | Undifferentiated, low entry barriers | Local firm | Local firm (sometimes under licence from or in agreement with, foreign producer) |
| (b) Well diffused | Differentiated, brand names important, marketing channels important | Local firm | Foreign buyer (retailer or producer) subcontracting to local firm |
| (c) (i) Well diffused | Vertically integrated into international production/distribution structure | Local firm | MNC with ICA* |
| (ii) Well diffused | Vertically integrated into international production/distribution structure | Foreign affiliate | MNC |
| (d) New and complex | Differentiated/and or internationally integrated | Foreign affiliate | MNC (export-oriented production or offshore assembly)† |

NOTES

* Industrial Cooperation Agreements (of the sort common in East–West co-production arrangements).

† Export-oriented production refers to MNCs which have located entire production processes in LDCs, or have geared import-substitution activity to export (e.g. VW in Brazil); offshore assembly refers to MNCs 'sourcing' selected components from LDCs, keeping other processes in developed countries.

available on some of these countries, but the two or three that have suggest that the role of MNCs has been underestimated. Not only have foreign firms played important roles in the export of high-technology products, the dynamic role of these products in total manufactured exports have caused their role to increase over time. To review the more recent evidence:

(i) *S. Korea.* Sung-Hwan Jo (1976) has presented a sectoral breakdown of the foreign share of exports for 1974; this is reproduced in Table 7.12. The concentration of foreign exports in high-technology sectors is striking (with the exception of transport equipment). Sung-Hwan Jo notes that the total contribution of foreign firms to exports (including non-manufacturing) has been rising over time: from 1·8 per cent in 1962 to 13 per cent in 1969 and 28 per cent in 1974. The indications are that, as Korea shifts increasingly into high-skill areas, this share will continue to grow.[28]

TABLE 7.12   Foreign share of S. Korean exports (1974)

| Sector | Total value ($m) | Foreign share* ( %) |
|---|---|---|
| *All manufacturing* | *3,866* | *31.4* |
| Food | 49 | 8.6 |
| Textiles and apparel | 1,537 | 12.2 |
| Lumber and wood | 280 | 2.1 |
| Chemicals | 389 | 57.3 |
| Petroleum and products | 101 | 56.2 |
| Clay and products | 84 | 73.9 |
| Metals and products | 120 | 84.2 |
| Machinery and parts | 77 | 93.4 |
| Electrical and electronic | 474 | 88.6 |
| Transport equipment | 121 | 0.7 |
| Other | 632 | 12.6 |

NOTE
* Foreign share is defined as the share in total exports of companies that are foreign-owned.
SOURCE
Sung-Hwan Jo (1976).

(ii) *Singapore.* The 1975 *Census* of Singapore provides, for the first time, the distribution of exports by ownership. As Table 7.13 shows, nearly 85 per cent is accounted for by foreign majority-owned enterprises and another 7 per cent by foreign minority-owned enterprises. The industrial breakdown of these exports is not given, but it is likely that MNCs are concentrated into the high technology areas into which the high labour costs of Singapore (next only to Japan in East Asia) are pushing it.

(iii) *Mexico.* A study of foreign firms' exports in Mexico by Jenkins (1979) finds a distribution, shown in Table 7.14, not dissimilar to that of S. Korea. There are, however, some interesting differences between the

TABLE 7.13   Distribution of value of exports of Singapore by owner (1975)

| Type of enterprise | Value of exports (Sing. $m) | (%) | |
|---|---|---|---|
| Foreign majority and wholly foreign | 6,058.2 | 84.2 } | 91.1 |
| Foreign minority | 500.6 | 6.9 } | |
| Wholly local | 641.8 | 8.9 | |
| | 7,200.7 | 100 | |

SOURCE
*Census of Industrial Production 1975*, Government of Singapore.

TABLE 7.14   Exports by foreign-owned corporations in Mexico distributed by industries, 1974

| | Exports of foreign-owned corporations (million pesos) | Distri- bution (%) | Foreign-owned Corporations' share of total Mexican exports (%) |
|---|---|---|---|
| Food | 100.6 | 1.9 | 9.2 |
| Drink | 76.8 | 1.4 | 31.1 |
| Tobacco | 0.1 | — | 3.1 |
| Textiles | 34.1 | 0.6 | 1.4 |
| Clothing and footwear | 173.9 | 3.3 | 24.2 |
| Wood | 3.1 | 0.1 | 1.1 |
| Furniture | 1.4 | — | 2.2 |
| Pulp and paper | 21.1 | 0.4 | 22.8 |
| Printing and publishing | 229.4 | 4.3 | 64.2 |
| Leather | 7.7 | 0.1 | 9.9 |
| Rubber | 26.8 | 0.5 | 38.0 |
| Chemicals | 1,364.4 | 25.7 | 40.0 |
| Petroleum and coal derivatives | 11.8 | 0.2 | 3.1 |
| Non-metallic minerals | 87.4 | 1.6 | 12.0 |
| Base metals | 206.9 | 3.9 | 26.4 |
| Metal products | 100.0 | 1.9 | 15.4 |
| Non-electric machinery | 371.5 | 7.0 | 33.4 |
| Electric machinery | 592.2 | 11.1 | 90.4 |
| Transport equipment | 1,765.9 | 33.2 | 95.5 |
| Other | 139.8 | 2.6 | 26.6 |
| Total | 5,314.8 | 100.0 | 34.1 |

SOURCE
Jenkins (1979).

two NICs: petroleum products are predominantly national in Mexico and foreign in Korea, while transport equipment is the reverse. These reflect deliberate strategies on the part of the respective governments rather than strengths of local/foreign enterprises. In most other sectors, the advantage of MNCs in high technology sectors is very obvious.[29] (iv) *Brazil.* Data on the foreign share of total Brazilian exports are not available, but Table 7.15 shows the distribution (in 1973) of exports by 318 leading enterprises which account for nearly two-thirds of total industrial exports. MNCs account for over half, and public sector firms (a peculiarly Brazilian feature) for 39 per cent of the total. The dominance of MNcs in the high technology sectors is perhaps expected,

TABLE 7.15  Brazil: Share of Foreign and Domestic Firms in Exports by 318 Leading Enterprises, 1973

| Industry branch | *Export shares ( %)* | | |
| | | *National* | |
| | *MNC* | *(Private)* | *(Public)* |
| --- | --- | --- | --- |
| Mining | 15.9 | 0.3 | 83.8 |
| Non-metallic minerals | 74.3 | 25.7 | — |
| Metal | 10.5 | 7.2 | 82.3 |
| Machinery (Non electrical) | 80.1 | 19.9 | — |
| Electrical equipment | 91.8 | 8.2 | — |
| Transport equipment | 85.6 | 14.4 | — |
| Wood | 55.7 | 44.3 | — |
| Furniture | — | 100.0 | — |
| Paper | 75.3 | 24.7 | — |
| Rubber | 92.4 | 7.6 | — |
| Leather | 29.8 | 70.2 | — |
| Chemicals | 84.1 | 0.2 | 14.7 |
| Petroleum | 7.2 | — | 92.8 |
| Pharmaceutical | 100.0 | — | — |
| Cosmetics, soaps, etc. | 90.6 | 9.4 | — |
| Plastics | 75.0 | 25.0 | — |
| Textiles | 16.0 | 84.0 | — |
| Clothing and footwear | 57.7 | 42.3 | — |
| Food | 75.9 | 14.1 | — |
| Beverages | 87.6 | 12.4 | — |
| Tobacco | 78.2 | 21.8 | — |
| Printing and publishing | 100.0 | — | — |
| Miscellaneous | 27.2 | 72.8 | — |
| Total | 51.4 | 9.8 | 38.8 |

SOURCE
Unpublished study prepared for the ILO by M. L. Possas.

though the magnitudes are surprisingly large: it is their role in the more traditional sectors (food, beverages, tobacco, clothing) which is astonishing. There is, moreover, no reason to expect that the role of foreign enterprises has declined since 1973: if anything, it has probably increased in the more advanced sectors.

(v) *India.* While direct evidence on the relative performance of Indian and foreign firms in very recent years is not available, circumstantial evidence (Lall (1980)) and a general knowledge of the country suggests that the bulk of the expansion of high-skill exports (engineering goods and chemicals) has come from indigenous enterprises. An unpublished World Bank study of Indian export performance puts the MNC share of engineering exports at 14 per cent. In this,the Indian case differs significantly from other LDCs. The rate of expansion has been slow until fairly recently, and export growth in general (see Bhagwati and Srinivasan (1975) has been bedevilled by inward-looking policies. Despite this, there are lessons to be learnt about how far indigenous firms can go on their own, especially in the context of the accumulation of technological learning and (in some cases) the launching of independent R and D efforts.

There are, therefore, interesting differences in the pattern of export growth of the NICs. The large Latin American countries have relied most heavily on the direct involvement of MNCs in both production and marketing of exports. The Far Eastern NICs have, with the exception of Singapore, been less dependent on MNCs for production and more so for marketing, though this balance is changing to a more Latin American pattern as they move into more complex activities (here South Korean automobiles may become a notable exception).[30] India has, on the other hand, tended to 'go it alone' to a much greater extent. Its exports have not done well in the NIC league (this may be changing), but whether this is due to self-reliance or to other policies is impossible to gauge. Yugoslavia and Israel may also offer insights into the capabilities of indigenous enterprises, but these may be difficult to generalise to the Third World at large.

Two phenomena in this context deserve much more intensive study than they have received: 'offshore assembly' in LDCs and 'Industrial Cooperation Agreements' in Eastern Europe.

*Offshore assembly.* Despite the tremendous publicity that this form of activity has received in recent years, little is known about its dimensions, growth, distribution and future potential—with the major exception of US activity (and, to a lesser extent, West Germany and Holland). Nearly all developed countries have legislation[31] which encourages offshore assembly or provision of components made domestically, and it is likely that firms in all of them take advantage of the provision. However, no comprehensive data on its use in the UK, France, Belgium, Sweden or Switzerland are available.

There are, however, indications that imports under offshore assembly provisions (OAPs) are growing rapidly, much more so than imports of manufactures as a whole from LDCs. For instance, while manufactured non-OAP imports into the US rose by 12 per cent per year in 1966–72, OAP imports from LDCs rose by 60 per cent per year. For West Germany the respective figures are 11 and 36 per cent, and for the Netherlands 2 and 39 per cent. In 1970–6, total manufactured exports of LDCs rose by 305 per cent, while the value of processing done abroad (in LDCs) for the US rose by 530 per cent. The last two years 1975–7 have seen a slowdown in the growth of US OAPs imports,[32] apparently as a delayed reaction to the recession, but the longer-term implications of this are unclear. Certainly the economics of comparative cost would seem to dictate a reversal to the early trend of rapid shift of processing abroad.[33]

Tables 7.16 and 7.17 show the growth and origin of OAP imports by the US. Their heavy concentration in terms of activity (metal products, mainly electronics) and origin (Mexico) may be noted. In comparison with OAP imports by Germany, however, they are fairly diversified in both: German OAP imports are concentrated in South Europe (mainly Yugoslavia) and in clothing.

A final set of data (Table 7.18) on US imports by MNCs may be of interest. This shows imports from 'related parties' (i.e. affiliates of US MNCs) abroad as a proportion of total US imports from several LDCs by industry. Most of such imports probably come under OAPs, but a part may not. As earlier figures suggested, MNC affiliate exports from LDCs are heavily concentrated in the high-technology sectors— electrical machinery, non-electrical machinery and instruments. In traditional items their participation is far lower. There are occasional exceptions: Mexico and Colombia, for instance, have high related-party exports to the US even in some traditional items, but these can be explained by their location (in particular the 'border industries' of Mexico) and the particular strategies of large US retailers.

*Industrial cooperation agreements.* UNIDO and UNCTAD have both recently launched several studies[34] of the process of technology exchange and contractual trade between DCs and Eastern European countries (and Yugoslavia). Some developing countries (e.g. India and China) are now exploring the feasibility of such systems, where

.

TABLE 7.16   US OAP imports—total and from developing countries (1966–76) ($m.)

| Year | Total value | | | Dutiable value | | | Value of US components | | |
|---|---|---|---|---|---|---|---|---|---|
| | 807.00* | 806.30* | Total | 807.00* | 806.30* | Total | 807.00* | 806.30* | Total |
| *A. Total OAP imports* | | | | | | | | | |
| 1966 | 889.8 | 63.2 | 953.0 | 776.5 | 29.0 | 805.5 | 113.3 | 34.2 | 147.5 |
| 1967 | 931.6 | 103.5 | 1,035.1 | 785.0 | 52.2 | 837.2 | 146.6 | 51.3 | 197.7 |
| 1968 | 1,432.0 | 122.4 | 1,554.4 | 1,206.2 | 57.5 | 1,263.7 | 225.7 | 64.9 | 290.6 |
| 1969 | 1,646.2 | 192.6 | 1,838.8 | 1,307.3 | 89.4 | 1,396.7 | 338.9 | 103.2 | 442.1 |
| 1970 | 2,004.2 | 204.0 | 2,208.2 | 1,570.5 | 101.3 | 1,671.8 | 433.7 | 102.6 | 536.3 |
| 1971 | 2,566.4 | 199.4 | 2,765.8 | 2,030.8 | 75.1 | 2,105.9 | 535.6 | 124.3 | 659.9 |
| 1972 | 3,090.5 | 318.3 | 3,408.8 | 2,410.1 | 130.3 | 2,540.4 | 680.4 | 187.9 | 868.3 |
| 1973 | 3,784.5 | 462.6 | 4,247.1 | 3,025.4 | 212.9 | 3,238.3 | 759.1 | 249.7 | 1,008.8 |
| 1974 | 4,828.1 | 543.7 | 5,371.8 | 3,818.6 | 240.4 | 4,059.0 | 1,009.5 | 303.3 | 1,312.8 |
| 1975 | 4,707.8 | 453.4 | 5,161.2 | 3,703.9 | 191.6 | 3,895.5 | 1,003.9 | 261.8 | 1,265.7 |
| 1976 | 5,247.5 | 471.5 | 5,719.0 | 3,976.2 | 197.0 | 4,173.2 | 1,271.3 | 274.4 | 1,545.7 |

*B. OAP imports from developing countries*

| | | | | | | | | | |
|---|---|---|---|---|---|---|---|---|---|
| 1966 | 60.5 | 0.2 | 60.7 | 31.3 | 0.1 | 31.4 | 28.9 | 0.1 | 29.0 |
| 1967 | 98.2 | 0.8 | 99.0 | 42.4 | 0.4 | 42.6 | 55.3 | 0.5 | 55.8 |
| 1968 | 215.9 | 5.8 | 221.7 | 94.8 | 2.9 | 97.7 | 121.1 | 2.9 | 124.0 |
| 1969 | 368.1 | 26.7 | 394.8 | 159.6 | 17.7 | 177.3 | 208.5 | 9.1 | 217.6 |
| 1970 | 502.2 | 39.3 | 541.5 | 226.9 | 19.0 | 245.9 | 275.2 | 20.3 | 295.5 |
| 1971 | 597.7 | 54.8 | 652.5 | 289.8 | 24.3 | 341.1 | 307.9 | 30.5 | 338.4 |
| 1972 | 945.5 | 120.0 | 1,066.5 | 500.9 | 46.4 | 547.3 | 445.6 | 73.6 | 519.2 |
| 1973 | 1,323.7 | 233.6 | 1,557.3 | 743.6 | 101.8 | 845.4 | 580.1 | 131.7 | 711.8 |
| 1974 | 1,948.9 | 401.2 | 2,350.1 | 1,131.6 | 171.4 | 1,303.0 | 817.3 | 229.8 | 1,047.1 |
| 1975 | 1,896.8 | 364.9 | 2,261.7 | 1,088.1 | 150.6 | 1,238.7 | 808.8 | 214.3 | 1,023.1 |
| 1976 | 2,430.5 | 376.5 | 2,807.0 | 1,395.0 | 153.6 | 1,548.6 | 1,035.5 | 222.9 | 1,258.4 |

NOTE
* Item number on US Tariff Schedule.

SOURCE
Helleiner (1977).

214 *Developing Countries in the International Economy*

TABLE 7.17   Origin of OAP imports from LDCs into the US, 1976 ($ thousand)

| | Mexico | Taiwan | Singapore | Hong Kong | Korea (Rep.) | Malaysia | Haiti | Brazil | El Salvador | Dom. Rep. | Philippines | Costa Rica | Total | (%) |
|---|---|---|---|---|---|---|---|---|---|---|---|---|---|---|
| **Schedule 1: Animal and vegetable products** | | | | | | | | | | | | | | |
| dutiable | 74 | 2 | | | | | | | | | | | 76 | (0) |
| duty-free | 116 | 2 | | | | | | | | | | | 118 | |
| total | 190 | 4 | | | | | | | | | | | 194 | |
| **Schedule 2: Wood and paper products** | | | | | | | | | | | | | | |
| dutiable | 5,668 | | | | | | 4 | | | 155 | | | 5,827 | (0.4) |
| duty-free | 18,964 | | | | | | 18 | | | 671 | | | 19,653 | |
| total | 24,639 | | | | | | 22 | | | 826 | | | 25,480 | |
| **Schedule 3: Textiles and textile products** | | | | | | | | | | | | | | |
| dutiable | 40,004 | 270 | 92 | 658 | 2,643 | | 6,440 | | 5,228 | 5,669 | 11,853 | 5,746 | 79,198 | (5.9) |
| duty-free | 90,760 | 500 | 30 | 1,350 | 2,260 | | 20,626 | | 12,649 | 14,408 | 1,339 | 13,245 | 157,167 | |
| total | 131,364 | 770 | 123 | 2,009 | 4,904 | | 27,067 | | 17,873 | 20,078 | 13,192 | 18,992 | 236,365 | |
| **Schedule 4: Chemicals** | | | | | | | | | | | | | | |
| dutiable | | | | | | | | | | | | | | |
| duty-free | | | | | | | | | | | | | | |
| total | | | | | | | | | | | | | | |

| | | | | | | | | | | | | | |
|---|---|---|---|---|---|---|---|---|---|---|---|---|---|
| **Schedule 5: Nonmetallic minerals and products** | | | | | | | | | | | | | |
| dutiable | | | | | | | | | | | | | 1,242 (0.1) |
| duty-free | | | | | | | | | | | | | 196 |
| total | | | | | | | | | | | | | 1,438 |
| **Schedule 6: Metals and metal products** | | | | | | | | | | | | | |
| dutiable | 406,829 | 231,605 | 128,589 | 97,101 | 63,455 | 70,265 | 4,471 | 63,387 | 26,938 | 1,967 | 3,011 | 1,467 | 1,099,085 (81.3) |
| duty-free | 353,785 | 32,558 | 54,999 | 38,728 | 75,813 | 47,248 | 18,633 | 12,765 | 7,049 | 5,635 | 2,596 | 1,101 | 650,910 |
| total | 760,615 | 264,163 | 183,588 | 135,829 | 135,269 | 117,514 | 23,104 | 76,153 | 33,987 | 7,602 | 5,607 | 2,569 | 1,749,995 |
| **Schedule 7: Misc. specified products** | | | | | | | | | | | | | |
| dutiable | 58,787 | 26,356 | 20,344 | 26,204 | 6,216 | 11,708 | 10,593 | 213 | 1,983 | 189 | 3,597 | 32 | 166,322 (12.2) |
| duty-free | 81,127 | 16,153 | 17,386 | 10,125 | 8,968 | 9,076 | 17,301 | 124 | 2,153 | 615 | 4,756 | 70 | 167,854 |
| total | 139,914 | 42,509 | 37,731 | 36,330 | 15,184 | 20,785 | 27,894 | 337 | 4,137 | 805 | 8,354 | 102 | 334,076 |
| **Total** | | | | | | | | | | | | | |
| dutiable | 513,204 | 258,233 | 149,025 | 123,963 | 72,314 | 81,973 | 21,508 | 63,600 | 34,144 | 7,980 | 18,461 | 7,245 | 1,351,650 (100) |
| duty-free | 544,948 | 49,213 | 72,415 | 50,203 | 87,041 | 56,324 | 56,578 | 12,889 | 21,851 | 21,329 | 8,691 | 14,416 | 995,898 |
| total | 1,058,152 | 307,446 | 221,440 | 174,166 | 159,355 | 138,297 | 78,086 | 76,489 | 55,995 | 29,309 | 27,152 | 21,661 | 2,347,548 |
| Distribution of dutiable value (%) | 38.0 | 19.1 | 11.0 | 9.2 | 5.3 | 6.1 | 1.6 | 4.7 | 2.5 | 0.6 | 1.4 | 0.5 | 100 |

SOURCE
As Table 7.16.

TABLE 7.18   US related-party imports as a percentage of total imports of selected manufactured products, from selected newly industrialising countries, 1977

| | Textiles 65* (%) | Non-electric machinery 71* (%) | Electric machinery 72* (%) | Clothing 84* (%) | Footwear 85* (%) | Scientific instruments 86* (%) | Total mfg (%) |
|---|---|---|---|---|---|---|---|
| Israel | 18.9 | 32.8 | 62.9 | 14.0 | 0.0 | 13.0 | 18.2 |
| Portugal | 2.8 | 24.7 | 78.4 | 0.4 | 0.2 | 82.5 | 12.5 |
| Greece | 3.7 | 52.2 | 99.1 | 5.0 | 0.8 | 2.2 | 7.8 |
| Ireland | 36.3 | 78.5 | 77.8 | 8.3 | 42.2 | 91.7 | 59.0 |
| Spain | 1.5 | 36.3 | 32.6 | 3.7 | 10.1 | 7.8 | 24.1 |
| Yugoslavia | 0.1 | 14.0 | 2.0 | 2.3 | 2.2 | 3.6 | 4.9 |
| Argentina | 0.5 | 39.1 | 76.1 | 2.9 | 0.8 | 10.0 | 9.2 |
| Brazil | 9.2 | 59.9 | 95.3 | 18.0 | 0.5 | 38.4 | 38.4 |
| Colombia | 1.5 | 16.8 | 3.9 | 15.7 | 81.2 | 87.8 | 14.1 |
| Mexico | 9.6 | 87.8 | 95.6 | 68.0 | 60.9 | 93.6 | 71.0 |
| Taiwan | 13.1 | 19.3 | 58.1 | 1.2 | 3.1 | 67.1 | 20.5 |
| Hong Kong | 4.9 | 68.5 | 43.4 | 3.4 | 3.6 | 30.4 | 18.1 |
| India | 6.1 | 30.5 | 58.7 | 15.8 | 6.1 | 16.7 | 10.1 |
| South Korea | 5.5 | 64.2 | 67.3 | 7.1 | 1.8 | 12.1 | 19.7 |
| Malaysia | 0.2 | 83.2 | 97.0 | 1.9 | 0.0 | 91.9 | 87.9 |
| Philippines | 28.9 | 69.7 | 31.7 | 53.4 | 0.0 | 27.0 | 47.5 |
| Singapore | 4.3 | 90.5 | 97.0 | 0.5 | 0.0 | 85.3 | 83.3 |
| Haiti | 2.9 | 33.7 | 36.5 | 24.8 | 77.2 | 97.9 | 28.4 |
| Total all Third World | 7.8 | 63.5 | 75.2 | 11.5 | 4.4 | 51.2 | 37.0 |

NOTE
* SITC category.
SOURCE
G. K. Helleiner and R. Lavergne, 'Intra-Firm Trade and Industrial Exports to the United States', forthcoming in S. Lall (ed.), 'Special Issue on the Multinational Corporation', *Oxford Bulletin of Economics and Statistics*, November 1979.

technology is purchased and paid for by goods exported to the technology supplier, in sectors where existing production techniques have been fully assimilated and where foreign marketing is exceptionally difficult. This is a different species of offshore assembly activity, where the control and technology resides with the local firm but exports benefit by having the brand name and marketing networks of the DC firms. We shall not, for lack of data or case studies in LDCs, go any further into this area.

## VI  CONCLUSIONS

There is a remarkable diversity of experience among the LDCs in their efforts to promote the export of manufactured products. In aggregate terms, the last two decades have witnessed a rapid and sustained growth in such exports, some of the striking features of which are as follows:

The increase is highly concentrated in a few semi-industrialised economies, which at some stage have switched from import-substituting to export-orientated policies. Of these, S. Korea, Taiwan, Singapore, Brazil and Mexico may be expected to continue their fast export growth, Hong Kong may be left behind, and India (still half way between the two strategies) may be able to recover some lost ground in the more capital-intensive and sophisticated range of manufactures.

The product range exported by the NICs has been diversified very dynamically. In recent years goods requiring complex technologies, sophisticated skills and large scale production have emerged as the fastest growing components of exports, though traditional labour-intensive items still constitute the large bulk of LDC exports. Some NICs are even appearing as competitors on international technology markets, with their local enterprises vying with the established multi-nationals in selling turnkey plant, consultancy services and other types of manufacturing knowhow in industries with stable technologies. In the future, we should expect to find a greater incidence of intra-industry trade between DCs and LDCs rather than inter-industry trade, with the dividing line between the two regions based increasingly on technological innovation (rather than on factor endowments or the possession of general skills).

The role of MNCs in the export expansion of NICs has been variable, both across industries and across countries. MNCs have been over-whelmingly important in high-technology industries like electronics and heavy machinery in all NICs (except India). In more traditional industries they have played a lesser part (except perhaps for the 'border industries' of Mexico), and here local firms, especially in the East Asian NICs, have taken the initiative, but often in collaboration with retailing groups from the rich countries. By country, MNCs have been most important for the export expansion of the large Latin American countries, less so for the East Asian countries, and least for India. Their role is probably growing in the Latin American and East Asian NICs as they shift to more sophisticated products.

This survey has not gone into the very important problem of protectionism in the industrialised countries, though some indications of import penetration into the OECD have been given. There is a large current literature on this, and the indications (unfortunately) are that the problems it is concerned with are going to grow rather than diminish.

As is usual with such reviews, let me end by mentioning a few areas of useful future research. First, it is becoming apparent, as Chenery and Keesing (1978) note, that different LDCs are manifesting different sorts of comparative advantage in international trade. While all NICs are diversifying and moving into higher-skill activities, their paths are not the same. India, for instance, is in much 'heavier' industry than S. Korea; Brazil is more capital-intensive than Taiwan. It would be interesting to analyse the different determinants of comparative advantage for each NIC separately, and to link these to the nature of the economy, the policies pursued and the extent of foreign investment permitted.

Second, it would be valuable to extend such a study of comparative advantage in manufactured trade to a study of exports of technology. This would explore, first, the different specialisations revealed by the different NICs, and, second, the determinants of technological development which underlie technology exports.

Third, we need more 'dynamic' analyses of the trade performance of NICs. We need, in other words, to explain the current *changes* in the pattern of manufactured exports rather than its static pattern in a given year. This would seem to confirm or reject the presumptions advanced above about the process of skill accumulation and technological improvement in the NICs.

Fourth, much more work needs to be done, at the level of primary research, into the activities of MNCs in relocating industry internationally. While there are some well-publicised cases of MNC export activity, like electronics, there are still major gaps in our knowledge concerning: the role of multinational buying groups; the 'offshore assembly activities' of MNCs from the UK, France,

Switzerland, Japan and the Scandinavian countries; the export performance of MNCs in general, by activity, in a large number of LDCs; the nature of the comparative advantage of MNCs over local firms in different industries. The feasibility of extending Industrial Cooperation Agreements of the East European variety to LDCs can also bear further study.

Finally, the relationship between the export growth of the NICs and that of other LDCs is a large grey area: have the former preempted the potential growth areas of the latter? Or are they moving up the spectrum and creating room at the bottom for the newcomers? How are NICs dividing their exports between DCs and other LDCs, and why?

The investigation of these questions can have important bearings on theory and policy. The state of knowledge on this whole area is still in a stage of infancy, and much remains to be done.

NOTES

1. This paper is revised from a survey prepared as part of a larger project for the National Economic Development Office, London, in December 1978. I am very grateful to NEDO for permission to publish it, and for providing unpublished material on the subject. Larry Westphal of the World Bank and Vincent Cable of the ODI kindly sent various working papers. Gerry Helleiner gave me access to his collection of papers and the benefit of his valuable comments. M. Hanawa provided research assistance. Oxford Analytica was the focal point for the work done for NEDO. To all these my thanks.

2. There is no generally accepted definition of NICs, but all the lists in use today include the four 'star performers' from South East Asia (Hong Kong, S. Korea, Singapore and Taiwan) and the two big Latin Americans (Mexico and Brazil). Most include India, and some include the South European countries (with Yugoslavia); the widest lists also include such potential competitors as Iran, Malaysia, Indonesia and the Philippines. I prefer to confine 'NICs' to the four South East Asians, the two Latin Americans and (with some hesitation) India.

3. The most comprehensive and useful tabulation of LDC exports is by UNCTAD (1978a). More analytical reviews are given in UNCTAD (1978e), Blackhurst *et al.* (1977a), Keesing (1979), Morton and Tulloch (1977) and OECD (1978c).

4. These totals include petroleum products and unworked non-ferrous metals. Total manufactured exports excluding these came to $27 billion in 1976.

5. This exclusion mainly affects countries like Venezuela, Saudi Arabia, Netherland Antilles, Trinidad and Tobago, Kuwait, Chile, Zambia, Zaire, the Bahamas and so on.

6. The figures, taken from Keesing (1979), are somewhat different from UNCTAD's, presumably because of different definitions of manufactures.

7. See de Vries (1977) on Latin America, Westphal (1978) on Korea, and Chenery and Keesing (1978) on LDCs generally.

8. Of course, as long as product diversification and upgrading are possible, this will not be a constraint to the *overall* expansion of LDC manufactured exports. Recent experience does not suggest that market saturation will be a general problem for NICs.

9. With two modifications: China may emerge as a major exporter of labour-intensive products if its present policy of barter arrangements with the West succeeds; and the OPEC countries may not enter steel and automobile markets because of political changes in Iran.

10. It may be noted that India, while a small exporter in terms of value of machinery, is 'going it alone' in terms of basing its effort on indigenous companies. Its exports are embodied in 'project exports' (turnkey power generation plants) to a much greater extent than other LDCs (except perhaps Yugoslavia) whose exports are largely 'sourced' by MNCs in a vertically integrated production structure. In terms of domestic technological capability, therefore, this may represent a higher level of achievement, as argued in in Chapter 8.

11. Similar points are made by Pack (1975).

12. TELCO now has an affiliate in Malaysia, and some six licensees in other LDCs, assembling its trucks; it is perhaps the first automotive multinational to emerge from the developing world.

13. Also see Stegeman (1977) on the steel industry in the EEC.

14. For a recent survey of the world chemical industry and the prospects for Third World entrants (mainly OPEC and Mexico) see *The Economist* 7 April 1979.

15. The subject of Third World multinationals has, however, received some attention. See, in particular, the papers by Wells and Diaz-Alejandro in Agmon and Kindleberger (1977), Wells (1978) and Heenan and Keegan (1979).

16. Hirsch's regression results also place pharmaceuticals and fertilisers in the 'poor man's goods' category, but he considers this erroneous and due to statistical problems (p. 12).

17. With the exception of Cline and Rapoport (1978) mentioned below.

18. The UK Departments of Industry and Trade have prepared a detailed tabulation of the RCA over 1964–74 of 380 UK manufactured products, according to rising, falling or stagnant trends (see 1977). It also calculates the 'disadvantage' of each in competing with imports. Such a calculation, if systematically and regularly carried out, could be a useful guide to policy makers.

19. See Stern (1975) and Yotopoulos and Nugent (1976), ch. 17, for a good reviews up to 1974, and Giersch (1977) for a review of work done at the Kiel Institut für Weltwirtschaft, which leads in research in this area.

20. Also see Goodman and Ceyhun (1977) for a testing of both approaches on US data.

21. However, see Rahman (1973) for an analysis which tends to support the conventional Heckscher–Ohlin theorem that developed countries have an advantage in capital-intensive and LDCs in labour-intensive products.

22. For more evidence on the significance of non-standardisation as a separate source of comparative advantage see Finger (1975a).

23. Similar points are made in a study of US 'disruptive imports' by Watkins and Karlik (1978).

24. See Birnberg (1978), Blackhurst *et al.* (1977, 1978), Hayes Committee (1979), Helleiner (1978), IMF (1978), and the World Bank (1978) for assessments of penetration, protectionism and future prospects.

25. Watkins and Karlik (1978) discuss this for the U.S. case and provide a useful list of products where U.S. industry is likely to be vulnerable in the near future.

26. For analyses of the comparative export performance of local and foreign firms based on sample data see Cohen (1975), Lall and Streeten (1977), McAleese (1978) and Morgenstern and Müller (1976). McAleese deals with exports from Ireland, the others with LDCs.

27. See also Helleiner (1977) for recent data on the US and Canada.

28. However, the rapid expansion of the large, integrated trading companies (ITCs) – a unique feature of the Korean economy, at least in the Third World – may reduce this share. In 1978, according to a *Financial Times* special survey (2 April 1979, p. 19), the 13 registered ITCs contributed 32 per cent of total Korean exports. In 1979, 12 registered ITCs will account for about 40 per cent of exports; these firms have, between them, nearly 300 overseas trading branches. The ITCs have been the only successful replication of the Japanese 'sogo shosha' enterprises.

29. Also see Newfarmer and Mueller (1975) for data on the role of U.S. MNCs in the exports of Brazil and Mexico. In these areas, US firms increased their manufactured exports by 85 per cent (Mexico) and 120 per cent (Brazil) faster than the countries' total export growths in 1966–72.

30. The main automobile producer in Korea is Hyundai, one of the large ITCs mentioned above, which has put together a 'package' of foreign technology, design and critical components. There is also a general Motors – Daewoo joint venture, with half the capacity of Hyundai, which will also enter export markets in the near future. See the *Financial Times* special survey (2 April 1979, p. 24).

31. See Finger (1975b).

32. I am grateful to Gerry Helleiner for this information.

33. See Finger (1975b, 1976, 1977) for an analysis of the competitive pressures making for overseas processing.

34. See UNCTAD (1975a), (1976), (1977) and UNIDO (1978). For a study of the role of MNCs in Eastern Europe see Wilczynski (1976).

REFERENCES

Agmon, T. and Kindleberger, C. P. (1977), *Multinationals from Small Countries* (Cambridge, Mass.: MIT Press).

Balassa, B. (1978), 'Export Incentives and Export Performance in Developing Countries: a Comparative Analysis', *Weltwirtschaftliches Archiv*, pp. 24–61.

Banerji, R. (1972), 'Major Determinants of the Share of Manufactures in Exports: a Cross-Country Analysis and a Case Study of India', *Weltwirtschaftliches Archiv*, pp. 345–80.

Baranson, J. (1971), 'International Transfer of Automotive Technology to

Developing Countries' (New York: United Nations Institute for Training and Research).

Bhagwati, J. N. (1978), *Anatomy and Consequences of Exchange Control Regimes* (New York: NBER).

Bhagwati, J. and Srinivasan, T. N. (1975), *Foreign Trade Regimes and Economic Development: India* (New York: NBER).

Birnberg, T. B. (1978), 'Economic Effects of Changes in the Trade Relations between the Developed and the Less Developed Countries', Yale University (1978), prepared for the Overseas Development Council (mimeo).

Blackhurst, R., Marian, N. and Tumlir, J. (1977), *Trade Liberalization, Protectionism and Interdependence* (Geneva: GATT), Studies in International Trade, No. 5.

Blackhurst, R., Marian, R. and Tumlir, J. (1978), 'Adjustment, Trade and Growth in Developed and Developing Countries' (Geneva: GATT), Studies in International Trade, No. 6 (mimeo).

Bloomfield, A. I. (1978), 'The Impact of Growth and Technology in Nineteenth-Century British Thought', *History of Political Economy*, pp. 608–35.

Boatler, R. W. (1975), 'Trade Theory Predictions and the Growth of Mexico's Manufactured Exports', *Economic Development and Cultural Change*, pp. 491–506.

Bokerman, H. (1978), 'Trade and Trade-Related Aspects of Industrial Collaboration Arrangements' (Geneva: UNCTAD) (draft).

Cable, V. (1977), 'British Protectionism and LDC Imports', *ODI Review*, no. 2, pp. 29–48.

Cable, V. and Weston, A. (1978), 'ODI Study of EEC Access Barriers Facing South Asian Exports and South Asian/EEC Commercial Co-operation', (London: Overseas Development Institute) (mimeo).

Chenery, H. and Hughes, H. (1973), 'Industrialization and Trade Trends: Some Issues for the 1970's', in H. Hughes (ed.), *Prospects for Partnership* (Baltimore: Johns Hopkins Press).

Chenery, H. and Keesing, D. B. (1978), 'The Changing Composition of Developing Country Exports' (Washington, DC: World Bank) (mimeo).

Cline, W. R. and Rapoport, A. I. (1978), 'Industrial Comparative Advantages in the Central American Common Market', in W. R. Cline and E. D. Dalgado (eds.), *Economic Integration in Latin America* (Washington, DC: Brookings Institution).

Cohen, B. (1975), *Multinational Firms and Asian Exports* (New Haven: Yale University Press).

Cortes, M. (1978), 'Argentina's Technical Development and Technology Exports to other LDCs' (Washington, DC: World Bank) (mimeo).

de la Torre, J. (1974), 'Foreign Investment and Export Dependency', *Economic Development and Cultural Change*, pp. 133–50.

de Vries, B. (1977), 'Export Growth in the New World Environment: the Case of Latin America', *Weltwirtschaftliches Archiv*, pp. 353–79.

Donges, J. B. (1976), 'A Comparative Survey of Industrialization Policies in Fifteen Semi-Industrialized Countries', *Weltwirtschaftliches Archiv*, pp. 626–51.

Donges, J. B. and Reidel, J. (1977), 'The Expansion of Manufactured Exports in Developing Countries: an Empirical Assessment of Demand and Supply Issues', *Weltwirtschaftliches Archiv*, pp. 58–87.

Fels, G. (1972), 'The Choice of Industry Mix in the Division of Labour between Developed and Developing Countries', *Weltwirtschaftliches Archiv*, pp. 71–121.

Finger, J. M. (1975a), 'A New View of the Product Cycle Theory', *Weltwirtschaftliches Archiv*, pp. 79–99.

Finger, J. M. (1975b), 'Tariff Provisions for Offshore Assembly and the Exports of Developing Countries', *Economic Journal*, pp. 365–71.

Finger, J. M. (1976), 'Trade and Domestic Effects of the Offshore Assembly Provision in the U.S. Tariff', *American Economic Review*, pp. 598–611.

Finger, J. M. (1977), 'Offshore Assembly Provisions in the West German and Netherlands Tariffs: Trade and Domestic Effects', *Weltwirtschaftliches Archiv*, pp. 237–49.

Frankena, M. (1973), 'Marketing Characteristics and Prices of Exports of Engineering Goods from India', *Oxford Economic Papers*, pp. 127–32.

Freeman, C. (1978), 'Technical Innovation and British Trade Performance', in F. Blackaby (ed.), *De-Industrialisation* (London: Heinemann).

GATT (1978), *International Trade 1977/78* (Geneva: GATT).

Giersch, H. (1978), 'Problems of Adjustment to Imports from Less Developed Countries' (Kiel: Institut für Weltwirtschaft) (mimeo).

Goodman, B. and Ceyhun, F. (1977), 'US Export Performance in Manufacturing Industries: an Empirical Investigation', *Weltwirtschaftliches Archiv*, pp. 525–55.

Hayes Committee (1979), 'The Newly Industrializing Countries and the Adjustment Problem' (London: Foreign and Commonwealth Office).

Heenan, D. A. and Keegan, W. J. (1979), 'The Rise of Third World Multinationals', *Harvard Business Review* (January–February) pp. 101–9.

Helleiner, G. K. (1973), 'Manufactured Exports from Less Developed Countries and Multinational Firms', *Economic Journal*, pp. 21–47.

Helleiner, G. K. (1975), 'Transnational Enterprises, Manufactured Exports and Employment in Less Developed Countries', *Economic and Political Weekly*, pp. 247–62.

Helleiner, G. K. (1976), 'Industry Characteristics and Competitiveness of Manufactures from Less-Developed Countries', *Weltwirtschaftliches Archiv*, pp. 507–24.

Helleiner, G. K. (1977), 'Intra Firm Trade and the Developing Countries' (Toronto: University of Toronto) (mimeo).

Helleiner, G. K. (1978), 'The New Industrial Protectionism and the Developing Countries' (University of Toronto: prepared for UNCTAD) (mimeo).

Helleiner, G. K. (1979), 'Structural Aspects of Third World Trade: Some Trends and Some Prospects', *Journal of Development Studies* (forthcoming).

Hirsch, S. (1977), *Rich Man's, Poor Man's and Every Man's Goods: Aspects of Industrialisation* (Tübingen: Mohr).

Hone, A. (1974), 'Multinational Corporations and Multinational Buying Groups: Their Impact on the Growth of Asia's Export of Manufactures', *World Development*, pp. 145–50.

Institut für Weltwirtschaft (1978), 'Analysis of the Determinants of consequences of a Selective as Compared to an Unselective Research and Development Strategy' (Kiel) (mimeo).

International Monetary Fund (1978), *The Rise in Protectionism* (Washington, DC).

Jenkins, F. (1979), 'The Export Performance of Multinational Corporations in Mexican Industry', *Journal of Development Studies*, pp. 89–107.

Katz, J. and Ablin, E. (1978a), 'Technologia y Exportaciones Industriales: Un Analysis Microeconomico de la Experencia Argentina Reciente', *Desarollo Economico*, pp. 87–132.

Katz, J. and Ablin, E. (1978b), 'From Infant Industry to Technology Exports: The Argentine Experience in the International Sale of Industrial Plants and Engineering Worlds' (Buenos Aires: IDB/ECLA), Research Programme in Science and Technology, Working Paper 14 (mimeo).

Kawaguchi, Y. (1977), 'The LDCs' Comparative Advantage and Industry Characteristics in Japan' (Washington, DC: World Bank) (mimeo).

Kawaguchi, Y. (1978), 'Non-Electrical Machinery Exports by LDCs' (Washington, DC: World Bank) (mimeo).

Keesing, D. B. (1979), 'World Trade and Output of Manufactures: Structural Trends and Developing Countries' Exports' (Washington, DC: World Bank) Working Paper 316.

Lall, S. and Streeten, P. (1977), *Foreign Investment, Transnationals and Developing Countries* (London: Macmillan).

Lall, S. (1979), 'Transfer Pricing in Assembly Industries: a Preliminary Analysis of the Issues in Malaysia and Singapore' (London: Commonwealth Secretariat) in *Industrial Cooperation*, Commonwealth Economic Papers, No. 11.

Lall, S. (1980), 'Developing Countries as Exporters of Technology', *Research Policy*, vol. 9 no. 1 (January), and Chapter 8, below.

Lipsey, R. E. and Weiss, M. Y. (1976), 'Exports and Foreign Investment in Manufacturing Industries' (New York: National Bureau of Economic Research), Working Paper 131 (mimeo).

Little, I. M. D., Scott, M. F. and Scitovsky, T. (1970), *Industry and Trade in Some Developing Countries* (London: Oxford University Press).

Lowinger, T. C. (1971), 'The Neo-Factor Proportions Theory of International Trade: An Empirical Investigation', *American Economic Review*, pp. 675–81.

McAleese, D. (1978), 'Outward Looking Policies, Manufactured Exports and Economic Growth: The Irish Experience', in M. J. Artis and A. R. Nobay (eds.), *Proceedings of the 1977 AUTE Conference* (Oxford: Blackwell).

Michaely, M. (1978), 'Income Levels and the Structure of Trade', paper presented to the Symposium on *The Past and Prospects of the Economic World Order* (Stockholm) (August).

Michaelet, C. A. (1977), 'International Subcontracting' (Paris: OECD) (mimeo).

Morgenstern, R. D. and Müller, R. (1976), 'Multinational versus Local Corporations in LDCs: an Econometric Analysis of Export Performance in Latin America', *Southern Economic Journal*, pp. 399–406.

Morrison, T. K. (1976), *Manufactured Exports from Developing Countries* (New York: Praeger).

Morton, K. and Tulloch, P. (1977), *Trade and Developing Countries* (London: Croom Helm).

Nayyar, D. (1978), 'Transnational Corporations and Manufactured Exports from Poor Countries', *Economic Journal*, pp. 59–84.

Newfarmer, R. S. and Mueller, W. F. (1975), *Multinational Corporations in Brazil and Mexico: Structural Sources of Economic and Non-Economic Power*, (Washington, DC: GPO).

OECD (1977), 'Midway Through Interfutures: International Division of Industrial Labour' (Paris) (mimeo).

OECD (1978a), 'Intermediate Results of the Interfutures Research Project: Long Term Perspectives of the World Car Industries' (Paris) (mimeo).

OECD (1978b), 'Midway Through Interfutures: Trade' (Paris) (mimeo).

OECD (1978c), 'The Impact of Newly Industrializing Countries of the Pattern of World Trade and Production in Manufactures' (Paris: Dept. of Economics and Statistics) (mimeo).

Pack, H. (1975), 'Export Prospects for the Mechanical Engineering Sector' (Washington, DC: World Bank) (mimeo).

Pack, H. (1978), 'The Capital Goods Sector in LDCs: a Survey' (Washington, DC: World Bank) (mimeo).

Pang Eng Fong and Lim, L. (1977), *The Electronics Industry in Singapore* (Singapore: Economic Research Centre).

Pavitt, K. *et al.* (1978), 'Technical Effort and Economic Performance: Some International Comparisons' (University of Sussex: Science Policy Research Unit) (mimeo).

Plesch, Phi Anh (n.d.), 'Developing Countries' Exports of Electronics and Electrical Engineering Products' (Washington, DC: World Bank).

Rahman, A. H. M. (1973), *Exports of Manufactures from Developing Countries* (Rotterdam: Rotterdam University Press).

Reidel, J. (1975), 'The Nature and Determinants of Export Oriented Direct Foreign Investment in a Developing Country: a Case Study of Taiwan', *Weltwirtschaftliches Archiv*, pp. 505–27.

Rhee, S. and Westphal, L. E. (1978), 'A Note on Exports of Technology from the Republics of China and Korea' (Washington, DC: World Bank) (mimeo).

Sang, Chul Suh (1975), 'The Development of a New Industry Through Exports: The Electronics Industry in Korea', in W. Hong and A. O. Krueger (eds.), *Trade and Development in Korea* (Seoul: Korea Development Institute).

Sciberras, E. (1977), *Multinational Electronics Companies and National Electronics Policies* (Greenwich: JAI Press).

Sharpston, M. (1975), 'International Subcontracting', *Oxford Economic Papers*, pp. 94–135.

Stegeman, K. (1977), *Price Competition and Output Adjustment in the European Steel Market* (Tübingen: Mohr).

Stern, R. M. (1975), 'Testing Trade Theories', in P. B. Kenen (ed.), *International Trade and Finance* (London: Cambridge University Press).

Stern, R. M. (1976), 'Some Evidence on the Factor Content of West Germany's Foreign Trade', *Journal of Political Economy*, pp. 131–41.

Stobaugh, R. M. (1971), *The International Transfer of Technology in the Establishment of the Petrochemical Industry in Developing Countries* (New York: UN Institute for Training and Research).

Sung-Hwan Jo (1976), 'The Impact of Multinational Firms on Employment and Incomes: The Case Study of South Korea' (Geneva: ILO) World Employment Programme, W.P. 12.

Tracy, M. (1977a), 'Tariff Preferences and Multinational Firm Exports from

Developing Countries', in W. G. Tyler (ed.), *Issues and Prospects for the New International Economic Order* (Lexington: Lexington Books).

Tracy, M. (1977b), *Trade Preferences for Developing Countries* (London: Macmillan).

Turner, L. and Bedore, J. (1978/79), 'The Trade Politics of Middle Eastern Industrialization', *Foreign Affairs* (Winter) pp. 306–22.

Tyler, W. G. (1972), 'Trade in Manufactures and Labour Skill Content: the Brazilian Case', *Economia Internazionale*, pp. 314–34.

Tyler, W. G. (1976), *Manufactured Export Expansion and Industrialization in Brazil* (Tübingen: Mohr).

UK Government (1978), 'Britain's Pattern of Specialization' (London: Department of Industry) (mimeo).

UK Government (1978), 'UK International Competitiveness and the Role of R & D' (London: Department of Industry) (mimeo).

UK Government (1977), 'Revealed Comparative Advantage in UK Manufactured Products' (London: Departments of Industry/Trade) (mimeo).

UNCTAD (1975a), *The Scope of Trade Creating Industrial Cooperation at Enterprise Level between Countries having Different Economic and Social Systems*, TD/B/490/Rev. 1.

UNCTAD (1975b), *International Subcontracting Arrangements in Electronics Between Developed Market-Economy Countries and Developing Countries* (New York: UN) TD/B/C.2/144, Supp. 1.

UNCTAD (1976), *Industrial Cooperation and Collaboration Arrangements in the Context of Industrial Re-structuring*, TD/185/Supp. 3.

UNCTAD (1977), *International Cooperation for Industrial Development, Re-structuring and Trade*, TD/B/C.2/179.

UNCTAD (1978a), *Supplement 1977 to the Handbook of International Trade and Development Statistics* (Geneva).

UNCTAD (1978b), *The International Market Power of Transnational Corporations: a Case Study of the Electrical Industry* (Geneva) ST/MD/13.

UNCTAD (1978c), *Transnational Corporations and Expansion of Trade in Manufactures and Semi-Manufactures* (Geneva) TD/B/C.2/197.

UNCTAD (1978d), *Dynamic Products in the Exports of Manufactured Goods from Developing Countries to Developed Market-Economy Countries, 1970 to 1976* (Geneva) UNCTAD/ST/MD/18.

UNCTAD (1978e), *Review of Recent Trends and Developments in Trade in Manufactures and Semi-Manufactures* (Geneva) TD/B/C.2/190.

UNIDO (1978), *Industrial Cooperation: Evolution of the Context, Problems and Approaches* (Vienna) UNIDO/ICIS. 68

Walter, I. (1978), *Trade and Structural Adjustment Aspects of the International Iron and Steel Industry: the Role of the Developing Countries* (Geneva) UNCTAD/ST/MD/16.

Watanabe, S. (1972), 'International Subcontracting, Employment and Skill Promotion', *International Labour Review*, pp. 425–9.

Watkins, S. B. and Karlik, J. R. (1978), *Anticipating Disruptive Imports* (Washington, DC: US Senate, Joint Economic Committee).

Weiss, F. D. (1978), *Electrical Engineering in West Germany: Adjusting to Imports from Less Developed Countries* (Tübingen: Mohr) Kieler Studien 155.

Wells, L. T. (1978), 'Foreign Investment from The Third World: the Experience of Chinese Firms from Hong Kong', *Columbia Journal of World Business* (Spring) pp. 39–49.

Westphal, L. (1978), 'The Republic of Korea's Experience with Export-led Industrial Development', *World Development*, pp. 347–81.

Wilczynski, J. (1976), *The Multinationals and East–West Relations* (London: Macmillan).

Wolter, F. (1977a), 'Factor Proportions, Technology and West German Industry's International Trade Patterns' *Weltwirtschaftliches Archiv*, pp. 250–67.

Wolter, F. (1977b), 'Adjusting to Imports from Developing Countries: the evidence from a Human Capital Rich—Natural Resource Poor Country', in H. Giersch (ed.), *Reshaping the World Economic Order* (Tübingen: Mohr) pp. 97–130.

World Bank (1978), *World Development Report 1978* (Washington, DC).

Yotopoulos, P. A. and Nugent, J. B. (1976), *Economics of Development: Empirical Investigations* (New York: Harper & Row).

# 8 Developing Countries as Exporters of Industrial Technology[1]

## INTRODUCTION

This paper presents a preliminary attempt to describe and assess the emergence of domestic enterprises in the Third World as exporters of capital and technology. The evidence, while scattered and incomplete, points to a clear trend: the more industrialised of the developing countries have experienced a considerable measure of technological progress in recent years, and have now developed the capability to generate and transfer a large range of industrial technologies. This has important implications for policies in respect of technological development and transfer in developing countries. It also has major implications for conventional theories about the role of developing countries in the international division of innovative effort and industrial skills, and so about their long-term comparative advantage in trade and production.

The copious literature that exists on the economics of technological innovation and diffusions,[2] on the one hand, and on technology transfers to, and its absorption by, developing countries,[3] on the other, has (with a few exceptions noted later) ignored the generation of technology by indigenous enterprises in poorer countries. It has, therefore, failed to recognise a number of significant changes which have been occurring in recent years and which may be summarised as follows.

(i) A significant amount of technological change is taking place in the modern industrial sectors of developing countries, particularly in those with relatively long experience of manufacturing and with broad-based capital-goods sectors. Such 'change' is defined broadly. It encompasses increases in productivity and efficiency from simple learning by doing (which is entirely expected), advances in the capability to completely appraise, design, construct and manage complex and advanced industrial processes (which is less so), and a manifestation of the ability to

228

adapt, change, improve and extend these technologies (which is unexpected). Developing countries are, in other words, increasingly able to assimilate, imitate and innovate in areas of medium to high technology.

(ii) The nature of technological change in developing countries is very different from that in industrialised countries. The skills and needs on which it is based guide and constrict its progress: but it *is* progress, and it calls for skills and resources which are not normally attributed to developing countries. The nature of this progress is discussed below.

(iii) Such progress has enabled a number of countries to emerge as exporters of technology in several forms and to diverse areas. This 'revealed comparative advantage' of developing countries calls for a rethinking of some modern trade theories which assign an importer's role to them in skill and technology intensive industries. It is not *general* requirements of skills and technology which increasingly determine comparative advantage between industrialised and developing countries, but *particular* forms of skill and technology, based on specific investments in R and D, organisation and marketing, within industries (regardless of whether they are 'high' or 'low' technology in conventional terms) that decides such advantage.

(iv) The basis of comparative advantage in technology exports by developing countries is threefold: the low cost of highly skilled manpower; the suitability of the technology to conditions in developing countries; and the 'unpackaged' nature of technology sales.

(v) Technological progress occurs within both indigenous and foreign firms in developing countries (this paper is concerned only with the former), but it is likely that the nature and strength of links with firms abroad negatively affects the speed, depth, and external benefits of such progress in indigenous enterprises. TNCs may be very effective agents of transmitting modern technology to developing countries, but strong ties with them (in the form of ownership and control) or a total technological dependence on them (in the form of continuous and passive licensing) can reduce the capability of indigenous enterprises to assimilate, improve and export certain forms of technology. It follows from this reasoning that developing countries should exercise greater selectivity and restriction in buying foreign technology than most of them currently practice. This prescription, for partially 'delinking' domestic technology from foreign technology, especially in capital-goods manufacture, is based on the need to protect investments in inherently new risky and costly activities in information creation.

## THE EVIDENCE

Technology can be transmitted across countries through a large variety of channels, ranging from official technical aid, migration, scientific communication and exports of equipment to licensing, direct investment, turnkey projects, training and consultancy services. This paper is concerned with technology exports *by indigenous enterprises in response to market forces*, and with technology in the sense of adding directly to the industrial capabilities of the host economy.[4] It concentrates on the following five forms of technology exports: setting up of entire production systems (turnkey projects); engineering consultancy for manufacturing industry; licensing of know-how and managerial/technical services; direct investment; and training schemes. Exports of capital equipment, though growing in significance and sophistication, are excluded from discussion, as are government ventures undertaken on a cooperative or technical assistance basis with other governments, outside the market framework.

The bulk of information used in this paper is on India, and it comes from periodicals rather than from academic studies. The main sources are the official weekly news bulletin of the government on trade, *Economic and Commercial News* (New Delhi) and the official periodical on the public sector, *Lok Udyog*; these are not referred to in detail because of the frequency with which they have been used. Jha (forthcoming) provided invaluable background on Indian technological development in the public sector. For other countries, sources are published articles and newspaper reports, references to which are given individually.

TURNKEY PROJECTS

The sale of turnkey projects by local enterprises in developing countries has grown impressively in recent years. The main exporters of complete industrial plants seem to be India, Argentina, Brazil and Mexico. Their relative importance is impossible to gauge with precision because of the lack of data, but the evidence at hand suggests that India is the most important, with Argentina some way, and the others much further, behind in terms of the number, range and sophistication of exports involved.

Indian exports of plant in relatively simple industries like textiles, sugar processing and cement have been common for some time now. Recent years have, however, witnessed the export of complete plants in sophisticated activities like large scale electrical generation;[5] complete automatic telephone exchanges;[6] electrical transmission equipment; pharmaceutical plants; fertiliser plants; oil transmission, blending and electronic control systems; steel plants (some of these were subcontracted to India by Russia); machine tool factories; assembly of light two-wheelers; and several other types of manufacturing plant. Both public and private sector firms are active, but the former seem to predominate in the 'heavy' end of the business.

The development of turnkey activity by Indian firms has been the next logical step from the export of individual items of capital equipment in those industries where the complexity of new manufacturing facilities makes it more economical and rational to order the entire plant from one supplier than to buy bits and pieces and put them together. The supplier then designs, makes and starts up the entire plant—clearly, the skill and technology required are far more advanced than the manufacture and export of individual items of equipment.[7]

Argentina has been exporting turnkey plants in meat refrigeration, fruit processing, cotton oil extracting, shipyard technology and baking facilities,[8] while Brazil and Mexico have been exporting turnkey plants for steelmaking.[9] Much of their export has taken place within Latin America, but the Brazilian firm Cia. Vale do Rio Doce is setting up a steel plant as far away as Egypt.

On the evidence available, other developing countries seem to have little or no exports of turnkey plant.[10] Countries like Taiwan, South Korea, Hong Kong and Singapore, which have grown rapidly by exporting labour-intensive products rather than domestically designed capital goods, do have a comparative advantage in technology in the manufacture of these labour-intensive products. They exploit this advantage mainly by means of direct investment (see below), since they lack a broad indigenous capital-goods production base on which to build up technology for the design and construction of complete factories (as they develop capital-goods production, however, there is little doubt that they will enter this area with the same dynamism that they have exhibited elsewhere).[11]

ENGINEERING CONSULTANCY

The growth of the size, complexity and specificity of a large number of industrial processes has made them 'consultancy-intensive': these include steel, nonferrous metals, power generation, mining and the continuous-process industries like oil, petrochemicals, chemicals, paper and others.[12] Consultants are essential to the evaluation, design, commissioning and construction of a large number of industries: in a sense they embody the 'pure' technology of setting up modern industry, choosing the technique of production, buying the capital goods and overseeing the construction.

A number of indigenous engineering consultants from developing countries are exporting their services. As the growth of consultancy skills is organically linked to experience of building capital goods and setting up plants, the same countries that export turnkey technology also lead in exporting consultancy technology. India, with over a hundred consultancy enterprises, has the widest range of such services, since it possesses the experience, not only of operating particular industries (which gives rise to consultancy specialised in those technologies), but also of constructing a wide range of investment goods (which gives rise to experience of a *family* of related technologies). Mexico, Brazil and Argentina follow with a more limited range of services.

Consultancy firms from India who are active abroad include large private companies like Dastur and Co. (exporting consultancy for iron and steel to several developing and industrialised countries), Dalals (chemical technology), Industrial Development Consultants (general consulting), and Tata Consulting Engineers (thermal power technology),[13] as well as several public sector consulting and manufacturing enterprises: HMT in machine tools; ITI in telecommunications; National Industrial Development Corporation, NIDC, in chemicals, diesel engine plants, machine tools, pumps, food processing, mining machinery, textiles, paper and industrial planning and forecasting, selling to developed as well as developing countries;[14] Engineers India Ltd, in fertiliser, petroleum and chemical industries, singly and in collaboration with TNCs (like Kellogg of the US and Snam Progetti of Italy) from developed countries; Rail India Technical and Economic Services Limited (RITES), in railway technology; Metallurgical and Engineering Consultants Ltd. (MECON), in metallurgical technology, which is providing services to several foreign enterprises, including Altos Hornos de Mexico, itself a technology exporter. Apart from manufacturing, Indian consulting firms are also exporting services in hotel management, civil works, construction of dams, townships and airports and in feasibility studies and project designs of all sorts.

Mexico has a well-known independent consulting firm, Bufète Industrial, for general industrial services, as well as a public sector firm, PEMEX, specialising in petroleum technology. The Brazilian state-owned PETROBRAS also sells petroleum technology; its

SONDOTECNICA sells general consulting services. There are other consulting organisations of indigenous origin in countries like Argentina exporting manufacturing knowhow, but lack of data prevents the citing of specific examples (Diaz-Alejandro (1977) mentions Argentinian consulting firms, along with Mexican and Brazilian ones, as operating abroad in Latin America).

In general, therefore, India seems to lead in the field of exporting engineering consultancy. Its firms span an enormous range of technologies and serve an impressive collection of countries, including some developed ones like Italy, West Germany, Hungary or the UK; they subcontract from established TNCs certain jobs they can perform more cheaply; and they serve as vehicles for exporting knowhow and capital goods developed and produced in India.

LICENSING AND OTHER SERVICES

There is little evidence on the sale of patents and trade-marks abroad by developing countries. It is possible that some industrial processes developed by local enterprises in developing countries have been sold as such to other countries in return for fees or royalties, but the incidence of this seems to be rather low. The sale of brand-names must, for obvious reasons, be even more limited.

The reason for this may lie in the nature of developing countries' comparative advantage. The technology that these export is the result not of major innovations in products or processes, but of imitating, adapting or improving on known technologies: their advantage thus lies in their accumulated experience and the low cost of the people who possess it. It is an advantage which is difficult to embody in a saleable design, patent or blueprint (though this may change as their improvement become more distinct).

As for the export of managerial and technical services (the transfer of disembodied knowhow), there is some evidence that this is taking place on a growing scale.[15] Managerial services are exported by hotel chains from India, for instance, while HMT has recently agreed to send over 100 technicians to Libya to help operate a machine-tool factory. Indian Railways has provided technicians to a number of countries in Africa, while Indian steel companies have provided personnel to Iran. It is very likely that similar exports take place within Latin America.

DIRECT INVESTMENT

This is one aspect of technology exports by developing countries—
'Third World TNCs'—which has attracted some attention in recent
work.[16] Some data on direct investments by developing countries—but,
especially for Asia, rather incomplete—are presented in statistical form
in Tables 8.1–8.3.

Table 8.1 shows Latin American parent companies and affiliates in
the region in 1976. Argentina seems to lead the field in Latin America in

TABLE 8.1  Latin American parent companies and their affiliates in the region,
1976

| | Location of affiliate | | Location of parent company | |
|---|---|---|---|---|
| Country | Number | Percentage of total | Number | Percentage of total |
| Argentina | 2 | 1.2 | 69 | 34.0 |
| Bolivia | 14 | 8.2 | 2 | 1.0 |
| Brazil | 25 | 15.3 | 15 | 7.4 |
| Colombia | 14 | 8.2 | 21 | 10.3 |
| Costa Rica | 5 | 2.9 | 3 | 1.5 |
| Cuba | 1 | 0.6 | 2 | 1.0 |
| Chile | 3 | 1.7 | 12 | 5.9 |
| Ecuador | 55 | 32.3 | 4 | 2.0 |
| El Salvador | 1 | 0.6 | 2 | 1.0 |
| Dominican Republic | 2 | 1.2 | 1 | 0.5 |
| Guatemala | 1 | 0.6 | 2 | 1.0 |
| Guyana | — | — | 1 | 0.5 |
| Honduras | 2 | 2.4 | 1 | 0.5 |
| Jamaica | 4 | 2.4 | 3 | 1.5 |
| Mexico | 3 | 1.7 | 19 | 9.4 |
| Nicaragua | 2 | 1.2 | 2 | 1.0 |
| Panama | 2 | 1.2 | 1 | 0.5 |
| Paraguay | 4 | 2.4 | 3 | 1.4 |
| Peru | 7 | 4.1 | 16 | 7.9 |
| Trinidad and Tobago | 1 | 0.6 | 1 | 0.5 |
| Uruguay | 9 | 5.3 | 2 | 1.0 |
| Venezuela | 6 | 3.5 | 21 | 10.3 |
| Binational | 4 | 2.4 | — | — |
| Total | 170 | 100.0 | 203 | 100.0 |

SOURCE
United Nations Centre on Transnational Corporations (1978) p. 231.

TABLE 8.2  Intraregional direct investment stock, Latin America, by host country and by country of origin, 1971 and latest available year ($m.)

| Countries of origin | Argentina 1974 | Brazil 1971 | Brazil 1976 | Chile 1974 | Colombia 1971 | Colombia 1975 | Ecuador 1971 | Ecuador 1976 | Mexico 1974 | Venezuela 1970 | Venezuela 1974 |
|---|---|---|---|---|---|---|---|---|---|---|---|
| Argentina | — | 7.5 | 13.3 | 0.1 | 0.1 | 0.9 | — | 4.5 | 5.3 | ... | 11.2 |
| Brazil | 9.1 | — | — | 5.2 | 0.4 | 2.0 | — | 4.4 | 7.2 | ... | 1.6 |
| Chile | — | — | — | — | 0.1 | 0.1 | 2.7 | 7.9 | — | ... | 0.7 |
| Colombia | 0.9 | 2.6 | 6.9 | 5.3 | 1.4 | 7.5 | — | 4.0 | — | ... | 1.2 |
| Mexico | 1.0 | — | — | 0.8 | 0.3 | 0.8 | — | 1.4 | 3.6 | ... | 4.7 |
| Peru | 0.9 | — | — | — | 4.6 | 4.7 | — | — | — | ... | — |
| Uruguay | 2.2 | 8.3 | 12.0 | 1.7 | 10.5 | 19.3 | 3.4 | 10.3 | 1.8 | — | 2.1 |
| Venezuela | 0.1 | 4.2 | 9.0 | — | 0.3 | 0.3 | — | — | 3.5 | — | — |
| Latin American Free Trade Area | — | — | 1.0 | — | 0.3 | 0.3 | — | — | — | — | — |
| Sub-total | 14.2 | 22.6 | 42.2 | 13.1 | 17.7 | 35.6 | 8.1 | 32.5 | 21.4 | 6.7 | 21.5 |
| Panama | 80.6 | 80.1 | 275.0 | ... | 36.4 | 53.7 | ... | 4.0 | 119.3 | ... | ... |
| Bermuda | ... | 12.2 | 39.0 | ... | 0.7 | 1.0 | ... | — | ... | ... | ... |
| Netherlands Antilles | ... | 75.2 | 192.0 | ... | 13.4 | 20.2 | ... | — | ... | ... | ... |
| Bahamas | ... | 21.7 | 66.0 | ... | 13.7 | 10.0 | ... | — | ... | ... | ... |
| Other | ... | — | 39.0 | ... | 1.2 | 3.9 | ... | — | ... | ... | ... |
| Total | ... | 211.8 | 653.2 | ... | 83.1 | 124.4 | ... | 36.5 | ... | ... | ... |

SOURCE
United Nations Centre on Transnational Corporations (1978, p. 246).

TABLE 8.3   Intra-regional direct investment stock,* Asia, by host and origin, 1976 ($m.)

| Origin | Host country or territory | | | |
| --- | --- | --- | --- | --- |
| | Thailand† | Indonesia | Philippines | Hong Kong |
| Malaysia | 5.0 | 42.7 | . . . | . . . |
| Hong Kong | 10.9 | 728.3 | 14.2 | . . . |
| India | 2.4 | 19.4 | . . . | . . . |
| Philippines | 0.9 | 272.1 | — | 3.4 |
| Singapore | 2.2 | 115.6 | . . . | 13.4 |
| Korea, Republic of | . . . | 107.4 | . . . | . . . |
| Thailand | — | . . . | . . . | 29.7 |
| Other Asian developing countries | 22.1 | 102.9 | 3.1 | 7.3 |
| Japan | 74.5 | 1,216.6 | 124.2 | 56.8 |

NOTES
* The data for Hong Kong, the Philippines and Thailand refer to assets as reported in the sources listed above; the data for Indonesia refer to approved projects as of 1976.
† 1975.
SOURCE
United Nations Centre on Transnational Corporations (1978, p. 247).

terms of the number of affiliates abroad (69), though the figures do not differentiate between investments made abroad by indigenous enterprises and by affiliates of TNCs. Colombia, Mexico, Brazil and Peru also have 15 or more foreign affiliates. The main recipient of foreign investment, by number of affiliates, is Ecuador, followed at a considerable distance by Brazil. Table 8.2 shows stocks of foreign investment by Latin American TNCs. The main recipients by value of intra-regional investment are Brazil, Colombia and Ecuador. The role of tax havens like Panama and Netherlands Antilles is curious: they seem to export enormous sums of capital, mainly to Brazil, but this is clearly simply a channelling of funds through them by enterprises from developed countries. The Latin American firms that go transnational seem to specialise in consumer products requiring low to medium level technology, like electrical products, food products and metal products.

In Asia (Table 8.3), Hong Kong seems to be the major investor abroad, and Indonesia the major recipient of Third World capital. The Philippines, Singapore and South Korea also invest in excess of $100 million each abroad—again, the precise final origin of the investments is not discernible. Part of these investments may be from TNCs from developed countries, but part are clearly from local enterprises: Hong

Kong textile firms have, for instance, gone to other countries to enlarge their access to Europe under the GSP scheme (which allocates quotas by country). A large number of Singapore firms operate in Malaysia to serve the local Chinese community by making noodles and pickles, as well as operating small engineering works and textile factories.[17] Some Korean firms have even applied to Portugal for permission to set up an electronics plant there.[18] As with Latin American firms, these transnationals seem to specialise in small-scale operations using well-diffused technology.

India is not a major direct investor in terms of the value of its capital abroad, though Table 8.3 understates its activity because it excludes Indian investments in Malaysia, its major host country. India had, by mid-1976, 134 direct investments abroad, of which 64 were already in operation and the rest were under construction. The largest number (36) were in Malaysia; the rest were scattered through Asia, Africa and even some in developed countries (for oil engines, hardboard, asbestos, cement and magnetic wires). There is apparently also a wholly owned HMT assembly plant for machine tools in Luxembourg, and a number of private Indian enterprises are actively exploring the possibility of investing in the Irish Republic. In general, India restricts its foreign investors to small minority positions, and to contributing their equity in the form of equipment and machinery from India.[19] The former requirement may account for the apparently small value of flows of capital from India.

The industries in which Indian private sector investments are made abroad range from relatively simple ones like textiles, flour mills, soft drinks, foundries and tanneries, to relatively complex ones like integrated palm oil extraction, steel products, paper products, diesel engines, pharmaceuticals, rubber products, light electrical equipment, auto components and so on. The technology used is 'mature' and the scale of operations generally small. The public sector firm HMT has also entered into joint venture agreements abroad to produce various types of machine tools; the most recent instance being an agreement with the Kenyan Industrial and Commercial Development Corporation.[20] It will not be at all surprising that other large public firms, now involved in exporting products, technology and personnel, also get involved in equity participation abroad. This would represent the entry of 'Third World TNCs' into a distinctly higher level of skills and technology.

The tendency so far has been, as represented by Wells (1977) and Lecraw (1977), to regard Third World TNCs as specialising in 'mature' or 'low' technology, small-scale production and 'low' marketing (i.e.

little product differentiation, competition by prices rather than by advertising) activities. While this is true of the majority of cases, there is a risk of associating these enterprises too generally with rather low levels of skill, simple products and out-dated technology. The technology used is certainly 'mature' in almost all cases, but the levels of complexity and skill involved in manufacturing operations may be quite high. Furthermore, some Third World TNCs are starting to enter capital goods industries where extremely complex techniques, large scales and the ability to keep pace with innovation, are required. There are limitations to their present capabilities, as will be noted below, but these should be more clearly defined than they are at present, and they will change over time.

TRAINING PROGRAMMES

The only information available on technology transfers by training schemes comes from India, where a large variety of activities are under way by private and public enterprises to help other developing countries. One of two training centres in Singapore is run by Tata's, a private enterprise. The government owned Central Machine Tools has helped to set up a metal working research institute in Iran as well as providing training facilities for Iranian engineers in India. The National Industrial Development Corporation is setting up industrial estates in Guyana; it is equipping a Technical Training Institute in Malaysia; and it has helped Iran to set up Technolog, an engineering consulting enterprise. Hindustan Machine Tools is establishing an advanced training centre in Iraq and planning an industrial estate to service a machine tool factory in Iran. Besides this, there is a constant exchange of personnel between Indian enterprises and technology institutions and other developing countries. The export of knowhow to set up training centres is the provision of technology to absorb technology: its importance is so obvious as not to require further emphasis. However, it is the ability of developing countries to provide this sort of technology that is worth remarking upon. Until now, such technology has been virtually monopolised by the industrialised world.

This concludes the survey of the evidence. To summarise, then, nearly every country which has reached a certain stage of industrial development exports some form of technology. There are, however, noteworthy differences between the exporters. (*a*) Small economies which have followed liberal trading policies and achieved high growth rates in exports of simple manufactured products (South East Asia) mainly export small-scale, relatively mature technology for the manufacture of consumer goods, mainly in the form of direct investment. (*b*) Large economies, which have followed protectionist import-substitution policies but liberal policies on direct investment by TNCs (the big Latin American countries), export technology by means of direct investment in sectors where local industry flourishes (Argentina being outstanding by virtue of the strength of its indigenous enterprise), but not in those high-skill areas where TNCs are predominant. They export relatively little technology in complex and high-skill industries by turnkey jobs or consultancy—the main exceptions are complex industries where the state has played an active manufacturing role. (*c*) India, with highly protectionist policies towards imports of goods, technology and foreign investment, combined with a heavy emphasis on the development of local enterprise and domestic science and technology, seems to be in a category of its own. It exports low to medium technology, for the manufacture of consumer, intermediate and light capital goods, by means of direct investment (though lack of foreign exchange has kept this channel constricted till recently); it also exports technology of much greater complexity and skill, often in direct competition with established TNCs, by means of turnkey projects and consultancy services.

It may be noted that in most cases technology exports have grown to complement exports of manufactured products. For products of relatively simple technology, technology has generally been exported by means of direct investment, often in collaboration with local importers, to forestall threats to established markets.[21] As products move up the skill/technology scale, technology exports occur more to promote sales of producer goods than to protect established markets for consumer goods. In some cases, however, where a great deal of broad industrial expertise has been built up (Dastur's of India), technology sales may be unrelated to sales of products from the home country, and may even displace them if the technology supplier sources its purchases on a world-wide basis (i.e. the experience accumulated through indigenous industrialisation may be saleable, even if the final product is not).

Since nearly all technology exports by developing countries have been based on 'minor' or imitative technological activity, the initial input of technology has had to come from the industrialised countries. For foreign-owned or controlled enterprises, this has generally come in the form of direct transfers of designs, capital goods, patents and knowhow from their parent companies. For locally owned or controlled enterprises (including 'joint ventures' with equal participation by foreign and local enterprises) the input has come in the form of licensing (with the technology supplier actively assisting in the initial transfer) or imitation (with the local enterprise 'going it alone').[22] This section is only concerned with locally controlled enterprises: here the role of licensing and foreign technology transfer has, at least till now, been much more significant than that of imitation. Once the initial transfer of licensed technology has taken place, of course, the enterprises have had to devote considerable effort to assimilating, adapting and reproducing it at home and, later, abroad. This process, and the limits on the complexity, novelty and market orientation of the technology exported, are considered in more detail below. At this point it may only be suggested that two factors seem equally crucial in building up technology exports: the *initial transfer* from abroad (usually by licensing or joint ventures) and the *subsequent assimilation and adaptation*. Given these, the competitive edge of developing country enterprises lies in the much lower cost of their skilled manpower which can effect technology transfer to other Third World countries. However, the mere process of importing technology, without the technological base to assimilate it, will not lead to local technological development; and local technological effort, without a measure of foreign input, may be wasteful and unproductive.

## THE NATURE OF DEVELOPING COUNTRIES' TECHNOLOGICAL CAPABILITIES

This section provides some tentative explanations of the growth and pattern of technological exports by developing countries. Such a task should ideally be undertaken after a thorough and detailed examination has been made of technological change within the enterprises that develop from being technology importers to being exporters. Clearly, technology exports are only the tip of the iceberg of innovative activity that is taking place in newly industrialising countries. Given the evidence available, however, and the relative paucity of studies of innovation in developing countries,[23] we must perforce rely on casual empiricism and *ad hoc* theorising.

There are severe problems inherent in the measurement and precise definition of technological change, which have been amply discussed in the literature,[24] and which are not relevant to the purpose in hand. Taking the evidence on technology exports as valid proof of a great deal of successful technological activity, what we are concerned with here is:

how 'innovative' is this activity? What skills and other inputs does it require? What determines its pace?

Developing countries are clearly imitators and adapters of technology, not major innovators, and even as imitators they have been among the laggards rather than leaders. This does not imply, however, that technical progress does not take place among the laggards. On the contrary, there are, given the initial foreign impetus in the form of new techniques, several types of change that occur, which can be represented by various types of 'learning' processes. These may be grouped into elementary, intermediate and advanced stages, each with two subcategories.

ELEMENTARY

(a) Simple 'learning by doing', whereby an imported technology is unchanged, but its utilisation is made more efficient simply through the experience of *workers*.
(b) 'Learning by adapting', whereby small changes are made within a plant to a given technology by *shop-floor technicians, managers* and *engineers*, to raise productivity within a given technology, or to adapt the product to particular needs. Both types of elementary learning may occur, given a certain level of skills, in every sort of industrial activity,[25] regardless of foreign or local ownership.

INTERMEDIATE

(a) 'Learning by design', whereby imported equipment and processes are replicated, and knowledge is gained by *design engineers* and *capital-equipment manufacturers* of industrial processes. A move from elementary to intermediate stages clearly requires the establishment of an indigenous capital-goods industry.
(b) 'Learning by improved design', the next step in the design of equipment, where productivity raising changes (albeit of a 'minor' nature) are made, or the equipment is scaled down, adapted to use local raw materials or to operate in local conditions and with given operating and maintenance skills. Here design engineers generally need the help of a separate *R and D* department. This step requires a greater degree of local autonomy and control over the process of basic design of capital goods.

ADVANCED

(a) 'Learning by setting up complete production systems', whereby the ability is acquired, not just to produce items of equipment, but to engineer and tailor entire factories or plants to specific needs. At this stage the industry acquires the capacity to provide *consultancy services* and undertake *turnkey jobs*. This stage requires a great deal of accumulated experience in using and reproducing particular technologies or families of technologies, based on manufacturing and designing capital goods.

(b) 'Learning by innovation', whereby R and D department or a separate research institution, extends into *basic research and development*, and is able to offer new processes or new products, or both. This 'basic' R and D may be of a different order of magnitude from 'basic' R and D done in advanced countries, since it may not be on the frontiers of new technology. However, it may still lead to processes (as has happened, say, for chemical products) or new products, which are different from those first imported into the country. This final stage requires not only an advanced and diversified level of manufacturing, but a substantial research effort and high scientific skills.

This three fold categorisation of 'minor' technological progress helps to illustrate the complex and diverse nature of current technological activity in developing countries. There are different levels of 'innovativeness' involved, rising in skill and manufacturing requirements with each stage. Different developing countries have, according to their strategies and sizes, gone up to different levels: India has gone the whole way, with several enormous independent laboratories scattered through the country engaged in 'basic' R and D, and with an expanding emphasis on in-house design and development facilities in many manufacturing enterprises. Other countries have gone less far, with most stopping at (or even before) the elementary level, and some larger ones going somewhat further in particular industries (note that we are talking of indigenous enterprises only). *Some* learning is always going on, almost by definition, but the capability to export technology only comes when the enterprise has 'learnt' a particular saleable skill, which others do not possess or which it can offer more cheaply than others.

Different forms of technology exports may require different types and levels of technological 'learning' by the enterprise concerned, and different stages of industrial development in the economy where it originates. For an economy with no local capital-goods production in the relevant activity, technology exports may be based upon elementary learning which gives the capability to put together, and efficiently (and cheaply) manage, a 'package' based on imported capital goods and consultancy services. In the main, such exports will take the form of direct investment for the production of standardised consumer goods and 'mature' intermediate goods.[26] In exceptional cases, however, they may also take the form of consultancy services in a particular activity based on long experience of a given industry. For an economy which does possess a capital-goods base in the sector concerned, technology exports may require elementary learning by the exporting enterprise where it is, again by direct investment, producing standardised consumer or intermediate goods abroad.[27] They may, however, require intermediate and advanced learning where exports take the form of direct investment for the production of capital goods, or of turnkey jobs, consultancy and other services for the setting up and running of diverse or complex production systems. The more diversified and highly skilled the content of technology exports by a country, the more developed are its capital-goods sectors, and the longer is its experience with different forms of industrial activity likely to be. Furthermore, the success of technology exports will depend not only on 'technological learning', narrowly defined, but also on the success of the enterprise in correctly organising its internal structure and coupling research, managerial, financial and marketing activities.[28]

The role of the capital-goods sector in generating, diffusing and stimulating technological progress has been emphasised since the writings of Marx by several scholars, most recently by Rosenberg (1976) and Stewart (1977). Clearly, only local capital goods can *embody* new techniques generated locally, and only they can *transmit* new techniques across industries. In their absence, only small adaptations can be made to imported production processes. The skills required for technical learning here are of *engineering and design* rather than those of science. Minor innovations in machinery-making seems to be based on practical engineering experience in designing new equipment. Science-based innovation becomes significant if major innovations—completely new products and processes—are envisaged. This requires more sophisticated and expensive R and D facilities, much larger scale, much more risk-bearing ability and a much longer waiting period, than developing countries can (and should) afford. However, the line between minor and major innovations is hard to draw, and countries like India may well be able to contribute some major innovations in the foreseeable future.[29]

In sum, the development of indigenous technological capability is dependent upon the following: the length of experience with industrial activity; the capability of the economy to assimilate technology (which is a function partly of the availability of skilled work force and partly of experience itself); the organisational and managerial capabilities of the firms concerned; the existence of a capital-goods sector (which depends largely on the size of the economy and the sort of industrialisation strategy pursued); and the technological policy followed by the government. We have already remarked on the first four factors; let us turn now to the last one.

The evidence presented in the previous section seemed to indicate that different policies pursued by developing countries had produced different patterns of comparative advantage in technology exports. Thus, even given large internal markets, relatively developed industrial sectors and reserves of skilled manpower, certain countries had not revealed a competitive ability in exporting indigenous technology as diverse or complex as others. This difference may be traced to the *protection and promotion given to the process of learning* at different levels by the governments concerned, in particular to the protection and promotion of learning within locally controlled enterprises *vis-à-vis* the import of technology via direct investment by TNCs.

Countries that have permitted a free inflow of technology by means of foreign-controlled affiliates have not exported technology of the diversity and complexity shown by those that have followed a deliberate policy of protecting the learning process in locally controlled enterprises. India has, for instance, reached a considerably higher level of sophistication in technology exports than Brazil, mainly because the former has fostered the absorption of technology by local firms, forced them to develop their own designs and protected the development of local in-house R and D facilities, while Brazil has done little along these lines in its capital-goods industries.[30] Interestingly enough, in Brazil itself (and in Mexico), where the government has stepped in by setting up state-owned enterprises (as in petroleum) or by providing state assistance (as in steel), local enterprises have developed the capability to sell technology abroad.

The heavy electrical equipment industry provides another interesting case in point. The performance of Bharat Heavy Electricals Limited (BHEL) has already been noted above: it has become a technology exporter of world class, not able to compete in the largest projects, but certainly a worthy entrant into the next level of competition. In Brazil, on the other hand, where a thriving indigenous sector existed in the 1950s, TNCs have made such enormous inroads into the 'high' technology heavy equipment section of the industry that domestic enterprises have virtually been wiped off the map.[31] Lack of official protection and technological support, and predatory pricing policies and takeovers by TNCs, have combined to limit local technological capability to the elementary level (implementing basic designs supplied from abroad), while in India this capability has developed to the level of providing large turnkey jobs and consultancy in international markets.

It is not difficult to understand the need for official protection and promotion of technological development. Learning at the elementary levels is, given a certain capability, *inherent to the production process*, regardless of who owns the facilities. Any progress to higher levels, however, requires the fostering of indigenous technological learning activity in capital-goods industries which go beyond implementing imported designs, and which require replicating facilities, expertise and skills already in existence abroad. Local design and research activities involve, in other words, considerable learning costs, and they also entail a certain element of risk and delay. Enterprises owned by TNCs or directly dependent upon them for skill-intensive basic design and development work in capital-goods production are unlikely to undertake these risks, delays and costs: given the availability of established and proven capabilities abroad, the private assessment of investing in further developing indigenous technology is likely to be negative. A similar assessment may also be made by locally controlled enterprises: thus, a policy of technological generation must incorporate measures not only for the local production of capital goods, but also for fostering local design, subsidising and cajoling expenditure on design and development, and providing, where necessary, back-up in terms of scientific infrastructure.

Even given all the right conditions for technology generation, however, the pace and limits of successful technological learning will differ from industry to industry. Developing countries' comparative advantage is greatest: where learning involves the design of discrete items rather than of continuous processes; when the techniques involved are not subject to rapid change; when the skills required are based on production/design activity rather than on science-based R and D; when the commercial application of technology does not depend on large-scale marketing and promotion abilities[32] (the acquisition of marketing knowhow seems to involve a longer learning process, and even more investment, than production technology); when minimum efficient scale does not entail very long production runs or very large orders; and when the technology can be subjected to adaptations, scaling down, or simplification, to suit the conditions of developing countries. These conditions indicate, very roughly, the areas in which learning is likely to be most successful in the initial stages of entry into world technology markets. In later stages, however, the advantage of developing countries may change and expand: the process is so dynamic, and evidence so limited, that it is difficult to forecast with any pretence to accuracy.

Under present circumstances, nevertheless, these considerations point to an evolving division of technological work between nations whereby the more industrialised of the developing countries, given their cost advantages and experience, increasingly undertake transfers to other developing countries of technologies which are intensive in *their* types of 'high' skills. These technologies may well be able to meet substantial portions of the needs of these newly industrialising countries. They can also enter developed countries to perform costly skilled jobs where their cheap manpower can provide a massive advantage (e.g. engineering consultancy in certain industries, 'software' components of various technologies, project construction management, detailed design work).

High technology firms in the industrialised countries can participate in the technological progress of developing countries in one or both of two ways: subcontracting certain skill-based activities to Third World technology firms, or establishing affiliates in developing countries directly to exploit their pool of low cost, experienced and skilled manpower. There are signs that both these courses are being adopted,[33] but they are, as is noted below, likely to follow upon, rather than lead, local technological progress.

COSTS AND BENEFITS

(a) This section starts by considering the situation for the *technology exporting countries*.

The *benefits* of building up an indigenous technological capability which is internationally competitive are numerous. There is the earning of foreign exchange resulting directly from technology exports, and indirectly from the stimulation of exports of capital goods, services and intermediate products over the longer run.[34] There is establishment of an international reputation and winning of goodwill, and there is the experience gained from foreign operations and skill accumulated by tackling unfamiliar tasks, all of which add cumulatively to export competitiveness. But these are, like the exports themselves, just the tip of the iceberg of the benefits from technological advance internally. The development of an independent capability to assimilate, adapt and improve on technology is such a major step forward in the progress of industrialisation that its benefits are difficult to assess quantitatively or even to describe with precision. They range from the building up of a scientific and technical infrastructure capable of rationalising and reducing the cost of technology imports and of producing more 'appropriate' technology,[35] the setting up of ancillary and small subcontracting industries,[36] the better use of local raw materials and the creation of new skills, to less tangible but equally important benefits resulting from a stronger sense of self-reliance and confidence.

However, the *costs* of striking out on a serious policy of technology generation should not be underestimated. There are enormous direct expenses involved in setting up a scientific infrastructure, and the Indian experience does not—so far at least—seem to justify the establishment of large laboratories divorced from the production enterprises. A considerable amount of progress can, however, be made by in-house design, research and development expenditures in manufacturing enterprises without recourse to external scientific establishments. The direct costs of promoting technological activity in manufacturing units, especially when the country possesses large numbers of trained engineers, are unlikely to be high. The indirect costs may, however, be considerable. The essential period of learning—with its inherent costs in terms of lost output, mistakes made, low quality, high prices, delays in reaching efficiency frontiers—before a technological capability is built up, is painful. The pangs diminish after a 'technological takeoff' occurs, but the first stages inevitably involve inefficiencies of various kinds.

In this context it should be noted that, where a developing country possesses the basic requirements for creating technology locally, the benefits are likely to be greater by localising technological development in *indigenous* rather than foreign enterprises. Affiliates of TNCs may be able to provide very modern and complex technology much faster and more efficiently than a local imitator can. The very nature of their technological links abroad, however, necessarily reduces the extent of learning locally. An economy which remains dependent on foreign sources for the bulk of its technological activity remains incapable of generating a certain amount of local technological capability which recent experience proves to be well within its long-term comparative advantage. There is a strong case for confining dependence on foreign technology to activities where local technology is incapable of keeping up with science-based or very rapidly advancing technology abroad.

It is possible, of course, that TNCs themselves can help to reduce the constriction placed by technological dependence by establishing R and D facilities in developing countries, employing nationals and producing products and processes suitable to their conditions. As noted above, this has already started to happen, but its scope is bound to be fairly limited and it can serve only to complement local efforts, not to replace them.[37] The broad-based and basic knowhow which is needed for technological development in industry as a whole cannot be provided by foreign laboratories—it is experience which only local efforts can generate. Moreover, local enterprise can probably ensure a broader diffusion of innovations and stronger linkages with domestic manufacturers than can research offshoots of TNCs. The contribution of foreign establishments is, paradoxically, likely to be greater the more advanced is local technological prowess, in the sense that a more experienced indigenous sector is likely to attract the relocation by TNCs of more complex and more basic R and D activities.

The contrast between TNC affiliates and local establishments should not, however, be drawn too sharply. There is a variety of intermediate positions between wholly owned foreign subsidiaries, on the one hand, and wholly local enterprises, on the other. Some of these may prove satisfactory, indeed the most effective, vehicles of local technological activity: a locally controlled joint venture may, for instance, be able to engage in significant indigenous technological activity while drawing upon its foreign partner for assistance in exceptionally difficult problems and for access to technological information from industrialised countries. Others may not be so beneficial: a foreign-controlled joint venture may not, for instance, be willing to shift basic design and development work from its established centres to a developing country, or even a locally controlled firm may not wish to invest in local R and D. This is an area where generalisations are extremely difficult, not only because of the anecdotal nature of available information, but also because of the inherently unpredictable *individual* factor—different entrepreneurs in identical situations wish to retain different degrees of dependence of foreign technology. It seems reasonable to argue, nevertheless, that official policies can successfully be adopted which, on balance, draw forth a greater degree of indigenous technological effort, and these would tend to favour the maximum possible degree of local control compatible with access to foreign technology.[38] The issue of correct policies will be discussed further below.

(b) Let us now turn to the *technology importing* countries.

The *benefits* of importing technology from other developing countries arise from its lower cost, greater appropriateness to local conditions, or both. The cost element is likely to predominate in sophisticated technologies where there is little adaptability but where the input of skilled manpower is very large, as with design and consultancy work. A number of firms from advanced countries (especially the UK) have admitted their uncompetitiveness in some fields of standard engineering consultancy by handing over, losing or subcontracting jobs to Indian firms. The significantly lower cost of Third World consultants fuelled allegations by countries like Saudi Arabia that Western contractors are 'ripping them off' by submitting grossly inflated bids.[39]

The appropriateness element is likely to be more important in turnkey jobs and direct investments. Facilities provided by developing countries are likely to be of smaller optimum scale, use more labour-intensive techniques, be better suited to supply conditions in developing countries, be more responsive to demands for exporting, for local control and local training, and produce goods more adapted to popular needs, than those provided by the industrialised countries.[40] The experience gained by developing countries in assimilating foreign technology can provide them with a significant edge in transferring the same technology to another country as compared with the original supplier. Take the well-known example, documented by Baranson (1967), of the Cummins diesel engine plant in India. Baranson's study, conducted in the early stages of assimilating the technology, came to rather pessimistic conclusions about domestic technological and local-supply capabilities. Indeed, his descriptions of the requirements for successful diesel-engine manufacture made it sound unlikely that a developing country could ever undertake it efficiently.[41] Yet within a decade the inefficient technology importer had turned into an efficient exporter: the same Indian firm is now operating affiliates abroad to make diesel engines. No doubt its accumulated learning has enabled it to transfer the technology at lower cost (to both parties) than had been incurred in the first instance, and than would have been incurred if the original TNC had made the second transfer.

The extra *costs* of buying technology from a developing country rather than a developed one arise precisely from getting small-scale 'appropriate' technology. These may be the out-dated nature of technology, lower quality of output, lower export potential and smaller financial and technological capabilities of the supplier. How important and widespread these costs are cannot be assessed now but, since developing country exports are not (with a few notable exceptions like the offshore assembly of electronic components) in high R and D, rapid-change, export-based products in any case,[42] these are unlikely to be very high. Existing data (for instance, Lecraw (1977) do not indicate that low quality is a problem with technology exported by Third World TNCs.

There are also the potential indirect costs of a new form of technological dependence, of getting predigested, adapted technology which can inhibit comparable efforts locally. This is a real problem. The answer to it lies in correct technological policies within each developing country. In so far as a significant element of such policies lies in 'unpackaging' foreign technology and promoting local training, enterprises from other developing countries have shown themselves much more willing to get 'unpackaged', and to provide training and support to local efforts, than the established TNCs. In fact, a number of transactions have started as export sales, and have developed into turnkey projects and into joint ventures at the request of the buyer: the exact opposite of the real TNCs, which have come in with a highly profitable package of technological and other advantages which they have, naturally, been reluctant to dismantle.[43]

This is not to argue that as Third World enterprises gain in size, spread and reputation, they will necessarily remain better 'corporate citizens' than the TNCs of the developed countries. It is possible that they may also resort to transfer pricing, market allocation, monopolistic pricing or local technology-inhibiting practices which are feared in the operations of the traditional technology suppliers. Two points should, however, be noted in this context. First, many of the undesirable practices associated with the established TNCs are based precisely upon the possession of a profitable monopolistic 'package' (of capital, organisation, brand-names, patents, skills, R and D, and the like): since Third World technology suppliers possess mainly specific skills and not a larger 'package', they *cannot*, by their very position, use monopolistic practices to the extent that developed-country firms can. Secondly, there may be greater moral and political pressures on Third World technology sellers to be sensitive to needs for local control, local technology creation and increased exports on the part of recipient countries (see Wells (1977)). A longer-term strategy should aim to reinforce and perpetuate these pressures to ensure that the unfortunate frictions that have arisen from past TNC operation are not experienced again.

In sum, therefore, the purchase of technology from developing countries seems to offer considerable economic benefits. It also offers benefits of a broader sort. In the context of present negotiations on the New International Economic Order, where the building up of a common bargaining position and awareness of interdependence by the developing countries is of prime importance, the growth of intra-Third World trade in technology is of obvious significance. It contributes to greater independence of Third World countries as a group, strengthens their position in buying technology and, most importantly, leads to a more acceptable division of effort (and hopefully more fruitful cooperation) between established and emerging industrialisers.

NOTES

1. This paper was presented to seminars at the Institut für Weltwirtschaft, Kiel, and the Science Policy Research Unit, Sussex; I am grateful to the participants for comments. I would also like to acknowledge information provided by Prem Jha, Surojit Ghosh, Jorge Katz, Isabel Molina and Rustum Lalkaka.
2. Recent summaries and discussions of the literature may be found in David (1975), Freeman (1974), Johnson (1975), Mansfield (1968), Parker (1974) and Rosenberg (1976).
3. See, for instance, articles by Cooper and Stewart in Cooper (1973), Baranson (1969), various studies by UNCTAD under the general title of 'Transfer of technology to developing countries', and surveys by Morawetz (1974) and Lall (1978).
4. Technology exports are also growing in the field of civil engineering, banking and tourism, but these are not considered here.
5. Bharat Heavy Electricals Limited (BHEL), a public-sector undertaking, is setting up generating capacity of 544 MW in New Zealand, a 2 × 120 MW thermal station in Libya (for about $150 million, the largest Libyan contract for generation awarded), power generation and distribution facilities worth $74 million in South Arabia and so on. It has the capability to execute complete hydro, thermal and even nuclear power plants, and all its contracts have been won in open tenders against established TNCs. See *Lok Udyog* (Oct. 1977) and Rafferty (1977).
6. Indian Telephone Industries (ITI), a public-sector firm, has recently won many export orders, including one for two automatic exchanges in Surinam. It is now about to design and manufacture electronic exchanges and sophisticated defence communication equipment.
7. The export of sophisticated capital goods, based on local design, by indigenous enterprises of developing countries is itself a remarkable phenomenon which requires empirical and theoretical analysis, though this paper cannot discuss it in any detail.
8. Katz and Ablin (1977, pp. 10–11). About 20 instances of turnkey sales have been recorded.
9. Diaz-Alejandro (1977) and information provided privately.
10. Countries like Spain and Israel undoubtedly do, but are now advanced enough to be counted as industrialised nations. (On Spain, see More (1975).) Countries like South Korea are very active in turnkey jobs in civil construction: see the *Financial Times*, 14 March 1978, p. 20.

11. After this paper was written, Larry Westphal of the World Bank prepared, jointly with Y. W. Rhee, a note in which he showed that Korea and Taiwan were in fact selling turnkey plant abroad. These projects were mainly in traditional sectors like cement, paper and metal products, and, for Korea, were largely handled by the large integrated trading companies which had strong official (financial and political) support and which had gained foreign experience through civil construction. I am grateful to Larry Westphal for this information. It modifies some of the remarks made below but does not affect the conclusion about India's rôle as the leading Third World technology exporter nor the analysis of the nature of technical capabilities in developing countries.

12. This section draws on the excellent paper by Roberts (1973).

13. *ECN*, 3 April 1976, and information supplied privately.

14. *ECN*, 19 June 1976. Roberts (1973, p. 53) notes that NIDC 'offers services to a wide range of industries largely based on the implementation of technologies developed in India'.

15. Outside the enterprise framework, of course, such technology is being 'exported' on a massive scale by migration.

16. See Diaz-Alejandro (1977) on Latin America, Lecraw (1977) on Indian firms in Thailand, and Wells (1977) on the internationalisation of firms from developing countries in general. The UN Centre of TNCs (1978) has collected some data on direct investment flows between developing countries, which are reproduced in Tables 8.1–8.3.

17. See Lall (1979).

18. Information supplied privately.

19. Large business houses in India are pressing for a relaxation of this restriction, in view of their growing technological capability and the country's large foreign exchange reserves. See India as Capital Exporter, *Economic and Political Weekly*, 17 December 1977, pp. 2078–80.

20. Reported in *The Financial Times*, 14 July 1978, p. 4.

21. See Lecraw (1977) and Wells (1977).

22. For the process of technology assimilation by Japan in the pre-Second World War period, and the interplay between importation, adaptation and (subsequently) innovation, see UNCTAD (1978).

23. The major exceptions are Jha (forthcoming) and Katz (1974, 1976, 1977, 1978).

24. See Mansfield (1968) and David (1975).

25. The second sort of 'elementary' learning may also require a great deal of technologically directed activity (as Katz (1974, 1976, 1977, 1978) has noted), in contrast to simple 'learning by doing' which occurs almost naturally with the accretion of experience. It is termed 'elementary' only because it takes place within the given context of an imported technology and does not cover the design of the technology itself.

26. This is illustrated by Lecraw (1977) and Wells (1977).

27. For an analysis of the significant relationship between elementary technological activity (adaptation, 'trouble-shooting', higher process productivity, all within a given technology) and commodity exports in Argentina, see Katz (1974).

28. This is discussed for industrialised countries by Freeman (1974), and for the case of a large selection of Indian public sector enterprises by Jha (forthcoming).

29. The independent science institutions in India seem to have contributed little by way of useful industrial technology—the bulk of the contributions have come from manufacturing enterprises. Whether this is due to lack of necessary links (Cooper (1974)) between science and production, or simply a longer 'learning' curve is difficult to say. Also see Prahalad (1977).

30. A detailed and perceptive analysis of the Brazilian capital-goods industry by Erber (1978) very clearly demonstrates how the lack of protection and promotion on indigenous design led to a decline in Brazilian technological capability, and to a loss of market share to TNCs. It is also likely that permitting local enterprises to maintain a passive dependence on foreign-licensed technology will also not develop any local capability: a more forceful policy on developing and using local technology seems to be required. Evidence of this for some small Andean countries is provided by Mytelka (1978). In India, by contrast, *Lok Udyog* (various) and Jha (forthcoming) show how technological capability was built up in various enterprises (and not in some others) by the policy of attracting highly skilled (often foreign-trained) engineers, setting up substantial R and D departments, diversifying the product range, entering export markets and rationalising the organisational structure. Impressionistic evidence shows a marked relationship between the setting up of R and D activities, in particular, and entry, after a brief lag, into the technology export market.

31. For a description of the Brazilian experience see Epstein and Mirow (1977), and for a more general analysis of TNCs in the electrical equipment industry see Newfarmer (1978).

32. This is why most exports of high technology by developing countries have taken place on a tender basis, to 'informed' buyers who are not as swayed by brand-names as the ordinary customer.

33. Dastur's of India, for instance, has undertaken engineering consultancies in developed countries like West Germany, as has the NIDC in Italy and the UK. A few foreign transnationals are establishing research laboratories in the more advanced developing countries like Brazil, Egypt and India mainly in the food-processing and pharmaceutical industries. However, this seems to be more to meet specific local needs than to exploit cheaper scientific manpower. Till now there has been little indication that head-office-based design and development functions are being relocated.

34. Such exports enjoy the great advantage that they are not in the category of labour-intensive goods where protectionism is rampant in developed countries, and where import-substitution efforts are likely to come first in other developing countries.

35. Some evidence on this point is provided by Lecraw (1977) for technology exports by means of direct investment by Indian firms in Thailand.

36. The promotion of local ancillaries is documented for the Indian case by Subramanian (1976) and by the various special reports on public enterprises published in *Lok Udyog*. On the Japanese experience see Watanabe (1971) and UNCTAD (1978).

37. Foreign R and D can stimulate local innovation by 'fallout' effects; but it may also retard it by attracting the best personnel or picking up promising findings.

38. This point is made by Mytelka (1978) with reference to the Andean Pact countries.

254 Developing Countries in the International Economy

39. See 'India Ready for More Saudi Contracts', *Financial Times*, 7 March 1977.
40. For an analysis of Indian firms as compared to large TNCs and wholly local firms in Thailand, see Lecraw (1977, pp. 455–6). He finds that Third World TNCs not only used more appropriate technologies, but also had higher capacity utilisation rates, achieved higher profits and reinvested a larger portion of their profits.
41. 'For example, in the manufacture of a diesel engine for commercial trucks, there are approximately 750 parts ranging from cylinder blocks to fuel injector pins. In the United States, close to 200 plants supply materials, raw castings, forgings, components and parts to the diesel engine manufacturers. To produce these parts, as many as 300 different materials are required, each with narrow standards on physical and chemical characteristics and shapes or finishes. Over 10,000 separate manufacturing steps are required to convert materials and castings into finished parts for a single model . . . [To build diesel engines] 8 to 10 volumes (3,000 to 4,000 pages) containing materials standards and manufacturing specifications are required. There are approximately 145 technical specifications, engineering information items, testing methods and engine-rebuild standards; 67 special manufacturing methods; 439 materials standards, 240 process standards; and 25 salvage procedure standards for rejected parts'. (Baranson (1969, pp. 29–31).
42. There are notable exceptions, however, apart from the obvious cases of textile factories set up to take advantage of GSP. Kirloskar's of India have set up a (joint venture) electric motor plant in Malaysia which started exporting to S.E. Asian countries, Australia and New Zealand within three years of starting production. Furthermore, some Third World investments in developed countries (especially Europe) are being undertaken precisely in order to export (to the EEC).
43. For a longer discussion see Lall and Streeten (1977).

REFERENCES

Baranson, J. (1967), *Manufacturing Problems in India: the Cummins Diesel Experience* (Syracuse: Syracuse University Press).
Baranson, J. (1969), *Industrial Technologies for Developing Countries* (New York: Praeger).
Cooper, C. (ed.) (1973), *Science, Technology and Development* (London: Frank Cass).
Cooper, C. (1974), Science Policy and Technological Change in Under-developed Economies, *World Development* (March) pp. 55–64.
David, P. A. (1975), *Technical Change, Innovation and Economic Growth* (London: Cambridge University Press).
Diaz-Alejandro, C. F. (1977), 'Foreign Direct Investment by Latin Americans', in T. Agmon and C. P. Kindleberger (eds.), *Multinationals from Small Countries* (Cambridge, Mass.: MIT Press) pp. 167–96.
*Economic and Commercial News* (various) (New Delhi: Trade Fair Authority, Government of India).

Epstein, B. and Mirow, K. R. U. (1977), 'Impact on Developing Countries of Restrictive Business Practices of Transnational Corporations in the Electrical Equipment Industry: a Case Study of Brazil' (Geneva: UNCTAD/ST/MD/9).

Erber, F. (1978), 'Technological Development and State Intervention: a Study of the Brazilian Capital Goods Industry'. Ph.D. Thesis, University of Sussex.

Freeman, C. (1974), *The Economics of Industrial Innovations* (Harmondsworth: Penguin).

Jha, P. (forthcoming), *Technological Development and Organization in the Indian Public Sector: an appraisal* (Bombay and Delhi: Oxford University Press (India)).

Johnson, P. S. (1975), *The Economics of Invention and Innovation* (London: Martin Robertson).

Katz, J. (1974), 'Technology, Dynamic Comparative Advantages and Bargaining Power' (Buenos Aires: Instituto di Tella) (mimeo).

Katz, J. (1976), *Importacion de Technologia, Aprendizaje e Industrializacion Dependiente* (Mexico: Fondo de Cultura Economica).

Katz, J. (1977), 'Technologia y Expertaciones Industriales: Un analysis Microeconomico de la Experiencia Argentina Reciente', with E. Ablin, *Desarrollo Economico* (April–June) pp. 89–132.

Katz, J. (1978), 'Creacion de technologia en el sector manufacturero Argentino', *El Trimestre Economico* (January–March) pp. 167–90.

Lall, S. (1978), 'Transnationals, Domestic Enterprises and Industrial Structure in Host LDCs: a Survey', *Oxford Economic Papers*, pp. 217–48.

Lall, S. (1979), 'Multinationals and Market Structure in an Open Developing Economy: the Case of Malaysia', *Weltwirtschaftliches Archiv* (June).

Lall, S. and P. P. Streeten (1977), *Foreign Investment, Transnationals and Developing Countries* (London: Macmillan).

Lecraw, D. (1977), 'Direct Investment by Firms from Less-developed Countries', *Oxford Economic Papers*, pp. 442–57.

*Lok Udyog* (various), Monthly Journal of the Bureau of Public Enterprises and the Public Sector, Ministry of Finance, Government of India, New Delhi.

Mansfield, E. (1968), *The Economics of Technological Change* (London: Longman).

Morawetz, D. (1974), 'Employment Implications of Industrialization in Developing Countries', *Economic Journal*, pp. 491–542.

More, J. L. M. (1975), 'Quince años de Inversiones Españolas en el Extranjero', *Informacion Commercial Española*, (March) pp. 91–107.

Mytelka, L. K. (1978) 'Licensing and Technology Dependency in the Andean Group', *World Development*, pp. 447–60.

Newfarmer, R. S., (1978), 'The International Market Power of Transnational Corporations: a Case Study of the Electrical Industry' (Geneva: UNCTAD/ST/MD/13).

Parker, J. E. S. (1974), *The Economics of Innovation* (London: Longman).

Prahalad, C. K. (1977), 'MNCs and Export Development', *Economic and Political Weekly*, Review of Management, 26 February, pp. 25–31.

Rafferty, K. (1977), 'India Takes on the Power Industry Giants', *Financial Times*, 26 September, p. 5.

Roberts, J. (1973), 'Engineering Consultancy, Industrialization and Development', in Cooper (1973).

Rosenberg, N. (1976), *Perspectives on Technology* (London: Cambridge University Press).

Stewart, F. (1977), *Technology and Underdevelopment* (London: Macmillan).

Subramanian, S. K. (1976), 'Field Survey on Ancillary Development in India', in Asian Productivity Organization, *Intra-National Transfers of Technology* (Tokyo) pp. 63–85.

UN Centre on Transnational Corporations (1978), *Transnational Corporations in World Development: a Re-examination* (New York: UN).

UNCTAD (1978), 'Case Studies in Transfer of Technology: Policies for Transfer and Development of Technology in Pre-War Japan'. (Geneva: TD/D/C.6/26).

Vernon, R. (1966), 'International Investment and International Trade in the Product Cycle', *Quarterly Journal of Economics*, pp. 190–207.

Watanabe, S. (1971), 'Subcontracting, Industrialization and Employment Creation', *International Labour Review*, pp. 51–76.

Wells, L. T. (1977), 'The Internationalization of Firms from Developing Countries', in T. Agmon and C. P. Kindleberger (eds.), *Multinationals from Small Countries* (Cambridge, Mass.: MIT Press) pp. 133–56.

# Subject Index

# Author Index